Presidential Popularity and the Economy

Presidential Popularity and the Economy

Kristen Renwick Monroe

PRAEGER SPECIAL STUDIES • PRAEGER SCIENTIFIC

New York • Philadelphia • Eastbourne, UK
Toronto • Hong Kong • Tokyo • Sydney

Library of Congress Cataloging in Publication Data

Monroe, Kristen R., 1946–
   Presidential popularity and the economy

   Bibliography p.
   Includes index.
      1. Presidents—United States—Election.   2. Elections—
United States.   3. United States—Economic conditions—
1945–   —Public opinion.   4. Public opinion—United
States.   I. Title.
JK524.M66   1984   324.973′092   83–13943
ISBN 0–03–063566–7   (alk. paper)

Published in 1984 by Praeger Publishers
CBS Educational and Professional Publishing
a Division of CBS Inc.
521 Fifth Avenue, New York, NY 10175 USA

Printed in the United States of America
on acid-free paper

To my mother, Gertrude Renwick Monroe

And to the memory of my father and my brother,
James O. Monroe and James David Monroe

Contents

LIST OF TABLES

LIST OF FIGURES

Acknowledgments

I am indebted to many generous critics who have commented on various drafts of this book or on the papers on which it was based. Bernard Grofman, William Keech, and Stephen Weatherford provided invaluable comments on early drafts of the entire manuscript. William Fleming, R. G. W. Lampros, and Robert Shapiro were most helpful in their comments on the preliminary theoretical ideas contained in the Epilogue. Conversations with David Easton and Duncan MacRae, Jr., and the late Joseph Tanenhaus provided valuable help and encouragement at the initial stages of research, and I am thankful for that. Participation in a research group on political support and alienation, first organized by Jack Dennis as a National Science Foundation-supported series of conferences and later transformed into a Study Group of the International Political Science Association, provided valuable contact with foreign scholars, chief among them Bruno Frey and his associates, and Rudolph Wildenmann. Participation in a conference on voter turnout organized by Richard Brody, Bernard Grofman, and Herbert Weisberg provided valuable comments on the conceptual framework presented in Chapter 2.

In addition to the above scholars, particular thanks are due James Alt for our conversations concerning the political importance of economic expectations, Donald Kinder and D. Roderick Kiewiet for our ongoing dialogue on the sociotropic voter, H. Mark Roelofs for friendly and stimulating disagreements over the extent to which the president controls economic policy making, and Dona Metcalf Laughlin for her assistance in the empirical analysis that appears in Chapter 4. Certain linkages between specific empirical findings and the more theoretical implications of the study, I owe to my association with Joseph Cropsey.

The task of collecting, coding, and analyzing the vast amount of data presented here was made much easier by the helpful assistance of several students it has been my pleasure to know at New York University: Dona Metcalf Laughlin, Laura Scalia, and Jo-Anne Hart. For their skill and patience with the word processor, I owe thanks to

Beatrice Lewis, Fernando Viana, Joanna Cowie, and Karen Dalton. For all of us, George Sharrard was a most generous ally in our battles with the computer.

The American Institute of Public Opinion and the Roper Center at the University of Connecticut at Storrs provided access to the Gallup data files; and Norman J. Cantor, former Dean of the Faculty of the Arts and Science at New York University, approved the purchase of Gallup data never released to the public. I, along with other scholars who may later use the raw data contained in Chapter 2 or Appendix A, owe them our thanks. Parts of this manuscript appeared in *Political Behavior*; I appreciate Paul Hoeber's kind permission to reproduce these segments here.

My thanks to the foregoing individuals and institutions is surpassed only by my gratitude to my family. For personal encouragement and support, I am deeply indebted to my mother, to my husband, and to young Alexander for his unique contribution.

None of the above individuals, of course, is responsible for any of the errors contained within. The faults of the study are mine alone.

Introduction

This book has a dual purpose. For the student and layman
interested in the economy's political significance, it summarizes in nontechnical language much of the recent scholarly
literature on presidential popularity and the economy. It
discusses the major economic changes that have occurred in
twentieth century America and analyzes the importance of
these changes for public support of incumbent presidents.
For the professional political scientist and political economist, this book presents the first comprehensive group
analysis of the economic influence on presidential popularity
to allow fully for the role of partisan loyalties. It argues
that an integrated rational approach is needed to detect the
complex process by which the economy influences presidential popularity. This approach allows for the conscious
calculation of self-interest that economists assume motivates
political behavior; it also allows for the inherited values and
more primitive ideological and often preconscious, or even
unreasoning, influences on political behavior stressed by
sociologists. Through an extensive review of the literature, the analysis suggests that much of the empirical
controversy in this area stems from hidden theoretical
disagreements between economists and sociologists over the
fundamental motivations underlying human behavior. This
conclusion is buttressed by a detailed empirical examination,
using Gallup Poll data, of the key theories of political
support for incumbent presidents. This empirical analysis
juxtaposes a nonrational cyclical model with an integrated
rational model of the public's political response to the
economy and demonstrates that an integrated rational approach is more useful than either cyclical or narrowly
rational explanations. The epilogue discusses the theoretical implications of this and outlines an economic
ratiocination model useful in explaining politicoeconomic
interactions.

The book begins with a prologue designed to serve as a
valuable review of economic trends in twentieth century
America. Special attention is paid to the critical differences
in economic conditions during the last 15 years in terms of
both the economic circumstances confronting government
policy makers and the government's response to the econo-

my. This section also presents evidence on the remarkable accuracy of the Gallup Poll in predicting voting behavior, a matter of natural concern to newcomers to the field, who will wish to know immediately the political significance of the Gallup Poll data on presidential popularity.

Chapter 1 is a critical analysis of the recent scholarly literature on presidential popularity and the economy, beginning with the early works on the economy's impact on voting. Because the early works were based on elementary statistical analysis, their inclusion serves primarily as historical interest and as a bridge between the theoretical origins of political economy and the later empirical examinations of many of these theories within political science. The 1950s and early 1960s saw a recurrence of the debate between economists and sociologists over the fundamental motivation behind human behavior. Since the economists had reached the limit of existing statistical expertise, this period was dominated by social psychological explanations of voting that stressed personal characteristics correlated with the vote. Only in 1971, when Kramer expanded Downs's theoretical work to construct a rational choice formulation of the relationship between the economy and congressional voting patterns, were the foundations laid for a more sophisticated analysis stressing rationality and the economic approach to political problems. With this work, the debate over economic influences on political support resumed with a vengeance. Many works analyzed both voting and public opinion measurements of popular support for political incumbents in the United States, Western Europe, Canada, and Japan. As survey researchers, following a sociological approach, began to employ microlevel survey data to bridge the gap between collective electoral behavior and the individual voter, the rational choice theorists designed ever-expanding detailed surveys to test some of the assumptions on which this earlier aggregate work had been based. The tension between the economic and sociological approaches, as well as some of the excitement of this period, is captured in Chapter 1.

As work in this area expanded, debate centered on certain controversies and research focused on a few crucial questions. What role do the political parties play in filtering individual perceptions of presidential performance on macroeconomics? Are Republican presidents expected to have different priorities on macroeconomic policies than Democratic presidents? When voters respond politically to economic conditions, do they act on the basis of their individual self-interest? Or do they act based on broader connections with the interests of one of their peer groups?

Do voters consider the public interest and national economic well-being when they respond politically to economic conditions? What is the media's role in shaping both public perception of the economy and the political response to economic change? Is unemployment more important than inflation? Is unemployment among certain groups more important politically than unemployment among other groups? Are the actual levels of unemployment and inflation politically relevant? Or is it the direction of economic change—the improvement or deterioration of employment and price levels—that matter politically? How important is economic reality compared to people's expectations and perceptions of reality? And finally, are the relevant economic conditions the macroeconomic phenomena, such as unemployment and inflation, on which scholarly and political attention has been focused so far? Or must we consider redistributive economic policies (such as taxation, income, and social welfare policies) and the relative political power of the groups affected by these policies if we want to determine the economy's full effect on presidential popularity?

Beyond asking which economic predictors influence presidential popularity, it is crucial to determine the relative importance of the economic and noneconomic factors in causing shifts in public response to the president. To what degree can changes in presidential popularity be attributed to public whim? Do all presidents enjoy a brief "honeymoon" period after their inauguration? Do dramatic international crises rally public support behind the president as a national leader, regardless of the president holding office? Is the decline in public support of recent presidents inevitable as long as Americans expect more of their presidents than any individual can deliver in this era of the post-imperial presidency? And finally, what shifts in popularity result from purely political acts by the president, acts having nothing to do with economic performance or economic policy? How troubled is the American public, for example, by corruption? How important is it that people believe their president to be a strong leader? And what role do partisan loyalties play in the process by which Americans give or withhold their support from presidents? Are Democratic presidents expected to follow certain policies? Because Democrats have different constituent groups, are they judged by standards of performance—in both the economic and the political realm—that differ significantly from the standards by which Republican presidents are evaluated?

These are some of the questions on which debate has centered. In Chapter 2 these questions are discussed in

considerable detail and are blended into a framework for
analysis that can serve as a heuristic tool. Chapter 2
presents an integrated rational approach to understanding
presidential popularity and the economy, an approach that
stresses rational behavior but that also allows for ideological
factors.

Chapter 3 begins the empirical examination of this approach by examining trends and cycles in group support
for American presidents from 1965 to 1980. This analysis
begins with a juxtaposition of two alternate models of political behavior: a cyclical and a rational model. The ideologi-
cally oriented cycle theory argues that shifts in presidential
popularity result from recurring patterns in public opinion
that are unrelated to specific presidential actions or events.
The rational choice theory explains these shifts through
specific presidential acts and events. The analysis in
Chapter 3 constitutes a simple demonstration of the superi-
ority of the integrated rational approach. Using Gallup
data on public support for the last four presidents, it
shows that in every case the high and low points of their
popularity can be traced to specific events or presidential
actions. Even this simple analysis reveals that the
so-called honeymoon period, so crucial to the cyclical theory
of presidential popularity, is highly specific to the individual incumbent. Chapter 3 thus demonstrates that while
there are, indeed, cycles in presidential popularity, these
cycles are neither as uniform nor as unresponsive to presidential actions as the cycle theorists suggest. And general
cycles by no means sufficiently explain the fluctuations in
presidential popularity. For this, presidential acts and key
events must be included in the analysis. Thus, a full
consideration of presidential popularity must encompass both
the rational and the cyclical components of political life.

Beyond addressing this theoretical concern, the analysis
serves an additional function: It provides specific political
information about presidential popularity and the economy.
What has been the public's general response to the president since 1965? Are there important differences among
groups? Have all four presidents enjoyed roughly equal
levels of political support? Were they all equally loved and
respected by different groups in society? If not, were
they given equal chances to prove themselves when they
took office? Did Johnson and Ford enjoy a longer honeymoon period because of the tragic and traumatic circumstances under which they assumed the presidency? Did
Nixon, who was disliked by so many people, enjoy the same
grace period after taking office as the relatively unknown
Carter? Has there been a trend since the Vietnam and

Watergate years toward a more critical, even cynical, evaluation of incumbents? Are we now in for a period of one-term presidents whom we expect to perform miracles and then cast aside in anger when they cannot live up to this impossible image? If the recent trend in public attitudes toward presidents is indeed more cynical, is this because the presidents themselves aroused unrealistic public expectations in their quest for office? These are the main questions discussed in Chapter 3.

In Chapter 4, analysis moves to a more systematic examination constructing a multivariate statistical model of group support for the last four presidents. This section is the first comprehensive group analysis of presidential popularity. It is important, in part, because it allows more fully for partisan loyalties than earlier works have done. Its development of systematic predictors of public response to leadership, corruption, and international crises should prove particularly useful to the professional political economist. Though these predictors are but crude first attempts, they strongly suggest the public's full political response to the president can best be detected through an integrated rational approach that stresses economic considerations but includes nonrational forces as well.

In Chapter 4 the political impact of cyclical and political influences is compared with the impact from economic predictors. The central question is: Are economic conditions or political and cyclical events more significant influences on popularity? To answer this question, a multivariate statistical model is developed. Based on the integrated rational framework presented in Chapter 2, this model provides a systematic examination of presidential popularity in terms of redistributive and macroeconomic predictors, political influences, and cyclical phenomena. How do these findings correspond with the traditional wisdom that increases in inflation and unemployment hurt popularity and increases in income help it? The most important general conclusion is that the economy's impact on popularity is strongly affected by political party affiliation. Differing public expectations concerning the economic priorities on the political parties cause strongly divergent public response to the economy. These expectations depend heavily on the political ties of the incumbent president. This underlying partisanship must be fully taken into account in order to detect the more complex economic influences that counteract each other at the aggregate level.

Beyond this, the analysis found economic predictors more important than political or cyclical predictors of presidential popularity. The single most important economic predictor is unemployment, particularly among white-collar workers and among married men. Actual macroeconomic conditions carry greater political weight than governmental redistributive policies, and the economy's political importance is equally strong for all economic classes in American society.

The centrality of party is particularly interesting given recent discussions of the weakening and decline of American political parties. My analysis suggests party ties remain strong but are subtle in their influences, working through public perceptions of differing party priorities. This, in turn, establishes different public expectations about economic performance, expectations that critically determine the public's political response to the economy. This response is not at all a class response in the Marxist sense, which argues that the two major parties in the United States do not differ on their economic priorities; nor is it a class response in a more limited sense, which suggests lower- or working-class respondents will be more concerned with unemployment and upper-income or occupational groups more concerned with inflation. Neither of these occurred.

Instead, a more explicit attempt to separate and analyze the political reaction to unemployment among those groups most dramatically affected by it—the young, blacks, and women—suggested a rather remarkable public concern for the economic well-being of the polity as a whole. Analysis suggested that a surprising number of voters respond to the president not so much on the basis of their individual situation, or even that of their immediate referent group, but rather on the basis of a judgment of the president's ability to alleviate unemployment for the nation as a whole. This finding confirms Kinder's sociotropic voter theory, confirmation which is particularly important since it comes from a time-series analysis using robust aggregate indicators of economic conditions and therefore is not subject to either of the methodological criticisms dealing with cross-sectional survey data levelled by Kramer or Sears et al.

Some of the findings presented in the analysis (such as unemployment's reverse influence, detected only in a group analysis and heavily dependent on public expectations of different party economic priorities) alert us to a provocative question of potential theoretical interest: Are there other anomalies concerning the economy's political impact and is there a way to resolve these anomalies by refining the traditional theory of political support? In other words, can my findings on the economy's influence on presidential popularity yield broader insights into political behavior? I believe so. In an epilogue I take the opportunity to step back and examine these findings in relation to others in the field. This examination reveals certain contradictions and anomalies, both in the form of specific empirical findings and in the models reflecting broader theoretical orientations to understanding politics. These contradictions and anomalies are important in pointing to the need for theoretical clarification within contemporary political economy. This clarification centers on distinguishing between an economic decision-making process and economic motivations or goals. It is the distinction between understanding political behavior as a result of an economic process of calculations, regardless of the goals motivating this behavior, and understanding political behavior as being caused by economic motivations. This distinction alerts us to a long-standing and hidden philosophical disagreement between the sociological and economic approach to social science over the fundamental motivations of human behavior. This disagreement centers on the need to revise our definition of rationality in social science and to construct a model of political behavior that integrates the sociological and economic approaches.

The epilogue represents a first attempt to do this. Discussion concentrates on four specific areas. First, I advance a theoretical clarification between the economic explanation as a decision-making process and as a motivation for political behavior. Second, I relate this to an extended historical debate between economists and sociologists over the fundamental motivations underlying political behavior. I will argue that this debate runs so deeply within social science that it affects much empirical work in hidden ways. To document this, I present two examples of how this hidden disagreement has led to empirical controversies that could be resolved by reference to a broader theoretical framework, a framework that is essentially an integrated rational framework. Third, I assert that the heart of the difficulty centers on the narrow definition of rationality utilized in political economy and in much of political science. The discussion in this epilogue concludes with a critique of the major politicoeconomic models. An outline of an economic ratiocination model is presented as a first effort toward wedding the economist's emphasis on rationality as a conscious calculation of costs and benefits with the social psychologist's emphasis on behavior derived from preconscious and subconscious impulses.

Prologue

For those not familiar with recent political economic interactions, a prefatory note is in order. This prologue addresses two central questions that naturally occur to those
new to the field. First, what can an examination of Gallup
Poll data on presidential popularity reveal about the public's
political response to the economy? And second, what has
been the pattern of economic activity in the United States
in recent years?

PRESIDENTIAL POPULARITY AS A POLITICAL
PHENOMENON: THE GALLUP POLL MEASURES OF
PRESIDENTIAL POPULARITY AND THEIR RELATIONSHIP
TO VOTING

Why should scholars, presidents, or the public care about
presidential ratings in a public opinion poll? The answer is
that polls predict voting. A first question, then, is how
accurately the poll data analyzed here predicted voting in
national elections from 1936 to 1980.[1]
    There are actually two questions here. The first asks
how well the Gallup Preelection Poll predicts voter behavior.
The second asks how closely this Preelection Poll on voting
intentions corresponds with the more frequent poll query on
presidential popularity: "Do you approve or disapprove of
the way President _____ is handling his job as
president?"[2]
    First, compare the Gallup predictions with actual voting.
Historical evidence suggest an extraordinarily close relation
between the Gallup estimates of voting intention and the

1

actual vote. The Gallup Poll has successfully predicted the victorious presidential candidate or Congressional party in all 22 elections since 1936.[3] (Table P–1). Gallup has also been remarkably accurate in predicting the percentage of the final vote in these elections. From 1936 to 1980 the average difference between the Gallup estimates and the final vote for the winning party or presidential candidate was only 2.3 percentage points.[4] From 1964 to 1980—the dates covering the period analyzed here—the average difference was only 1.9 percentage points.

Because of this, Gallup polls are widely accepted as indicating public reaction to the president even in non-election years. This raises the second question: How

TABLE P-1. Gallup Predictions and Election Results, 1936-1980

Year	Gallup Final Survey		Election Result		Percentage Deviation
1980	47.0%	Reagan	51.0%	Reagan	-4.0
1978	55.0	Democratic	54.6	Democratic	+0.4
1976	48.0	Carter	50.0	Carter	-2.0
1974	60.0	Democratic	58.9	Democratic	+1.1
1972	62.0	Nixon	61.8	Nixon	+0.2
1970	53.0	Democratic	54.3	Democratic	-1.3
1968	43.0	Nixon	43.5	Nixon	-0.5
1966	52.5	Democratic	51.9	Democratic	+0.6
1964	64.0	Johnson	61.3	Johnson	+2.7
1962	55.5	Democratic	52.7	Democratic	+2.8
1960	51.0	Kennedy	50.1	Kennedy	+0.9
1958	57.0	Democratic	56.5	Democratic	+0.5
1956	59.5	Eisenhower	57.8	Eisenhower	+1.7
1954	51.5	Democratic	52.7	Democratic	-1.2
1952	51.0	Eisenhower	55.4	Eisenhower	-4.4
1950	51.0	Democratic	50.3	Democratic	+0.7
1948	44.5	Truman	49.9	Truman	-5.4
1946	58.0	Republican	54.3	Republican	+3.7
1944	51.5	Roosevelt	53.3	Roosevelt	-1.8
1942	52.0	Democratic	48.0	Democratic	+4.0
1940	52.0	Roosevelt	55.0	Roosevelt	-3.0
1938	54.0	Democratic	50.8	Democratic	+3.2
1936	55.7	Roosevelt	62.5	Roosevelt	-6.8

Source: Gallup Election Handbook

closely do responses to the monthly Gallup polls on presidential approval correspond with Gallup preelection surveys of voting intention?[5]

Table P–2 provides data on contemporaneous polls on presidential popularity and voting intentions from 1948 to 1980. These data suggest popularity and voting intentions are closely related. In four of the nine presidential elections during this period the popularity of the incumbent president was higher than the support he or his party's nominee received in the poll measuring voting intentions. In five of the nine elections the opposite pattern occurred.[6] The discrepancy between voting and approval ratings ranges from 2 to 13 percentage points. Presidential popularity averages 0.67 of a percentage point higher than voting intention when voting intention is calculated assuming a two-man race; it is 2 percent higher when voting intention is recorded assuming a three-man race.[7]

The evidence in these two tables thus confirms that the Gallup Poll measures of voting intentions correspond closely with actual voting behavior. Furthermore, the presidential popularity polls correspond closely with contemporaneous measures of voting intentions. Precisely because they correspond so closely with the voting intention polls that so accurately anticipate voting behavior at election times, the public opinion polls indicating presidential popularity are the best regular feedback available to the president concerning mass public reaction to his performance.[8] Thus, the polls are important indicators of public approval and, as such, should be studied as an independent political phenomenon.

ECONOMIC CONDITIONS IN VIETNAM AND POST-VIETNAM PERIOD

A second major concern centers on the nature of economic conditions between 1965 and 1980. Did the economic problems confronting presidents during this period differ in any important way from those confronting earlier presidents? What economic policies were followed? How successful were these policies believed to be at the time?

The first part of the period was characterized by economic expansion, propelled by the real growth in gross national product that occurred between 1960 and 1965. Most of the post-1965 growth originated in the government spending for the Vietnam War and the Great Society programs. These led to continual growth and economic boom until the cutbacks in both war and welfare programs under Nixon.

TABLE P-2. Presidential Popularity and Voting Intentions, 1948-1980

President	Dates of Polls	Popularity of Incumbent President	Voting Intention			Difference
			Incumbent or Party Candidate	Opposition Candidate	Third-man Opposition	Popularity Minus Voting Intention
Carter	August 15-18, 1980	32%	45%	39%[a]	13%[a]	-13
			39	38		- 7
Ford	June 11-14, 1976	45	37	55[b]		+ 8
Nixon	June 23-26, 1972	56	54	37		+ 2
			45	32	18[b]	+11
Johnson	Late August 1968[c]	35	29	45[d]	18[c]	+ 6
Johnson	June 4-9, 1964	74	77	18[e]		- 3
			70	27[e]		+ 4
Eisenhower	October 18-23, 1960	58	48	49[f]		+10
Eisenhower	July 12-17, 1956	69	61	37		+ 8
Truman	October 9-14, 1952	32	40	47[g]		- 8
Truman	March 9-24, 1948[h]	35	39	47	7[i]	- 4

[a]Two vote polls taken: Carter-Reagan and Carter-Reagan-Anderson; [b]Two vote polls taken (June 16-19, 1972): Nixon-McGovern and Nixon-McGovern-Wallace; [c]No date given; Johnson-Nixon-Wallace; [d]Johnson-Nixon-Goldwater; Vote poll taken (June 11-16, 1964): [e]Vote poll taken (June 11-16, 1965): Johnson-Nixon; [f]Vote poll taken (October 30-November 4, 1960): Nixon-Kennedy; [g]Vote poll taken (October 28-November 1, 1952): Stevenson-Eisenhower; [h]Both polls taken only in Southern States; [i]Three Man Race: Truman-Dewey-Wallace.

The economic problem of the 1965–1980 period culminated in the 1974–1975 recession, a recession that introduced Americans to stagflation. Although the stagflation was worldwide, its psychological impact was intensified for Americans by the balance of payments deterioration and the recognition that the United States no longer enjoyed economic preeminence and invulnerability. A further shock to the economic confidence of the country came from the ineffectiveness of the traditional tools of fiscal and monetary policy to direct the economy throughout the postwar period.

As a result of these factors, public psychology concerning the economy shifted during the 1965 to 1980 period. Americans began to grapple with three disquieting ideas. First, the United States was now only one of several key nations in the world economy. Second, the market mechanisms had significantly restructured the United States economy from a producer to a service economy.[9] Third, the extensive welfare programs designed to cushion the poor during economic downturns had succeeded enough to prevent the decreasing prices usually found during a recession but had also built inflation into the American economic system. Even worse, the basic mechanisms of the market had been so altered by government social welfare policies that the traditional economic theories concerning government action during recession needed drastic reformulation (Okun 1981.)

These were the psychological responses to economic fluctuations. How did the actual economic trends and cycles between 1965 and 1980 compare with the long-term economic trends and cycles? In particular, how did the 1965–1980 period compare with the long-term economic pattern of inflation, unemployment, and income, the three economic phenomena that most directly concern presidents?[10]

Unemployment

Did the unemployment facing presidents in the Vietnam/post-Vietnam period differ significantly from that facing earlier presidents? Yes. Annual figures on unemployment, summarized in Figure P–1, show three distinct periods: the 1890s until the Depression, the Depression and World War II period, and the postwar period. During the first period, fluctuations in employment were sudden and extreme. The high unemployment of the 1930s Depression was followed by the low unemployment of World War II.[11] The immediate postwar period saw unemployment hover near 3.5 percent.[12]

Figure P–1.   Unemployment 1890–1970

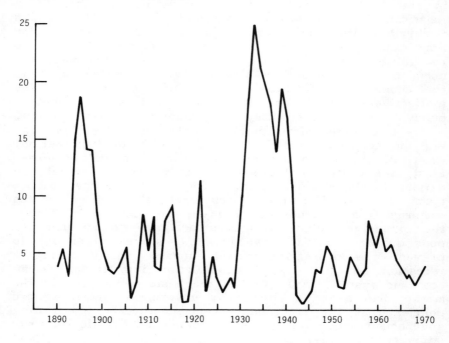

Source: U.S. Department of Commerce, Bureau of The Census, *Historical Statistics of the United States, Bicentennial Edition, Colonial Times to 1971, Part I.*

These changes were due at least in part to the institutional reforms taken in response to the 1930s Depression, reforms that altered the pattern of unemployment by removing the extreme fluctuations of the earlier pre-1930s period. Unemployment between 1965 and 1980 corresponds to that of the immediate post-World War II period in its smooth and gradual movement. The average unemployment after 1965, however, was somewhat higher than the average rate between 1945 and 1965, with the main difference between the 1965–1980 period and the earlier postwar period being the gradually increasing rate of aggregate unemployment, particularly after 1974.[13]

Patterns of Group Unemployment

What was the unemployment pattern among different groups?[14] The range of group unemployment between 1947/

1948 and 1965 is striking. It demonstrates the economy's differentiated impact, with women, blacks, and the young suffering much more than others during economic distress.[15]

Figure P–2. Group Unemployment Rates, 1948–1965

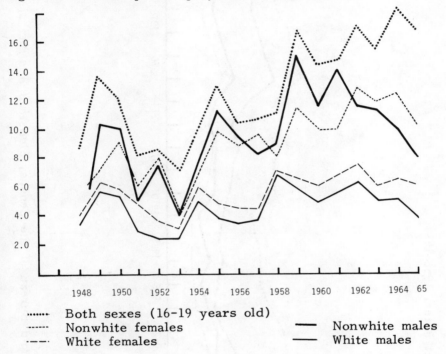

.... Both sexes (16-19 years old)

------- Nonwhite females   ——— Nonwhite males

-- -- White females   ——— White males

Source: Bureau of Census, *Statistical Abstract of the United States.*

How do the 1945–1965 group unemployment rates compare with those of the 1965–1980 period? In contrast to the 1954–1965 period, aggregate and female unemployment correspond closely between 1965 and 1980.[16] (See Figure P–3.) Male unemployment rates are generally low for 1965–1980, remaining under 5 percent during Ford's term in office. The differential between white and nonwhite unemployment is again striking, with white unemployment usually at least 4 percentage points below the nonwhite rate.

The close relationship between aggregate and female unemployment demonstrates the sharp change in the composition of the labor force during the postwar period. The tremendous increase in female workers was unprecedented

Figure P-3. Group Unemployment Rates, 1956–1980

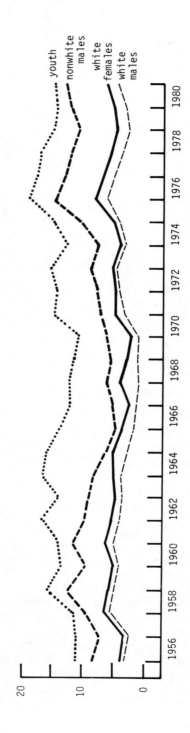

Source: Department of Labor and Bureau of the Census, *Statistical Abstract of the United States, 1980.*

8

and contributed a new set of complex unemployment problems for presidents.[17]

Inflation and Income

Historically, price increases accompany wars. This was
true during this period, as the two highest inflations of
this century occurred during and after the two World Wars,
either as the economy geared up for war or adjusted from a
wartime economy. Other periods of high inflation depend
on how the government financed the war or on the international economy (see Figure P–4).

Figure P–4. Changes in Consumer Prices, 1913–1980

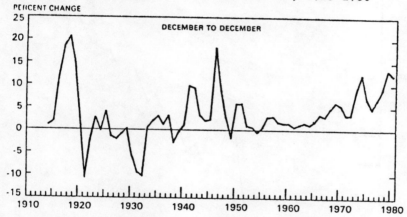

Note: Percent change for 1980 is from December 1979 to
November 1980 at a seasonally adjusted annual rate.
Source: 1981 Economic Report of the President, Depart-
ment of Labor.

Differences between the Korean and Vietnam inflations
show the range of government flexibility in dealing with
inflation and suggest why the public quite properly holds
the government responsible for inflation. During the
Korean War, taxes were increased dramatically early in the
war. Wartime controls on production, equipment, wages,
and prices were instituted. As the war progressed and it
became apparent that the war was smaller in magnitude than
had been expected, the controls were gradually lessened.
Wartime inflation actually fell from 6.6 percent during the
first year of the Korean involvement to 1.6 percent during
the last year.

Figure P–5.   Patterns in Income, 1929–1970*

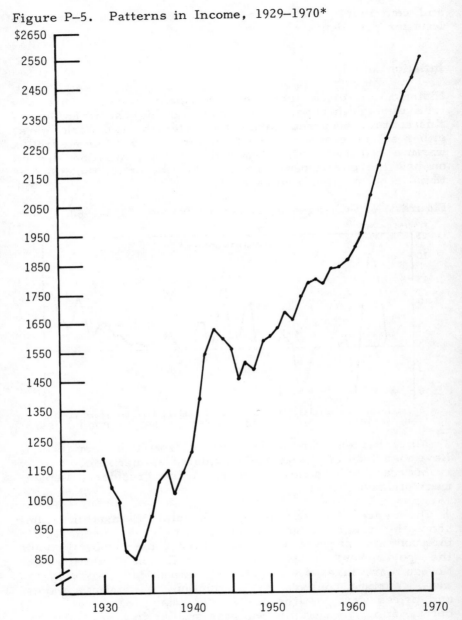

*Per capita disposable income (1958 dollars).
Source: U.S. Department of Commerce, Bureau of Census, *Historical Statistics, Bicentennial Edition, Colonial Times to 1971*, Volume 1, 225.

The Johnson administration did not follow this traditional scenario. President Johnson refused to adopt wartime price controls or to increase taxation to pay for the Vietnam War.[18] Because of his refusal to finance the war directly and immediately, the Vietnam inflation was greater than the Korean inflation and extended over a longer period of time.[19]

Wars also affect incomes. During the 1929–1965 period income increased in all years except the 1930s, the 1957–1958 recession, and right after wars.[20] Per capita disposable income was $1,274 in 1929. The level fell between 1929 and 1933, when it was $343 less than it had been in 1929. Income rose between 1934 and 1938, when it again declined: at $1,105 it was $131 less than 1929 disposable income. It was not until 1940, when World War II was in full force in Europe, that income exceeded pre-Depression levels.

After the war the economy faltered, with income declining from 1945 until 1948, when it once again began to increase. Despite outlays for the Korean War, the 1944 income level was not surpassed until 1953. Income faltered in 1954 as the transition was made from a wartime to a peacetime economy. Except for the 1957–1958 recession, income increased steadily throughout the rest of the period.

CONCLUSION

Overall, what was the economic situation facing both policymakers and voters between 1965 and 1980? The 1965–1980 period had less sudden dramatic economic shifts than the pre-World War II era. The 1957/1958 and the 1974/1975 recessions were the most serious periods of economic downturn in the postwar period. Stagflation, the major economic problem between 1965 and 1980, arose because of two factors: (1) the decision not to increase taxes to finance the spending for the Vietnam War and the Great Society programs, and (2) a worldwide recession that resulted largely from high oil prices. The domestic policymakers were reasonably held to blame for the former but not the latter problem. Just how much these economic downturns affected the political fortunes of incumbent presidents is the subject of the rest of this book.

NOTES

1. In the analysis presented here I have examined data collected by the American Institute of Public Opinion (AIPO), the oldest American polling agency. This poll,

referred to throughout as the Gallup Poll, is the best-known and probably the most influential poll politically.

2. Comparing the Gallup Poll predictions of voting with the actual vote in elections will determine the accuracy of the poll in predicting a behavioral phenomenon—voting—from an attitudinal expression of public opinion. Comparing the relationship between the Gallup Poll expressions of approval or disapproval for the president with the Gallup measurements of voting intentions will determine the degree to which the regularly collected presidential popularity series can be used as a proxy for voting intention, as it is now widely used by politicians, the press, and the public.

3. Consider the 1980 election when many voters remained undecided or lukewarm in their support, making a final vote choice or shifting their votes in the last days of the campaign, and leaving most pollsters and commentators surprised at the size of the Reagan victory. How did Gallup fare in predicting this election? In the October 25–26 Gallup survey, taken just prior to the presidential debate, Carter held the edge: Carter 45 percent, Reagan 42 percent, and Anderson 9 percent, with 3 percent undecided and 1 percent intending to vote for a fourth candidate. After the debate on October 28 the pattern shifted, with both Carter and Anderson losing support: Reagan 44 percent, Carter 43 percent, Anderson 8 percent, undecided 4 percent, and 1 percent intending to vote for a fourth candidate. A follow-up poll on October 30-November 1, in which the undecided voters were asked to give their probable vote choice, showed a stronger shift to Reagan. This final Gallup Poll gave Reagan 47 percent, Carter 44 percent, Anderson 8 percent, with 1 percent intending to vote for a fourth candidate. The actual results of the November 4 election were: Reagan 51 percent, Carter 41 percent, Anderson 7 percent, and other minor candidates 1 percent.

4. Table P–1, which contains data from the Gallup Poll Election Handbook, documents this in detail. For each year I have presented Gallup's final preelection survey estimates of the percentage of the vote Gallup believes will go to the winning presidential candidate or, in off-year elections, to the party that Gallup predicts will control Congress. By comparing this figure with the actual election results, it is possible to determine both how accurately Gallup predicted the election and what the average difference was between the final vote and the Gallup estimates of that vote.

5. Contemporary histories and biographies of decision makers suggest that both politicians and the public believe there is a strong overlap between actual voting behavior,

the Gallup Poll reelection estimates of voting intention, and the more frequently observed sample of presidential popularity measured by the approval question. Table P–2 tests the accuracy of this belief. A comparison of responses to contemporaneous polls that ask about both presidential approval and voting intentions in the approaching election will determine how closely the monthly responses measuring presidential popularity reflect stated voting intention. It also will provide information on the effect of an opposition candidate, someone who provides a real alternative to the incumbent, on public attitudes toward the president. This, in turn, can yield indirect evidence on the importance of party ties in the voting process by providing information concerning voters who dislike the incumbent but will vote for him anyway, either because of party loyalty or because they dislike his opponent even more.

The importance of this can be seen by considering the 1980 election. Carter received a popularity rating of only 32 percent in the poll conducted August 15–18, 1981, the latest in which both presidential popularity and voting intentions were measured. Yet despite the low rating they gave him, 45 percent of the poll respondents said they intended to vote for Carter rather than for Reagan.

6. In three of these nine presidential elections, however, the incumbent was not running for reelection. When these three are omitted from the calculations, we find that in the remaining six elections the percentage of respondents approving of the president was lower than the percentage who stated they intended to vote for him. In the other three presidential elections, the pattern was reversed: people approved of the president, but said they did not intend to vote for the incumbent when presented with an alternative candidate.

7. This is calculated by adding the amount of the total percentage by which approval overestimated or underestimated voting and then dividing by the number of elections.

8. Presidential popularity polls are watched closely by the president and his staff, who use them to gauge public reaction to specific policies. Sharp declines in popularity polls conducted after major policy decisions are duly noted. In some cases, policies may be altered because of strongly adverse public reaction. In other cases, a president may note the cost to his popularity from following a particular policy, but still decide, perhaps for ideological or personal reasons, to stand by the unpopular policy. It is rare, however, for the president and his staff to be unmindful of

the potential political costs of a particular policy.

Yet another use is made of the Gallup polls, which is not considered directly here. This is the widespread interpretation of the popularity poll as indicating the public's response to specific policies advocated or pursued by the incumbent administration. Many times Gallup will attempt to separate the public's response to the president's personality from its response to specific policies associated with him. This is done by asking the same respondent to evaluate the specific policy in addition to giving his general approval rating for the president. We can then compare, for example, public responses to the general approval question: "Do you approve or disapprove of the way President Carter is handling his job as president?" with responses to: "Do you approve of President Carter's policies?" Doing so suggests the American voter closely identifies the president with key policy questions; unfortunately, the data on presidential popularity are too irregular to allow a systematic examination of this linkage. The connection between presidential popularity and public preference on policies, although widespread, seems less reliable than the connections between voting, voting intentions, and presidential popularity. The problem becomes complicated because a voter's general approval of a president may be rooted in prior attachments that, though nonpolicy-related in formation, still color the voter's evaluation of a president's specific policies.

There is much literature suggesting this is true. (See, for example, Lee Sigelman and Pamela Johnston Conover's [1981] analysis of how prior partisan feelings and preferences affected public responses to Carter's handling of the Iranian hostage crisis.) Thus while the polls are interpreted by the press, the public, and the administration itself as providing critical information on voting intentions, on the public's personal response to the president as an individual, and on the public's response to some of the president's most important policies, establishing the validity of this linkage is tricky and lies beyond the scope of this analysis.

9. See Ginzberg 1981.

10. Any historical discussion of economic data will be limited by the reliability and consistency of available data series. In replicating data, minor inconsistencies may occur for many valid reasons: e.g., because different base years were used to calculate from the same economic series, because comparisons of economic change were made on a month-to-month, quarter-to-quarter, or fiscal-versus-calendar-year basis, or because the government later recal-

culated and revised particular economic series.

11. The impact of the Great Depression was evident in the unemployment statistics throughout the 1930s. The annual rate rose from 3.2 percent to 8.7 percent in 1930, and by 1931 it had increased to 15.9 percent. Bad as this seemed at the time, over the next five years an unemployment rate of just under 16 percent would look unbelievably good. In 1932 unemployment was 23.6 percent. In 1933 it reached 24.9 percent. The rate held at more than 20 percent for two years. It then dropped to 16.9 percent in 1936 and 14.3 percent in 1937, before shooting up again to 19 percent in 1938. Only with the advent of World War II did unemployment return to its pre-Depression rate: 9.9 percent in 1941, 4.7 percent in 1942, and 1.2–1.9 percent during the rest of the war.

12. In the immediate postwar period unemployment increased slightly but never rose much above the relatively moderate range of 2.9 percent (1953) to 6.8 percent (1958). With the exception of the 1958 recession and the low unemployment periods around the Korean War (2.9 percent in 1953, 3 percent in 1952), the usual unemployment rate from 1946 to 1965 hovered around 3.5 percent.

13. The period between 1945 and 1965 had only two years, 1958 and 1961, when unemployment went above 6 percent. In contrast, the 1965–1980 period saw unemployment above 6 percent briefly during Nixon's presidency and throughout most of the Ford and Carter presidencies. The 1965–1980 period ended with an unemployment rate of nearly 9.7 percent.

14. Obviously, group patterns generally will reflect the aggregate trends of overall economic fluctuations, with the highest levels of unemployment occurring in 1958 and 1961 for all groups. The group patterns in the 1947–1965 period and the 1965–1980 period, however, differ in important ways.

Because the aggregate figures on unemployment are made up of data on unemployment among all groups, the logical inference is that the general unemployment pattern reflects the pattern of all groups. Unfortunately, it is not possible to actually test this because the historical data on unemployment among different groups do not extend back as far as the data on aggregate unemployment. For example, the earliest figures for male/female unemployment are from 1947; the earliest figures for any age or racial breakdowns are from 1948. All we can do, then, is examine the pattern of unemployment among different groups from 1947/1948 through 1980, first, to contrast the different patterns of group unemployment over time, and second, to determine whether the group unemployment problems confronting presidents during the 1965–1980 period differed substantially from those facing presidents holding office earlier in the post-World War II period.

15. As a base, consider aggregate unemployment. This ranged from 2.9 to 6.8 percent between 1947 and 1965; the lows occurred during the Korean War and the highs during the 1957/1958 recession. For women, the range is much greater: 3.3–7.2 percent, with the highest unemployment rates occurring in 1954 (6 percent), 1958 (6.8 percent), and 1961 (7.2 percent), and the lowest rate occurring in 1953. When we look at racial groups, the differential between white and black unemployment is obvious. The range for white males is 2.5–6.1 percent. For black males, the contrast is striking: a range of 4.8–13.8 percent. Black females have rates slightly higher than black men and much higher than white women. The unemployment range for black women is 4.1 percent (1953) to 10.8 percent (1963). The group with the highest unemployment, however, is the young. Their unemployment rate never dropped below 7.6 percent, and was usually double-digit throughout this period, reaching 17.2 percent in 1963.

All of these data come from the annual figures on unemployment, expressed as a percent of the civilian labor force, as presented in the *Historical Statistics of the United States—Bicentennial Edition: Colonial Times to 1971, Part I* (Washington, D.C.: U.S. Department of Commerce, Bureau of the Census, 135.5).

16. Both range from 3.5 percent (1968) to 8.5 percent (1975).

17. Figure P–2 graphs the percent rate of the labor force participation from 1949 to 1972 for both men and women, controlling by age.

Labor force participation among civilians has fluctuated between 53 and 65 percent. The participation rates for men 25 to 54 years of age have stayed remarkably constant at slightly over 90 percent. The rate for younger men has fluctuated a bit more, from about 83 to 88 percent. The rate for all civilians, roughly 60 percent throughout the period, has been similarly constant, reflecting the heavy role played by the 25-to-54-year-old male in the labor force. And the participation of both sexes over 55 years of age has declined slightly from 43 to 38 percent. The biggest change occurs among women. Only slightly more than 45 percent of women 20-to-24-years old participated in the labor force in 1949. By 1972 the rate was nearly 60 percent. In 1949 only 35 percent of the women between the ages of 25 and 54 were working; by 1972 over 50 percent of these women were in the labor force.

18. The refusal to increase taxes probably originated in Johnson's quite accurate perception that the country would choose to cut back on his Great Society programs if faced with increased taxes.

19. For a detailed analysis of the economics of spending, see Thurow (1980). For a discussion of wage and price controls, see Russell (1983).

20. See Weatherford (1977) for a discussion of the public's political response to recession.

Political Support for Incumbents

Why do we support political incumbents? How much impact does the economy have on this support? Is its impact differentiated by socioeconomic class? How crucial are party stands on economic issues in this process? Early works provide only partial answers to these questions.

Most early works on the economy's political impact examined only voting. Not until the late 1950s did refined statistical techniques allow more extensive analysis of public opinion support for incumbents. This book will pull together and build on the collective findings from those earlier works to address these questions concerning the economy's influence on presidential popularity.

The first part of this chapter, summarizing early works on the public's political response to the economy, is essentially an intellectual history of the development of the political economy literature as it applies to voting. The few works from this period that measured public opinion expressions of incumbent popularity are also included. This discussion, which is chronological and by author, will serve as an historical introduction to the field for the newcomer and as a review to be skimmed and used as reference for those already familiar with the subject.

The second part of this chapter discusses the most significant recent econometric analyses of electoral behavior, beginning with Kramer's important work published in 1971. This section is more analytical, relating recent findings on one specific area to those in another. It emphasizes the substantive points of agreement and highlights areas of controversy or uncertainty about the way in which the economy influences incumbent popularity.

The third section focuses on survey analyses of voting behavior or public opinion expressions of support for political incumbents or political parties. It includes analyses of incumbent popularity in the United States, Western Europe, Canada, and Japan and asks how closely the manner in which the economy influences popularity in the United States corresponds to the pattern in other political systems.

The last section is a detailed discussion of the most important recent work analyzing microlevel responses to the economy. It begins with an analysis of Fiorina's retrospective voting model as it has been applied to microlevel data. This application spurred other work using cross-sectional data to bridge the gaps between our knowledge of political economy at the collective electoral level and at the level of the individual voter. In analyzing the individual voter's response, we will ask more specific and detailed questions about how economic considerations enter into the voter's political calculations. This type of analysis can trigger innovative theoretical work, as is seen in the theory of the sociotropic voter; but it is also subject to certain potential methodological limitations, as is equally evident in the debate over the sociotropic voter.

THE ECONOMY AND VOTING: THE EARLY WORKS

From Rainfall and the Populists to Business Curves and Congressional Voting

The first analyses of economic influence on voting were impressionistic, dealing with general feelings about how people voted when times were bad. Throughout the 1920s and 1930s most analysts used only simple correlations and tabulations or compared data series listing the number of votes with a subjectively derived index of economic well-being or general business activity. There was little effort to allow for the simultaneous impact of many economic variables or for the effects of political incumbency or "coattails." There was little concern with theory; most works were in the nature of ad hoc empiricism. Table 1-1 lists these works, by author and year published, identifies the main variables used in the analysis, and summarizes the findings on the economy's impact on voting.

John Barnhart's (1925) analysis of the connection between annual rainfall and voting for the Populist party is one of the earliest works to describe the impact of economic hardship on an emergent political party. Barnhart compares maps of population, drought, and agricultural conditions in Nebraska in the 1880s and 1890s to determine the effect of economic hardship resulting from drought on the decline of the Republican party and the rise of the Populist party. He concludes that although not decisive, the "drought made a bad set of agricultural conditions worse" and put the farmer in a "receptive frame of mind" for the arguments of the Populist party.[1] Thus, he judges the economy a factor in voting.

Stuart Rice (1928) determines the proportion of total Republican candidates in the New Jersey Assembly over 48 successive elections. He then compares this pattern with an unspecified business curve and finds that fluctuations in Republican party voting follow the ups and downs in this business cycle. On the basis of this simple correlation of time-series data, Rice concludes there is a relationship between Republican voting and economic prosperity, with Republican voting increasing during periods of economic well-being and decreasing during recessions.

Clark Tibbitts (1931) uses a cross-sectional analysis of voting in 94 congressional districts in the Northeast in 1882 and 1884 to determine whether the popularity of political parties is related to economic conditions at the time of the election. On the basis of the Harvard curve of business activity, he chooses the elections of 1882 and 1884 as examples of economic prosperity (1882) and economic depression (1884). Tibbitts acknowledges the importance of presidential races on congressional elections by weighting his variables to allow for deviations from the trend.[2] He finds that party voting does vary with business conditions. While noneconomic factors do influence voting, the incumbent has an advantage in elections occurring during or just after periods of expansion, while elections during a depression will result in loss of votes for the incumbent party.

W. A. Kerr (1944) asks whether prosperity increases votes for the conservative party, defined as the Whig party prior to 1856 and the Republican and Prohibition parties thereafter. He explains this conservative vote from 1840 to 1940 by the following indicators: per capita real national income, cost of living, and wholesale price index.[3] He concludes that there is only modest support for the hypothesis that prosperity leads to increases in the conservative vote, but he offers no explanation as to why this is so.

Albert Rees and his colleagues (1962) consider the economy's influence on cross-sectional congressional voting from 1946 to 1958. They measure economic well-being by calculating the state-insured unemployed (as a percentage of those covered by unemployment insurance) and by the net income per farm in the state. Each variable is expressed in terms of deviations from its 13-year state average. Using simple bivariate tabulations, Rees et al. determine whether low unemployment and high farm income are associated with party voting in 41 states. They find a positive relationship between Republican voting and high employment for slightly more than half of the cases.[4] They find no relationship between voting and farm income. They conclude that Democrats do slightly better in elections when economic conditions are poor and Republicans do better when times are good.

From FDR and Farm Wages to Presidential Voting and Price Levels

W. F. Ogburn and Lolagene Coombs (1940) explain cross-national changes in the Roosevelt vote from 1932 to 1936 through the average wage in manufacturing and wholesale trade, and the average value of farm per person employed in farming, weighted by the proportion of the population living on farms and in towns. They find a substantial positive relationship between the economy and changes in Roosevelt's vote in three states and substantial negative relationships in two states.[5] They conclude there is no systematic relation between prosperity and the change in Roosevelt's vote.

Harold Gosnell and William Coleman (1940) consider income and changes in the presidential vote in 65 Pennsylvania counties from 1928 to 1936. Economic well-being is measured by an index of salary income for manufacturing plus the value of principal crops for agriculture, weighted by the relative importance of agriculture and industry and the number of people employed in each group within the county. They find a weak relationship between the decline in this index and the shift in votes for the Democratic presidential candidate from 1928 to 1932 and again from 1932 to 1936. When rural and ethnic composition of the population is controlled, the strength of the relationship increases. Gosnell and Coleman conclude that economic fluctuations do affect voting for the incumbent party's presidential candidate.

Louis Bean published several works throughout this period. *Ballot Behavior* (1940) examines changes in the

House of Representatives from 1894 to 1934. To determine the effect of prosperity and depression on votes for the incumbent party, Bean compares House votes with changes in general business activity.[6] He finds the incumbent party lost 15 of the 19 elections held during economic downturns, with losses occurring in all 9 midterm elections but only in 6 out of 10 presidential elections. Bean concludes that a decline in business activity hurts the party in power, but that a president's popularity and other noneconomic factors may offset the impact of the economy in presidential years. Bean's later work on economic influences on voting largely substantiates his claim that business depressions are of primary importance in producing changes in party control.[7]

Johann Akerman (1947) considers depressions and presidential voting from 1868 to 1945. Akerman categorizes presidential elections as occurring in peak or trough years. He looks at the fate of the incumbent president's party and concludes that 16 out of the 20 elections in his sample support the hypothesis that a presidential party will be ousted during a depression but maintained in prosperity.

F. A. Pearson and W. I. Myers (1948) consider whether people vote for the incumbent during economic prosperity but against the president's party during or after a depression. Their sole indicator of economic well-being is the "general price level." Following Kerr, Pearson and Myers classify presidential elections from 1828 to 1924 into low- or declining-price periods versus high- or rising-price periods. They find the incumbent party candidates won 11 of the 13 elections held in low- or declining-price periods, and lost 16 of the 18 elections held when prices were rising or high. They conclude that the economy influences presidential voting.

Thomas Wilkinson and Hornell Hart (1950–1951) consider the importance of economic prosperity for presidential and congressional voting. Their indicator of economic prosperity, a poorly defined index of general business activity,[8] fails to explain either the popular presidential vote for the party in power from 1844 to 1948, or changes in the House membership of the party in power from 1856 to 1948.

The 1950s and 1960s:
Economists versus Sociologists

Three impressions emerge from the above. First, there is much confusion. These early works demonstrate, as V. O. Key put it, that "people did, indeed, appear to vote their

TABLE 1-1. The Economy and Support for Political Incumbents: Early Works

Author	Date	Main Variables Used in Analysis	Findings	General Conclusion: Does the Economy Affect Voting or Popularity?
Barnhart	1925	Populist party vote, drought, agricultural conditions.	Economy affects voting.	yes
Rice	1928	New Jersey congressional voting, business curve.	Fluctuations in Republican voting do follow business cycle.	yes
Tibbitts	1931	Congressional voting, business conditions.	Party voting varies with business conditions.	yes
Ogburn and Coombs	1940	FDR vote, 1934-1936 wages, farm values.	No systematic relationship between prosperity and changes in FDR vote.	no
Gosnell and Coleman	1940	Presidential voting, income.	Weak relationship between income and Democratic vote is increased when rural and ethnic factors controlled.	yes
Bean	1940, 1948	Congressional voting, business activity.	Recession hurts incumbent party. Economy less important in presidential election years.	yes
Kerr	1944	Conservative party voting, income, cost of living, wholesale price index.	Weak association between prosperity and conservative vote.	yes, but not much

24

Akerman	1947	Presidential voting, Depression.	Depression hurts incumbents.	yes
Pearson and Myers	1948	Presidential voting, general price level.	Economy influences presidential voting.	yes
Wilkinson and Hart	1950-1951	Presidential and congressional voting, general business activity.	No relationship between economy and presidential vote or changes in House membership.	no
Rees et al.	1962	Congressional voting, unemployed, net income per farm.	Republican voting affected by employment but not by farm income.	mixed

pocketbooks. Yet the demonstration created its embarrassments because it also established that exceptions to the rule were numerous."[9] Second, the sophistication in the data analysis is quite primitive, with most authors failing to describe data sources or the constructions of their indicators of economic well-being. Third, and most importantly, virtually none of these authors develops explicit underlying assumptions about why and how the economy should affect voting. They offer ad hoc empiricism unsupported by developed theoretical work.

These early works were part of a widespread movement in social science, between 1920 and 1950, to develop generalizations about why people vote as they do. The usual method is illustrated in the economic analyses of voting described here. Statistical associations were made between aggregate votes and some objective measure of social conditions (such as the state of the economy) or census characteristics (such as the percentage of urban, ethnic, or particular religious groups). The limits of existing statistical techniques were, with a few exceptions, reached in the late 1950s. At this point we see a switch in the approach to analyzing the economy's political impact.

The 1960s were dominated by works inspired by *The American Voter* (1960). Voting, including the analysis of the economic influences on voting, is no longer explained through objective conditions measured by aggregate data. Now the emphasis is on survey research data that allow the respondent to report both his subjective perceptions of the economic situation and his vote intentions. Along with this emphasis is a shift away from the implicit assumption that the voter is a rational actor who calculates the benefits and costs of voting. Analysis moves toward explanations of voting that stress party identifications inherited from parents or associated with membership in an ethnic or religious group. These identifications may provide rational reasons for voting for a party or candidate, but only in a looser sense, more removed from the individual's own immediate calculations of benefits and costs.

There are some notable theoretical exceptions to this trend. *An Economic Theory of Democracy*, by Anthony Downs (1957), provides an elaborate framework for voting that assumes the existence of a rational economic man in politics. V. O. Key's (1966) posthumous work (with Milton Cummings) argues that supposedly irrational party identifications do, in fact, embody intuitive calculations of advantage. And Riker and Ordeshook's *A Theory of the Calculus of Voting* (1968) advances a utility-maximizing explanation of both the decision to vote and the decision not to vote. Not until Gerald Kramer's important empirical work on congressional voting, however, do we find a return to the systematic empirical analysis of economic influences on electoral behavior. The description of current work in this area thus must begin with an analysis of this significant study.

RECENT ECONOMETRIC ANALYSES OF ELECTORAL BEHAVIOR

Kramer's Rational Choice Formulation and Stigler's Response

Gerald Kramer's (1971) work has an importance beyond that of its own substantive contributions. First, its use of more sophisticated statistical techniques demonstrated the importance of such techniques for careful empirical analysis. Kramer thereby reopened empirical debate in this area, particularly for analysts using aggregate data. Second, Kramer presented an explicit theoretical framework for his statistical model and reintroduced the rational actor into empirical work in this area. Last, Kramer influenced rational choice theorists, who had traditionally concentrated on formal models, to conduct empirical tests of rational choice propositions using aggregate or survey data.[10] So Kramer both redirected the theoretical underpinnings of empirical work using rigorous statistical analysis of aggregate data and encouraged formal rational choice modelers to test their propositions against empirical data.

Kramer constructed a multivariate statistical model of voting in congressional elections from 1896 to 1964. Initially, he found fluctuations in unemployment have no appreciable influence on elections, while fluctuations in real per capita income are influential. His later reanalysis of the data qualified these findings somewhat and suggested that both income and inflation are important.[11]

The traditional democratic view of the rational voter is of one who gathers information on party platforms and candidates' issue positions and past voting records, and then votes for the candidate or party he believes will benefit him the most. Kramer rejects this view as unrealistic because it requires the voter to invest too much time in gaining information. He instead posits a rational actor who votes on the basis of the most easily available information, which Kramer believes is the past performance of the incumbent party. This should give the voter some indication both of what the party would do if elected and of how effective its policies are.[12] Kramer's underlying assumptions can be summarized as follows:

1. The rational actor will view voting as a choice between two alternatives on economic policies and, eventually, between two alternative sets of economic conditions.
2. Past economic performance reflects actual policies of a party or incumbent.[13]
3. The party controlling the presidency is the incumbent party.
4. Voters view congressional candidates as essentially party members, i.e., as Democrats or Republicans rather than individuals.

These premises suggest to Kramer that variations in party popularity will reflect public response to the incumbent party's policies. He does note that his model might be better applied to a parliamentary system where there is stricter party voting, but he assumes that American voters generally hold congressional candidates responsible for what a presidential administration does to the economy.

Finally, Kramer assumes a satisficing model in which a voter satisfied with the incumbent's performance will vote to retain him and/or his party; conversely, a voter dissatisfied with the incumbent's performance will vote against him or his party to register disapproval or to give the opposition a chance.[14] Kramer's specific hypotheses to test are (1) that an increase in income will help the incumbent party, and (2) that an increase in prices and unemployment will hurt the incumbent party.

Kramer's dependent variable is the party's share of the vote in congressional elections from 1896 to 1964. All minor party votes are counted as anti-incumbent.[15] Kramer considers congressional voting in relation to (1) changes in unemployment from the preceding years, (2) relative change in per capita real income (monetary income deflated by a cost of living index), (3) changes in money income (treated similarly to real income), and (4) changes in the price level (measured by the consumer price index). The signs for all economic variables are governed by incumbency; the incumbency variable equals +1 if the president is a Republican and -1 if he is a Democrat.[16] Kramer introduces a coattails parameter into the analysis of presidential elections; he ignores the coattails at the state or local level. Kramer varies the economic predictors introduced into his model. He omits 1912 because of the Progressive-Republican split, and omits 1918, 1942, and 1944 because of the distorting impact of wars on the price and income series.

Kramer's general conclusion is that economic fluctuations are "important influences on congressional elections, with economic upturn helping congressional candidates of the incumbent party, and economic decline benefitting the opposition."[17] In the analysis of variance, Kramer finds that economic fluctuations account for approximately one-half of the variance in congressional vote.[18] This seems to overstate the actual findings a bit. Kramer does find a significant influence from real income, with rising per capita real income helping and declining income hurting the incumbents substantially. But when real income is held constant, the other economic predictors (inflation and unemployment) have no significant independent influence. Kramer finds little advantage to being an incumbent except in periods of economic success. Presidential coattails, however, can help congressional candidates. Table 1-2 summarizes Kramer's and other recent works.

Kramer's work reopened the debate about the economic influences on electoral behavior with great fanfare, evoking a strongly critical response from George Stigler. Stigler (1973) reanalyzes Kramer's data, making several modifications:

1. He shifts the independent variable to exclude minority party votes and expresses the incumbent's share of the congressional vote as his share of the total vote. This has little affect on results.
2. Stigler extends the time period to 1970 and drops the years prior to 1900 (for which Kramer includes unemployment in his model) because reliable unemployment data are unavailable before 1900.
3. Stigler reintroduces the war years omitted by Kramer, arguing that these are not that unusual and that Kramer is inconsistent on this point by failing to omit 1898, 1950–1952, and 1962–1964 as war years. This shift of years analyzed does not affect the findings.
4. Stigler uses two-year rather than one-year units to calculate economic change since this time period corresponds to the congressional term. This alteration drastically affects results, causing unemployment and real income to lose significance.[19]
5. Stigler also analyzes changes in income in relation to changes in the share of the vote, arguing that measuring changes in both can better detect the

impact of new economic conditions and avoids the problem of average popularity of each president. This modification tends to lead to a loss of significance for prices but confirms the significance of income changes.

Stigler's criticisms have not been sufficiently acknowledged in later works by political scientists. At the very least, his modifications demonstrate how extremely sensitive empirical results are to slight modifications in definition and choice of years analyzed. This is particularly important in light of the small number of observations found in most time-series analyses (N = 34 for Kramer). For example, in one calculation Stigler inadvertently omitted 1944 and 1946 instead of 1942 and 1944 from the model, and the regression coefficient for real income lost all significance.[20] Thus changing one observation reduced the regression coefficient below statistical significance. Since much of the debate in this area has been over empirical findings rather than theoretical differences, Stigler's demonstration of the substantive importance of such seemingly minor changes makes his a major contribution.

Stigler is not content with this methodological criticism, however. He offers findings from other empirical data to support his claims that the economy does not influence voting at this level. Using cross-sectional data, Stigler looks first at changes in the Republican share of the vote for 70 congressional districts from 1958 to 1960. He regresses this on candidate incumbency, the share of the rural-farm population in the district, and unemployment rates in 1960. He finds only the farm variable important, and that just in counties with large farm populations. Second, Stigler looks at changes in the Republican share of the vote from 1966 to 1968 in 40 whole-county congressional districts. He compares these changes with candidate incumbency and with changes in employment. Again, he finds no significant relationships. Finally, Stigler examines the change in the Republican share of the vote in the 1950 election in 62 whole-county congressional districts. Again he compares this change with candidate incumbency and changes in unemployment, and again finds no significant relationship.

Thus, in both his time-series and his cross-sectional analyses, Stigler reaffirms Kramer's finding that unemployment in itself has no electoral importance. He disagrees with Kramer's conclusions on income, however, arguing that fluctuations in real per capita income also lack important electoral impact. Stigler is not surprised by these findings. Perhaps influenced by his neoclassical economics background, he argues that it would be unreasonable for a voter to give much weight to short-term economic fluctuations. He finds no difference between essential Democratic and Republican policies on unemployment and steady rates of growth of real income. Furthermore, he argues, the parties do not differ in their intellectual or political capacities to deal with macroeconomic policies of this kind. Therefore, Stigler concludes, it is illogical to expect voters to shift their allegiance on the basis of short-term fluctuations in general aggregate economic conditions. In light of the paucity of theoretical work in this area, Stigler's questioning of the implicit assumptions underlying most empirical work was an even more important contribution than his empirical challenges to Kramer.

The Debate Intensifies: Arcelus and Meltzer versus Bloom and Price and Goodman and Kramer

Francisco Arcelus and Allan Meltzer's (1975) analysis of congressional voting presents an elaborate theoretical framework for analyzing the costs and benefits of different economic policies. This framework is particularly sensitive to general economic considerations, as well as to the intricacies of trade-offs among economic policies. Their approach assumes the rational actor and their empirical analysis stresses a two-step process: the decision to vote and the decision about the preferred candidate or party. They assume that both steps depend on rational calculations about costs and expected benefits.

Arcelus and Meltzer analyze voter turnout from 1920 to 1969, expressed as the number of votes cast for House elections divided by the voting age population. They also analyze the Democratic and Republican votes, each expressed as the percent eligible to register who vote Democratic (or Republican), divided by the total voting age population. (Unlike Kramer, they do not treat all minor party votes as anti-incumbent votes.) They conclude there is an identifiable and stable partisan vote for the House. They find a coattails effect in so far that an incumbent president increases his party's congressional votes, but this coattails effect does not work through the president's impact on the economy. Rather, they find that the economy affects participation rates instead of voting. Changes in unemployment have little systematic effect on either the participation rate or individual party strength. A similar lack of effect was obtained for agricultural prices, stock prices, and "other economic variables."[21] Inflation is the exception: an increase in its rate lowers the Democratic, but not the Republican, share of the vote.

Arcelus and Meltzer conclude that "with the possible exception of inflation, aggregate economic variables affect neither the participation rate in Congressional elections nor the relative strengths of the two major parties."[22] They agree with Stigler that this lack of influence may be the result of considering short-term fluctuations and that voters may be sophisticated enough to consider long-term as well as immediate economic factors.

Commenting on this work, Saul Goodman and Gerald Kramer (1975) criticize Arcelus and Meltzer for "their model, the data they apply to it, the statistical method they use to estimate it, and the way they interpret their results."[23] After reanalyzing the Arcelus and Meltzer data and correcting for what they argue are errors, Goodman and Kramer conclude that unemployment, inflation, and real income do indeed influence congressional elections and that this economic influence works not merely through participation rates, but in ways that are "broadly (though not completely) consistent with the notion that the electorate punishes the party in power according to its economic performance."[24]

In another comment, Howard Bloom and Douglas Price (1975) advance an asymmetrical voting hypothesis concerning economic conditions and congressional elections. They find that a decline in real per capita income hurts the party of the incumbent president in congressional elections. Bloom and Price conclude that there is an asymmetrical economic influence on voting in that voters respond to negative changes but not to positive ones. In other words, voters assign political blame but not reward for economic conditions.

Later work by Arcelus (1978) takes account of Bloom and Price's (1975) criticisms and tests whether prosperity and recession have asymmetrical effects on voter behavior. His conclusions substantiate his earlier findings that economic fluctuations affect voter participation rates rather than actual shifts in voting between the two parties.[25] This finding concerning the importance of the economy for voter turnout is confirmed by Rosenstone (1982), whose analysis of microlevel survey data from both the November 1974 Current Populations Survey (CPS) and an aggregate time-series data from presidential and midterm elections since 1896 suggests that unemployment, poverty, and the decline in economic well-being all affect voter turnout negatively. Rosenstone concludes: "When a person suffers economic adversity his scarce resources are spent holding body and soul together, not on remote concerns like politics. Economic problems both increase the opportunity costs of political participation and reduce a person's capacity to attend to politics."[26]

In a related work, although one that falls outside the specific debate, Ray Fair (1978) analyzes an election function for the United States Congress. In contrast to both Kramer and Stigler, Fair finds that the growth rate of real income is the only significant economic predictor of congressional voting. He discounts lagged models, arguing that voters are myopic, i.e., they consider only the current state of the economy, as represented by the current growth of real income.

One must take care in evaluating the debate among these different authors. Goodman and Kramer are impressive in their thorough reexamination of the data and in the force with which they reaffirm the validity of Kramer's earlier findings. Their argument occasionally becomes tendentious, however, with strongly worded conclusions resting on relatively minor statistical quibbles.[27] Bloom and Price are much less comprehensive in their criticism. But their comment is more useful substantively because it raises the issue of whether voters blame and reward incumbents or merely punish them. The importance of turnout as an intervening variable, noted by both Arcelus and Rosenstone, alerts us to the necessity of building into our models intervening factors which may lessen or enhance the economy's direct importance for political support. And Fair's finding that voters are myopic is a cornerstone in the literature of political business cycles.

Congressional Voting

Edward Tufte (1975) seeks an economic explanation for the traditional midterm congressional losses suffered by the incumbent president's party. His model assumes voters use midterm elections to register approval or disapproval of the president's performance, especially his ability to manage the economy. Tufte proposes a two-stage model. The first stage explains the magnitude of votes lost in the congressional election by the president's party in terms of both the Gallup Poll evaluation of the president at the time of the election and the economy's performance in the year prior to the election. (The economy's performance is measured by the yearly change in real disposable income per capita.) Tufte's second stage compares the actual vote loss with the number of seats lost by the president's party. After testing his model for midterm elections from 1938 to 1970, Tufte concludes that a change of $100 in real disposable personal income per capita in the year prior to the midterm election is associated with a national change of 3.5 percentage points in the midterm vote. An increase of 10 percentage points in the Gallup Poll is associated with a national change of 1.3 percentage points in congressional voting. His model explains 91.2 percent of the variance in national midterm elections.[28]

Gavin Wright (1974) looks at voting during the New Deal era to determine whether government expenditures affect elections. He concentrates analysis on income, unemployment, the number of people on relief per state, the number of people in the state holding WPA jobs, and the percent of the state's farm population. He obtains mixed results showing that government spending has only an indirect political significance. In a cross-sectional analysis of changes in the Democrat's share of the congressional vote in 1936, 1938, and 1940, Wright finds the main expenditure effect works through income changes, which significantly affected the 1936 and 1938 elections. WPA employment was significant in all three elections. Wright argues that these results "confirm the [political] relevance of the allocation of aggregate spending."[29] However, changes in income did not have any impact on the 1940 election. And there is even less evidence that voting was affected by direct government spending.

James E. Pierson (1975) analyzes congressional elections and economic conditions within congressional districts, using both district-level aggregate data and survey data for the 1974 elections. His economic predictors are prices (CPI), per capita personal income, and real personal per capita income.[30] Despite the fact that he is analyzing the change in the vote from 1972 to 1974, no proxy variable is included for the Watergate scandal. Pierson finds no significant relationship between economic variables and voting at either the aggregate or the individual level; indeed, according to his results, voting in congressional elections is virtually independent of district economic conditions. He therefore concludes that the economy's political impact, noted in so many previous studies, must be related to voters' estimation of national economic conditions.

Walker Pollard (1978) considers economic influences on presidential voting at the state level from 1952 to 1972. Pooling time-series and cross-sectional data, he analyzes the impact of per capita personal income and inflation on changes in the share of per capita personal income and inflation on changes in the major party vote. Pollard analyzes each economic predictor according to (1) its growth rate, (2) deviations from its normal growth rate, and (3) lagged forms of the predictor, with exponentially declining weights to give greater weight to the most recent economic events. He introduces several control variables to allow for the political influences that have definitively been established as important for voting: (1) changes in party strength or identification, adjusted for trend; (2) changes in partisanship due to social issues; (3) changes in partisanship due to war or peace; and (4) any change in the party of the incumbent president.

Pollard concludes these political variables are more important than the economic ones. He finds income has no effect on voting and inflation has only a minor effect. In accounting for the lack of economic influence, Pollard notes the unreliability of income data series at the state level. While it is possible that Pollard's nonfindings can be attributed to data problems, they are more likely the result of intermixing different levels of analysis. The dependent variable is measured by aggregate voting for the president at the state level, as is income. But inflation is measured by national aggregate data. The political dummy variables are measured by survey data at the regional level, and the incumbency variable, which is used to adjust all forms of the economic variables, is based on the Republican share of vote in each state. This intermixing of levels of analysis, without adequate theoretical explanation or justification, plus the inclusion of several political dummy variables that closely approximate the dependent variable, lead to specification error that quite probably would make it difficult to find any independent economic effects on voting.

Kernell's (1977) work on congressional voting does not directly consider the impact of economic conditions. Using a negative voting model, Kernell argues that voters evaluate presidential performance when voting in midterm elections. Furthermore, people who disapprove of a president's performance, whatever their party affiliation, will turn out in greater number than those who approve of the president's performance. Kernell does not attempt to measure the political importance of economic variables in his negative voting analysis. He establishes only that midterm congressional voting is influenced by presidential popularity. In later work on presidential popularity (not voting), Kernell (1978) does consider the political importance of economic variables. He finds that while changing prices have a

TABLE 1-2. The Economy and American Voting: Recent Works

Author	Date	Main Variables Used in Analysis	Findings	General Conclusion: Does the Economy Affect Voting or Popularity?
Kramer	1971	Congressional voting, unemployment, income, prices.	Voting affected by income changes, not by inflation or unemployment if income held constant.	yes
Stigler	1973	Congressional voting, unemployment, income, prices, rural-farm population.	Voting affected by farm population, not affected by unemployment or inflation; income effect mixed.	no
Wright	1974	Congressional voting, income, government expenditures (WPA jobs, relief), farm population.	Main influence of expenditures is through income. Federal employment significant.	yes
Arcelus and Meltzer	1975	Congressional voting, voter turnout for congressional elections, unemployment, agricultural and stock prices, other unspecified economic variables.	Inflation affects Democratic vote. Economy affects voter participation rates not actual vote choice.	mixed
Goodman and Kramer	1975	Reanalysis of Arcelus and Meltzer data.	Economy affects participation and voting.	yes
Bloom and Price	1975	Congressional voting, unemployment, income and inflation.	Economic deterioration hurts incumbents, but improvement does not help them.	an asymmetric effect
Tufte	1975	Midterm congressional voting, disposable income, president's popularity.	Congressional voting affected by income and president's popularity.	yes

Pierson	1977	Congressional voting, district level data on prices and income.	Congressional voting not affected by local economic conditions.	no
Arcelus	1978	Uses earlier Arcelus and Meltzer data to test for asymmetric effect of economy.	Economy affects voter turnout, not vote choice.	no
Pollard	1978	Presidential voting, income, inflation, party identification and partisanship, change in incumbency of president.	Some influence from inflation, none from income; political variables more important than economic.	little
Kirchgässner	1981	U.S. presidential vote (1896-1976). Various lagged periods for economic events: inflation, rate of real income growth, unemployment, party.	Inflation is the single most important predictor. No party differences mediate the economy's impact, but being an incumbent helps. Voters have a high but not an infinite discount rate for the economy.	yes
Hibbing and Alford	1981	Congressional voting, individual and aggregate data on economic conditions.	Income changes and voter's subjective economic conditions affect voting only for Congressional incumbents in president's party.	yes but only for incumbents
Lau and Sears	1981	Microeconomic conditions, votes for Carter.	Economic affects only voters who blame president for economic woes.	yes if president blamed
Rosenstone	1982	Presidential and mid-term elections since 1896 and 1974 CPS data, unemployment, poverty, economic decline.	Economic adversity reduces political involvement, lowers voter turnout.	yes

strong impact on popularity, unemployment has a weak effect, and then only for some presidents. We might infer from this that the economy affects presidential popularity, which then affects midterm congressional voting in the negative fashion described by Kernell. This evidence is too removed to be considered more than speculative, however, and Kernell makes no such assertion himself.

The Hibbing and Alford (1981) study of congressional voting considers both individual and aggregate level data to examine the economy's impact on voting for incumbent congressmen from the president's party. They find that changes in real disposable income and the voter's subjective evaluation of his individual financial well-being significantly affect congressional races involving in-party incumbents but do not affect elections where the incumbent is not running for re-election. They conclude that the assignment of responsibility for economic management of the economy is crucial. The critical factors here appear to be the combined membership in the president's party and actually having been in Congress. This assigns the president key responsibility but makes it clear that simply sharing the party label is not sufficient to incur blame (or reward) for existing economic conditions.

The Hibbing and Alford findings are more policy-oriented and retrospective than are conclusions reached by Kuklinski and West (1981), who also look at congressional support. These findings, however, suggest support for senators will be more responsive to economic conditions. They argue that the essential pattern of evaluation is a prospective rather than a retrospective one. That is, people use present conditions to form expectations of future economic conditions rather than using voting as a simple referendum indicating pleasure or discontent with past performance.

Similar findings are reported by Lau and Sears (1981) in their microlevel analysis of support for President Carter. Only when voters blamed the president for their individual economic hardships, were personal economic grievances politically significant. These findings, which suggest different public responses to the perceived economic priorities of the two main political parties, essentially confirm the findings of Kinder et al. concerning the political importance of collective economic judgments. While Lau and Sears do not extend the empirical demonstration offered by Kinder and Kiewiet or by Hibbing and Alford, their arguments are particularly interesting in drawing attention to the social psychological literature on the importance of attributions of causality in determing political responses to the economy, a phenomenon that may have a unique American tone in its emphasis on individualism and self-reliance (see Brody and Sniderman 1977).

The literature summarized above demonstrates the importance of Kramer's work in reopening discussion of the political importance of aggregate economic conditions. Kramer's importance is broader still, however, since his work also stimulated sophisticated econometric analysis both of voting in countries other than the United States and of incumbent popularity.

THE ECONOMY AND INCUMBENT POPULARITY:
THE PUBLIC OPINION POLLS

Support for American Presidents from FDR to Ford

Early findings on the economy's impact on presidential popularity, usually measured by Gallup Poll data, are as mixed as the findings on voting. Wesley Clark's (1943) early analysis finds Roosevelt's popularity affected by income and relief expenditures, but his techniques and data are too unsophisticated to produce definitive results. John Mueller's (1970, 1973) econometric analysis of wars, unemployment, and popularity is the first important recent analysis. Mueller finds unemployment affects popularity, but only after he assumes the public blames but does not reward the president for economic changes. This asymmetrical effect corresponds to the findings on voting noted by Bloom and Price and confirmed by Arcelus. However, Hibbs's (1974) technical reanalysis of Mueller's data suggests these findings are unreliable when subjected to rigorous statistical tests and that the relationship Mueller noted is not definitive.

Jong Lee and Jeffrey Milstein (1973) explain presidential popularity during the Vietnam War through inflation, unemployment, and the number of Americans killed in action. In later work, Lee (1975) expands analysis to include press attention, presidential activity from 1948 to 1973, and several political proxy variables. He finds inflation, income, and unemployment significantly influence popularity, with voters more likely to punish the Republicans for unemployment and the Democrats for inflation.

Henry Kenski (1977a, 1977b, 1977c, 1979) has contributed several works to the debate. Unfortunately, his results concerning the impact of inflation and unemployment on popularity are mixed, and occasionally even contradictory. His final conclusion seems to be that the relationship between these economic predictors and popularity is not a

TABLE 1-3. The Economy and Presidential Popularity

Author	Date	Main Variables Used in Analysis	Findings	General Conclusion: Does the Economy Affect Voting or Popularity?
Clark	1943	Roosevelt popularity, national income, federal relief expenditures.	Economy affects popularity particularly among those on relief.	yes
Mueller	1970, 1973	Presidential popularity, unemployment, public attitudes on wars.	Increase in unemployment hurts president's popularity but decreases do not help it.	yes, asymmetric effect
Hibbs	1974	Reanalysis of Mueller's data: unemployment, public support for wars and presidents.	Wars, unemployment not affect popularity.	no
Lee, Lee and Milstein	1975, 1973	Popularity, income, inflation, unemployment, political variables.	Income and inflation affect popularity. Democrats more likely to be punished for inflation and Republicans for unemployment.	yes
Stimson and LeGette	1975	Popularity, time, economy, war, international rally events.	Popularity simply decreases over time.	no
Stimson	1976	Presidential popularity, time.	Popularity erodes over time.	no

40

Author	Year	Variables	Findings	Economic effect
Kernell	1977	Presidential popularity, prices, unemployment.	Popularity affected by inflation and weakly by unemployment.	yes
Kenski	1977, 1979	Presidential popularity, inflation, unemployment.	Several studies, findings contradictory. Suggests any relationship may not be linear.	unclear
Monroe	1978	Popularity, inflation, unemployment, stock market, military expenditures, income.	Inflation and military expenditures affect popularity.	yes
Kernell	1978	Popularity, time, unemployment, political events, inflation.	Inflation and unemployment have only a weak impact, political variables important.	yes, but slight
Zeller and Carmines	1978	Truman's popularity, unemployment and time.	Unemployment little impact.	no
Shapiro and Conforto	1980	Popularity, economic conditions, and perceptions of these conditions.	Perceptions important.	yes
Golden and Poterba	1980	Presidential popularity (Gallup). Rate of change in urban worker consumer price index, unemployment, real disposable income, incumbency variable, duration in office, Watergate, fiscal, monetary, and transfers policy.	The economic stimulus needed to gain even small popularity gains is substantial, e.g., over $5 billion of increased spending to purchase one point of popularity. Concludes that there is little evidence that fiscal, monetary, or transfers policy are affected by electoral cycles.	yes

TABLE 1-3. Continued

Author	Date	Main Variables Used in Analysis	Findings	General Conclusion: Does the Economy Affect Voting or Popularity?
Monroe and Levi	1983	Gallup popularity of presidents. Survey estimates of economic expectations, 1950-1975. Inflation, income growth, military expenditures, and war proxy.	Expectations of economic growth affect presidential popularity. Inflationary expectations have no political consequences but the mere existence of uncertainty over future inflation hurts presidential popularity.	yes

42

linear one. Work by James Stimson and Caroline LeGette (1975), and later by Stimson alone (1976), agrees with Kenski's speculations on linearity. Stimson and LeGette argue that presidential popularity is almost exclusively the result of temporal approval cycles having less to do with the characteristics or actions of specific incumbents than with unrealistic public expectations early in a president's term. After examining the importance of the economy, wars, and international rally events, they conclude that these factors have only a slight impact on popularity. Their analysis concludes that the most important cause of fluctuations in presidential popularity is the passage of time.

The Stimson argument that popularity fluctuates in a particular pattern over time regardless of presidential actions has been seriously challenged. In an analysis that assumes a more sophisticated, lagged economic-memory pattern, Monroe finds the economy an important predictor of popularity while Stimson's cyclical variables are not (Monroe 1978). Samuel Kernell (1978) argues that Stimson's time variable is merely a surrogate for other phenomena that can be operationalized more fully. He expands on Mueller's work suggesting that voters assign political blame but not reward to the president, and finds presidential popularity is strongly affected by inflation. Unemployment and income have only a weak impact and then only for some presidents. Minor work by Zeller and Carmines (1978), which unfortunately ignores the considerations raised by Kernell and Monroe, examines Truman's popularity in terms of time and unemployment. They find unemployment has little independent effect on popularity. Recent work by Monroe and Levi (1983) confirms Monroe's earlier findings on the economy's political importance, with economic expectations and economic uncertainty being key determinants of presidential popularity.

Public Support for Incumbents Outside the United States

Several works by Bruno Frey and various colleagues consider popularity in different national contexts, one of which is the United States. They find trends in American presidential popularity significantly related to the economy, when they allow more fully for the effects of personality and the traditional decline in presidential popularity over time. Their substantive results shift somewhat, however, depending on the specific analysis, but it usually transpires that changes in unemployment, changes in prices, and income growth all have a significant influence on popularity. An increase in the unemployment level causes presidential popularity to decline by about 3.5 percentage points, a rise in inflation results in a decrease of about 1.5 percentage points, and an increase in the growth rate of nominal disposable income increases popularity by roughly 0.5 percentage points. In later work, Frey (1979) finds unemployment, real disposable income, and changes in price significantly affect presidential popularity between 1953 and 1976. Frey does not include political variables in this model but still argues for their inclusion. This work strengthens his earlier admonition to incorporate political variables into econometric analyses, a judgment reached also by Robert Shapiro and Bruce Conforto (1980) in their analysis of the link between aggregate economic conditions and the voter's perception of changes in his individual and family economic situation.

It is worthwhile to note several important works on the economic influences on incumbent popularity in other countries. Most of these works focus on aggregate responses to incumbents. Analyses of British government popularity or party support are not definitive, although many are technically sophisticated. Samuel Brittan (1962), David Butler and Donald Stokes (1969), and C. Goodhart and R. Bhansali (1970) find the economy has a strong political impact. Henry Burant (1965) is more qualified in his conclusions. Bruno Frey and Hermann Garbers (1971) suggest that the British Gallup popularity series may simply represent an autoregressive process with random shocks and that any relationship detected between unemployment and popularity actually originates in popularity.

Later work by Frey and Schneider (1982) proposes a two-sector politicoeconomic model that includes both the popularity function of the government and a government response function.[31] When this model is applied to Germany, the United States, and the United Kingdom, economic variables, such as unemployment, income, and changes in prices, are found to significantly influence popularity.[32] Political factors, such as the depreciation in popularity and an autonomous election cycle, are also significant.

Perhaps one of the most thorough analyses of British government and opposition popularity is by W. Miller and M. Mackie (1973). Their conclusion, that "the apparently strong link between . . . unemployment and inflation and government popularity in the 1959–1967 period was not in reality so strong as has been thought," downplays the idea that voters choose between "competing teams of economic managers" and calls for more sensitive statistical techniques to detect the complex relationship between the economy and political popularity (Miller and Mackie 1973).

Work on French political parties by Rosa and Amson (1976) finds that increases in inflation and unemployment tend to increase the vote for leftist parties, while rises in real income decrease the leftist vote. (The parties are treated here as a bloc, despite any interparty conflicts.) Lafay (1977) finds that rising inflation and unemployment decrease support for the incumbent French prime minister, and Lewis-Beck (1980) confirms this finding in his analysis of support for both the French prime minister and the president between 1968 and 1975. According to Lewis-Beck, "adverse economic conditions hurt the prime minister somewhat more than the president" because the president is able to deflect some of the blame for economic deterioration to the prime minister.[33] Unfortunately, Lewis-Beck fails to provide any theoretical explanation of why or how this happens. Nor does he consider why the reverse phenomenon does not occur, i.e., why the prime minister does not receive more credit for improved economic conditions. While Lewis-Beck's analysis is more sophisticated than earlier analyses in its inclusion of a variable for time in office (a significant influence) and the war in Algeria (no effect), his and other works on French politics are essentially atheoretical replications of empirical analyses done in the United States. Lewis-Beck later expands his analysis of European political support to include the French and Italian multiparty systems (Lewis-Beck and Bellucci 1982). They find that deteriorating economies significantly increase the leftist legislative vote. These models, that divide votes into government and opposition, predicted actual vote share and forecasted the 1980 Communist party support in Italy as well as the 1981 French victory by the Socialists.

Frey (1978, 1979a, 1979b) and Frey and Schneider (1978) look at cross-national popularity functions in the United States, the United Kingdom, the Federal Republic of Germany, and Sweden. The results are not totally consistent. The first works (1978 and 1979a) suggest that while the time in office and political factors specific to each incumbent do have important political effects, the economic impact on incumbent popularity is always substantial. Although in subsequent work, Frey argues for inclusion of both political and economic variables in a politicometric analysis, he fails to incorporate them into his first empirical estimations of the popularity function. In still later work done with Schneider (1980) on German and American popularity functions, he concludes that the specific popularity level of governments or presidents must be included in the

TABLE 1-4. The Economy and Political Support: Cross-National or Non-U.S. Recent Works

Author	Date	Main Variables Used in Analysis	Findings	General Conclusion: Does the Economy Affect Support?
Miller and Mackie	1973	Popularity in Britain, unemployment, and inflation.	Relationship not as strong as earlier works had thought.	weak
Rosa and Amson	1976	French party support, inflation, and unemployment.	Increases in inflation and unemployment help leftist vote; increases in income hurt it.	yes. Class effects strong
Lafay	1977	Support for French prime minister, inflation and unemployment.	Inflation and unemployment hurt support for prime minister.	yes
Frey, Frey and Schneider	1978, 1979, 1980, 1981, 1982	Popularity, unemployment, inflation, private consumption expenditures, various political variables.	Effect varies in different countries. In U.S. unemployment affects popularity; prices and income affect popularity only after an individual president's personality and honeymoon decline are allowed for.	yes
Lewis-Beck	1980	Support for French prime minister and president, inflation, unemployment, time, and Algerian war.	Inflation and unemployment hurt the prime minister more than the president.	yes. Effect varies by office

Author	Year	Variables	Findings	Economy matters
Inoguchi	1980	Japanese support for Liberal Democrats and government, income prices, time in office and frequency of elections, structural variables.	Economy affects support for government and incumbent party; greater impact seen in public opinion data than in voter turnout.	yes
Paldam and Schneider	1980	Danish popularity, inflation, unemployment, real wages, balance of payments, and direct taxes.	Economy key for 4-5 quarters. Socialists more affected by unemployment, and Liberals and Conservatives by taxes.	yes. Important party effects. Political climate limits economic impact.
Hibbs and Vasilatos	1981	Inflation, unemployment, real income growth, support for Pompidou and Giscard d'Estaing.	Public sensitive to relative rather than absolute economic performance. Real growth more important than nominal economic conditions (income versus inflation), therefore government policies which cut back unemployment, real output, and income growth to control inflation are not likely to increase public support for French incumbents.	yes
Hibbs and Madsen	1981	Swedish support for governing parties, unemployment, income, tax transfer policies.	Inflation, unemployment, and tax gap key predictors.	yes
Schneider, Pommerhene and Frey	1981	Voting in Swiss referenda, labor market, inflation, and income.	Inflation and income affect voting; unemployment little impact.	mixed
Lewis-Beck and Bellucci	1982	French and Italian multiparty voting, economic conditions, time in office.	Deteriorating economies affect leftist legislature vote.	yes

47

equation and that unemployment is the most important macroeconomic predictor of popularity, one that has a negative impact. Changes in prices and income are also significant, but government expenditures, taxes, and the national balance of payments do not specifically affect popularity.[34] Frey and Schneider discount the use of both lagged and expectations models since they find no strong indication that German and American voters consider the recent past or expected future state of the economy in their assessment of the government's performance. They do argue for class effects, finding that in the United States "high income recipients value price stability relatively more strongly than full employment [and] low income recipients value full employment relatively more. . . ."[35] Although they reach no specific conclusions on the importance of party affiliation of the incumbent president, their work does support the importance of this variable since they break down their American data into separate periods for the Eisenhower, Kennedy/Johnson, and Nixon/Ford administrations. (Here the level of statistical significance often falls below 95 percent, however, because of the smaller sample size.)

Takashi Inoguchi (1980) analyzes economic conditions and mass public support in Japan from 1960 to 1976, a period in which the Liberal Democratic party dominated the political scene. Inoguchi measures support by both electoral turnout and public opinion polls indicating approval of the ruling Liberal Democrats and the government. In his analysis, annual changes in income and prices are the economic predictors, tenure in office and frequency of elections are the political predictors, and he uses several base variables, e.g., trend in support for the Liberal party and the government, to measure the structural components of the system. He finds that economic conditions do significantly affect mass public support for the government and the incumbent party, with support for the government being more affected by economic conditions. Prices are slightly more important in the short term, while changes in income, even during a period of continuous economic growth, have the most important political impact in the long term. Inoguchi finds that the economy has a greater impact on public opinion measures of support than on voter turnout. Here he may be said to side with Goodman and Kramer in their debate with Arcelus and Meltzer, although the fact that turnout is so strongly influenced by the economy gives support to Arcelus and Meltzer's basic thesis.

Hibbs and Madsen (1981) analyze the importance of

macroeconomic conditions on aggregate political support for Swedish governing parties from 1967 to 1978. The authors assume and test the idea that voters evaluate relative rather than absolute economic performance, with mass political support for the government based on its cumulative performance records. They conclude that management of the economy is central in electoral shifts, with contemporaneous economic performance, as measured through the 1979 Jonung and Wadensjo model, being less important than the cumulated impact of deviations from the customary or expected economic performance. They test predictors of political support that include the rate of change in popularity, the rate of unemployment, the growth rate of per capita disposable income, and the difference between the growth rate of posttax, posttransfer per capita disposable income and pretax, pretransfer per capita earnings. (This variable measures "the wedge between the growth streams of final disposable income and original market income opened up by the state tax and transfer policies.")[36] The cumulated deviations, inflation, unemployment, and the tax gap were the crucial predictors of electoral support. Similar work on France by Hibbs and Vasilatos (1981) found the public sensitive to relative rather than absolute economic performance.

Martin Paldam and Friedrich Schneider (1980) look at government and opposition popularity in Denmark from 1957 to 1978. They divide their analysis into two separate time periods to reflect the shifting political climate in Denmark. For the 1957–1968 period, they find the government held responsible for changes in inflation, unemployment, real wages, the balance of payments, and direct but not indirect taxes. Voters tend to forget economic events within four to five quarters. The economy's impact on party support is more varied, with Socialist popularity more influenced by unemployment, and that of the Liberals and Conservatives by prices and taxes. The results for the 1972–1978 period are more mixed, and Paldam and Schneider draw only tentative conclusions for this period. In later work, Paldam is engaged in a study of the stability hypothesis presented here. To this end, he has expanded his economic analysis to include 145 national elections held in Australia, Belgium, Canada, Denmark, Eire, France, Germany, the Netherlands, Italy, Japan, New Zealand, Norway, Austria, Sweden, the United Kingdom, and the United States.[37]

An inquiry by Schneider, Pommerhene, and Frey (1981) into voting in Swiss referenda finds the condition of the labor market had little impact between 1951 and 1976. This finding is hardly surprising, since Switzerland had virtually no unemployment until 1974. Inflation had a negative impact, and the growth of real income a positive impact.

Group-Level Analyses

Several group-level analyses are worth discussing more fully. Work by Schneider (1978) is the first published analysis of U.S. popularity among different economic groups. Schneider begins his two-part analysis with a monthly examination of presidential popularity from April 1969 through October 1976. His goal is to determine the exact relationship between approval of the president and the economic and noneconomic influences, defined here as personality factors. He finds that both kinds of influence are important. Popularity is "significantly and quantitatively" affected by inflation, unemployment, and growth of per capita disposable income.[38] An increase of 1 percent in unemployment is associated with decreases in popularity of about 4 percent, and 1 percent in the annual growth rate of inflation with a 2 percent decrease in popularity.[39] Schneider does not include income and unemployment in the same analysis because of multicollinearity, and also because he believes that unemployment is the more important predictor.

The second part of Schneider's work tests his models with data on popularity among different income and occupation groups during the same 1969–1976 period. This kind of analysis is particularly important since, as Schneider notes, members of different income and occupation groups are not affected uniformly by macroeconomic changes, and therefore their political response to those changes should differ. In fact, Schneider does find that unemployment has a stronger negative impact on presidential popularity among lower- and middle-income groups than among the upper-income classes. Conversely, inflation has a stronger effect on presidential popularity among upper-income voters. Schneider finds that the economy's political significance varies even more according to occupation.[40] He gives no explanation of why this is so, however, but merely offers the general conclusion that "the impact of a changing economic situation on presidential popularity differs considerably among various groups of society."[41]

Schneider's work resembles Mueller's, Kenski's, and Kernell's in stressing both economic and political influences on popularity but, in fact, his political analysis contains little not found in these earlier works. To detect all of the specific characteristics attributable to each president—the president's party affiliation, the electorate's perception of his relationship with Congress and the bureaucracy, the size of the president's majority when he entered office, and his personal appeal on the media—he uses only one dummy variable: a simple linear variable with ascending values of 1, 2, 3, . . . for each month of a president's term.[42] Although this resembles Mueller's coalition-of-minorities variable, it lacks the theoretical logic and specificity of Mueller's variable. And it does not allow for the nonlinear fluctuations in popularity over time that were first identified by Stimson.

Similarly, Schneider's Watergate dummy variable is set equal to 1, 3, 5, 6, 10 . . . . 10 for March 1973 through August 1974, and zero at other times. No rationale is given for this choice of sequence. Nor does Schneider make any attempt to find a more solid, impartial indicator based on the number or timing of disclosures about Watergate, such as Kernell's measure of Watergate disclosures in several major newspapers.

A recent group-level analysis by Jonung and Wadensjo (1981) focuses on public support for the Swedish Social Democratic party from January 1970 to June 1979. It is worthy of detailed comment because of its sensitivity to, and creative capturing of, political reality. The authors divide their analysis into two periods: the period when the Social Democrats held power (January 1970 to September 1976) and the period when the party was out of power (October 1976 to June 1979). They focus on the political response to the economy among men and women and among different income, age, and employment groups. Income is categorized as low, middle, or high, with no further details given on the precise breakdowns. The age groups are: 16–24, 25–39, 40–49, 50–64, and 65–70 (the last group shifts to 65–75 and 65–80, depending on the time period analyzed). Respondents are categorized according to employment status to include housewives, students, pensioners, business owners, and public and private sector employees.

Unlike Schneider, Jonung and Wadensjo do not confine their inquiry to the economy's importance for political support among different groups. They also seek to explain differing group political responses by allowing for group differentials in economic conditions, in particular, by their measures of unemployment and inflation. Total labor force unemployment is considered, as are unemployment rates for both men and women, for those in age groups 18–24, 25–54, and 55–74, and for insured industrial workers. Different inflation rates are measured by the consumer price index (CPI) and the food price index. The logic behind their breakdown is as follows: Voters in a particular socioeconomic or age group should respond more strongly to the unemployment rate for their group than to the average unemployment rate. Older voters, particularly pensioners, are held to be more sensitive to inflation, although it is also argued that they might be less affected by short-term economic fluctuations in general since they have more experience and presumably longer economic memories. Groups whose employment status should provide stronger ties to the labor market, e.g., business owners, are expected to respond more strongly to unemployment than to inflation. The authors also argue that housewives and students should respond more to unemployment than to inflation, although their rationale for the housewives' expected response is never made clear.[43]

Jonung and Wadensjo find that empirical results are strongly influenced by whether the Social Democratic party is in power or not. When the Social Democrats hold power, unemployment has a strong importance among all groups except the oldest voters; its political impact is greatest among middle-income and young people. The kind of unemployment does not seem to affect this relationship much, although loss of jobs by insured industrial workers is more important than total unemployment to judge from the R^2. (Many of these divergencies can be explained by sampling errors in the labor force survey.)

Jonung and Wadensjo draw no definitive conclusions from the findings on inflation, which are mixed. A few surprises are noted: Male support for the ruling Social Democratic party is affected more by food prices, whereas women's support is related to consumer prices. Support among housewives and students seems to be affected as much by prices as by unemployment. Pensioners are more affected by inflation than by unemployment.

The second part of this work analyzes support for the Social Democratic party during the period when the party was in opposition. Here the relationships are reversed, as expected: Rising inflation and unemployment enhanced the party's popularity. The authors' general conclusion is that there are important group differences in public response to the economy, and that analyses that estimate only aggregate patterns will miss these significant group divergences.

Recent work by Hibbs (1982) analyzes political support among British occupational classes from late 1962 through 1978. Hibbs adopts the traditional view of class, arguing that macroeconomic fluctuations will evoke differing group political responses because the economic burdens and rewards are distributed unevenly throughout society. He cites public opinion data supporting the view that "lower status groups are likely to exhibit greater concern about unemployment and less concern about inflation than higher status groups"[44] and accepts Schneider's view that the public's preferences and objective economic interests concerning macroeconomic conditions and policies are class related.[45] His analysis selects occupational position, rather than income, as the best way to detect class response to the economy. His model assumes voters evaluate the cumulative performance of the governing party and compare it with the prior performance of the party in opposition. Without identifying it as such, Hibbs thus appears to accept a retrospective voting model as developed by Fiorina, in juxtaposition to the prospective voting model assumed by the more traditional policy-oriented analysts and those who stress the importance of expectations, e.g., Alt, or Kuklinski and West. Hibbs also assumes voters' economic memories are oriented heavily to current and recent events, and that memories fade in a geometrically declining lag structure. Hibbs's logit model includes government specific constants and shifting signs to allow for incumbency. It also makes endogenous the honeymoon effects and the time trends noted by the other analysts, thus putting the ad hoc dummy variables and time-trend terms of earlier models into a more mathematically precise model.[46]

Hibbs tests his model using quarterly data from 1962 through 1978, the period of the Macmillan-Home to the Wilson-Callaghan cabinets. He includes two unemployment measures—the level of unemployment and the percentage rate of the change of unemployment rate—to distinguish between the unemployment rate and the movement into or out of recession. He also analyzes both the CPI inflation (P) and the rate of acceleration of prices ($P_t - P_{t-1}$). He argues that the price acceleration term ($P_t - P_{t-1}$) measures inflationary surprises. He includes the growth rate of real personal, disposable income and a variable on the exchange rate, the change in the dollars-per-pound rate of exchange.

The findings suggest to Hibbs that there is considerable variation in the political response of occupational classes and that these are in line with the traditional wisdom in the area: Non-manual, middle-class voters support Conservative governments more than Labour governments, while the working class, especially semiskilled and unskilled workers, is more supportive of Labour governments. (Hibbs omits any earlier consideration of partisan affiliations in affecting this process.) He finds no erosion of class political alignments over this period, as Butler and Stokes[47] and Crewe, Sarlvik and Alt[48] have found.[49] He concludes that there is "no evidence of a persistent decline in the fundamental occupational class assignment of political support for Labour and Conservative governments."[50]

Hibbs concludes that British voters have extended economic memories, as do American voters, and that it takes almost five years for a government's record to be evaluated only on its own basis and not in juxtaposition to and with a discount factor that contrasts it to the previous government's economic record.[51]

Hibbs finds the rate of change of unemployment small compared to the unemployment level, which has important political consequences. The same is true for income. Hibbs finds the class responses as anticipated. He writes off several slight discrepancies in this as probably reflecting the inclusion of widows and state pensioners in the semiskilled- and unskilled-worker category. Exchange rates had a mixed political impact. He argues that, although there are no good time-series data on class preferences concerning the desired trade-off between inflation and unemployment, "it is clear that the politically acceptable short run macroeconomics policy trade-offs in Britain differ considerably across occupational classes. . . ."[52] When Hibbs translates his logit coefficients into percentage terms, he finds the political responses to macroeconomic changes among occupational classes are substantial. The cross-class variations are consistent with Hibbs's earlier findings. Working-class support is more responsive to macroeconomic conditions under Labour than Conservative governments. Middle-class support responds to economic conditions more during Conservative administrations. Hibbs argues that this suggests the decline in class loyalties noted by earlier analysts was generated not by a weakening in general class loyalties, so much as by the lower economic classes responding more to the economic distress during the Wilson-Callaghan governments.[53] In other words, working-class loyalties to Labour conflict with extreme working-class sensitivity to economic downturn and magnify the usual political response to economic downturn. Hibbs concludes that downward movements in class-based political support occur only during Labour governments, and presumably only Labour governments in office during hard economic times. The pattern of this decline is thus cyclical rather than secular to Hibbs.

Hibbs (1982b) performed a similar analysis for American class and occupational groups. This work offers some advance in the handling of political variables in a technically proficient econometric model. Hibbs analyzes quarterly Gallup data from 1961 to 1979, looking only at occupational and partisan groups. His economic predictors include aggregate unemployment, the rate of inflation, and the rate of change in per capita disposable personal income. Political variables include the number of Americans killed in Vietnam, a measure of Watergate events, and a rally variable similar to Mueller's. Analysis of the same econometrically sophisticated lagged logit model described above finds that Republicans are more sensitive to inflation and Democrats more sensitive to shifts in unemployment, income, and Vietnam casualties.[54]

Despite the technical precision of the Hibbs model, his analysis of American data suffers from some of the same defects as his British analysis and as Schneider's earlier work. None of Hibbs's work moves beyond an aggregate measure of unemployment, for example, failing to compare white-collar unemployment rates with presidential popularity or government support among white-collar workers. And neither work considers political responses to the president among groups that we know traditionally bear a disproportionate share of economic hardships: blacks and young people. Finally, neither the Hibbs nor the Schneider model develops a broad theoretical concept for their noneconomic variables, with the Watergate variables, for example, remaining simply an ad hoc construction to measure a temporary phenomenon in American political life.

Hibbs's British work was subject to a critical formal critique of the honeymoon period by Keech, who argued that there may be a honeymoon period whose length is absolute rather than relative to and dependent on the evaluation of the other party's economic performance. A formal critique of the model, while useful technically, ignores other more basic criticisms of Hibbs's work. First, his model omits any provisions for a partisan filter even though Hibbs acknowledges its tremendous importance in affecting the underlying support for both Labour and Conservative support. Secondly, his British model omits all political factors, and the American model includes few of these factors. The work reflects sophisticated technical skills but surprising obtuseness in political factors. Finally, Hibbs ignores much of the earlier work in this area. His criticism of earlier studies for focusing only on aggregate survey data is appropriate for most early works; but Hibbs ignores the earlier empirical works on occupational class by Schneider, Jonung and Wadensjo, and Alt's work on expectations, as well as Weatherford's theoretical criticism of the distinction between class and status, a distinction that may be particularly important in Britain. Hibbs contrasts his lagged model with "previous studies

TABLE 1-5. The Economy and Popularity: Recent Group-Level Analyses

Author	Date	Main Variables Used in Analysis	Findings	General Conclusion: Does the Economy Affect Popularity?
Schneider	1978	Presidential popularity, growth of per capita disposable income, inflation, proxy variable for each president, and Watergate.	Unemployment, income, and inflation affect popularity.	yes. Strong class effects with inflation more important for upper income/occupation groups, and unemployment for lower income/occupation groups.
Jonung and Wadensjo	1981	Support for Swedish Social Democratic party, group income, and unemployment.	Important class effects, although students and housewives as greatly affected by prices as by unemployment.	yes. Important class effects.
Hibbs	1982	British support, unemployment (levels and rate), inflation and price acceleration, growth of real personal, disposable income, and a variable on exchange rates.	Important class effects. Public has extended economic memories.	yes. Class effects are crucial.

| Hibbs | 1982 | U.S. partisan and occupational group support for president, unemployment, rate of inflation, rate of change in per capita disposable personal income, number of Americans killed in Vietnam, Watergate, and rally proxies. | Republicans are more sensitive to inflation; Democrats to unemployment. | yes. Partisan ties are central. |

embodying the unrealistic assumption that only current performance, evaluated absolutely, affects mass support for governments."[55] Again, however, this ignores much earlier work in the area. Stigler, Tufte, and Kramer, for example, each examined the discreet change in economic conditions between the election and the date when a party takes office. Monroe's Almon distributed lag model assumed economic memories are cumulative and gradual with more recent events having the greatest impact.[56] There is a vast literature on modeling inflationary expectations that is technically proficient and politically astute. Hibbs ignores this work, as he does Alt's important work on the political importance of economic expectations in Britain.

THE ECONOMY AND MICROLEVEL POLITICAL RESPONSES

Fiorina's Retrospective Voting Model

Analysts have recently begun using survey data to test the theoretical propositions of mathematical models of microeconomic influences on voting. Morris Fiorina's (1978) application of his retrospective voting model (1974) to microeconomic influences on congressional and presidential voting from 1952 to 1974 is one of the best examples, and is the one that spurred much work in this area.

Fiorina defines economic retrospective voting models as those in which voters evaluate a past performance, with good economic conditions causing them to accord approval to incumbents and bad economic conditions causing them to blame incumbents. He classifies Kramer's model as a retrospective voting model. Disagreeing with Stigler's negative conclusions on retrospective voting, Fiorina argues that whether people vote retrospectively is still an open question. He suggests that econometric studies of retrospective voting have relied too much on voting data. Fiorina argues that many important questions in this area cannot be answered using aggregate or macro data; we need, instead, to measure individual microlevel responses to the economy, which requires the use of survey data. In particular, Fiorina points to the Survey Research Center's (SRC) election studies as an untapped source of insight into such questions as which political party is considered strong on which economic policies and which economic issues voters consider most important.

Fiorina analyzes the SRC American national election studies from 1952 to 1974 to answer the following three questions: (1) Is there an individual-level basis for the party prospers in good times and suffers in poor times, regardless of whether it is actually responsible for these economic conditions, Fiorina compares presidential voting with responses to perceived changes in an individual's economic situation. He finds a weak relationship when looking at percentages. When he employs a logit model to test the monotonicity of the relationship between perceived economic situation and support for the incumbent party, however, Fiorina finds mixed results. Presidential votes appear to be related to an individual's current economic situation. How the individual perceives his own economic situation has some relationship to voting in on-year congressional elections, but no relationship to midterm congressional voting. Fiorina therefore disagrees with Tufte's conclusion that midterm elections are referenda on the incumbent administration's economic performance.

Fiorina next considers whether people believe there are important differences between the two parties on economic issues. He finds what he calls "circumstantial evidence" that they do. Employment, wage levels, and farm policies are considered Democratic issues; and voters concerned with these issues tend to vote Democratic. Government spending and taxation are held to be Republican issues. But inflation and prices are not seen as issues on which the parties differ. This evidence supports Stigler's theoretical speculations. Still, Fiorina is reluctant to draw definitive conclusions about the electoral importance of perceived party differences on economic issues because a voter may first choose a party and then accept its economic policy preference as his own. When Fiorina tests for this possibility by controlling for party identification, he finds that the control does diminish the basic relationship, particularly for Republicans, but does not wipe it out.

To determine whether it is an individual's personal economic situation or his assessment of overall economic conditions that influences his vote, Fiorina adds to his analysis questions on prices and on the individual respondent's unemployment status and his estimate of societal unemployment. He finds that the individual's perception of both his own economic situation and overall economic conditions affects presidential voting. Neither has a very strong influence on congressional voting, however, although here the evidence is inconclusive. And neither has any influence at all on midterm congressional elections.

Fiorina's general conclusions on the economy's influence on voting thus are mixed. He finds that voters do believe elections affect the economy. He disagrees with Arcelus and Meltzer in finding no relationship between economic strong influence on congressional voting, however, although here the evidence is inconclusive. And neither has any influence at all on midterm congressional elections.

Fiorina's general conclusions on the economy's influence on voting thus are mixed. He finds that voters do believe elections affect the economy. He disagrees with Arcelus and Meltzer in finding no relationship between economic conditions and participation, and with Tufte in finding no relationship between the economy and midterm congressional elections. He discovers evidence that an individual's economic situation affected presidential voting and congressional voting until 1960, but not thereafter, although much of this evidence is what he terms "circumstantial." He concludes that definitive answers in this area must await better information on voter expectations concerning the future economic situation and on whether individuals blame and reward the incumbent administration for particular economic conditions.

Fiorina's stress on expectations was followed up by work by James Kuklinski and Darrell West (1981) on the importance of economic expectations for voting in House and Senate elections. Kuklinski and West argue that a retrospective voting model may not accurately capture voter's politicoeconomic behavior and that a prospective model stressing expected future economic conditions may be more useful. They pose two questions: First, they ask whether there is a difference between voters' past economic experience and future economic expectations that is politically relevant. Their a priori reasoning argues in favor of the comparative political importance of expectations. They cite the aggregate studies by Arcelus and Meltzer[57] and Stigler[58] as essentially claiming voting is a forecasting process and Fair's (1978) work suggesting that the voter's discounting of past economic conditions is high, a claim also substantiated by most of the political business cycle literature.

Their second question addresses the public's assignment of economic responsibility and economic blame. Here Kuklinski and West focus on the possible differences between economic influences on House and Senate elections. They argue that earlier analysts have concentrated too much attention on House elections and cite extensive literature suggesting why Senators are more susceptible to economic voting than are Congressmen. Work by Erickson (1971) and Fenno (1975) on the greater importance of incumbency in the House suggests Senators are held more responsible for national problems and House members more as ombundsmen and providers of individualized services.

Work by Hinckley (1979) and Abramowitz (1979) finds Senate elections more competitive than House elections and suggests to Kuklinski and West that all issues, including economic ones, will be debated more vigorously in Senate elections. This they take to counter Kramer's claim that voting on economic grounds simplifies issues, i.e., they argue the economy will have a greater impact when the discussion of economic issues sensitizes the voter to his own economic position.

These propositions are tested by an empirical examination of 1978 CPS data. This analysis does find a divergence between individual respondent's perceptions of past economic conditions and their estimates of future economic conditions. Economic expectations have a strong impact on Senate elections but a limited impact on House voting, which is more affected by partisan identification and region. In their conclusion, Kuklinski and West argue that the limitations on the ability of political incumbents to control economic outcomes through macroeconomic policies may be one reason for the lack of economic influence on congressional voting, although their own work cites data suggesting that voters do hold Congress just as responsible for the economy as the president.

Microlevel Survey Data: The Linkage Between Collective Electoral Behavior and the Individual Voter

Works by Jeffrey Wides (1976) and Ricardo Klorman (1978) are similar to Fiorina's in their use of microlevel survey data to bridge the gap between the analysis of collective electoral behavior and that of individual voters. Wides's work concentrates on the electoral implications of individual perceptions of the trend in personal and family finances. In analyzing the SRC American national elections studies for 1964, 1968, and 1972, Wides discovers that a perceived improvement in personal finances is related to support for the incumbent presidential candidate. This relation is even stronger when he controls for party identification. Wides's study is important because of its emphasis on economic perceptions and its use of Katona's (1963) work on the psychological analysis of economic behavior. It is preliminary, however, and has been encompassed by Klorman's later work.

Klorman (1978) considers the impact of personal finances on voting for the presidency, Congress, governorships, and other state and local offices. Using SRC American national election data from 1956 to 1974, Klorman divides respondents into those who felt their personal and family financial situations had improved, worsened, or shown no change during the last year. Voting patterns for these three groups of respondents are then analyzed to test whether perceived economic improvement leads to voting for the party of the incumbent president and perceived deterioration leads to voting for the opposition party's candidates.

Using a simple correlation analysis, Klorman finds a relationship between the perceived trend in family finances and voting in about half of the elections analyzed. The influence varies considerably, however, depending on the office; voting in presidential and gubernatorial elections is more influenced by the economy than is voting in other elections. The relationship between the economy and voting is generally stronger in presidential election years. Klorman qualifies his conclusions, however, by noting that although there is some relationship between voting and perceived changes in the individual's economic situation, the perceived trend in family finance does not play an overwhelming role among the short-term forces that are responsible for deviations in the normal vote.

Stephen Weatherford's work (1978) on class differences in the political response to recession is another example of a sophisticated analysis of survey data that accepts the rational actor as its underlying premise. Weatherford considers the general hypothesis that economic downturn leads to dissatisfaction with political incumbents, and argues that the process by which this occurs is a subtle one in which economic effects are mediated by class status at a number of stages. He finds clear differences between the economic policies of the two political parties, and adopts the classical Phillips curve argument of a trade-off between unemployment and inflation, with the Democrats opting to increase employment in order to help the working class, and the Republicans concentrating on lowering inflation to aid the middle class.

Using SRC panel data from 1956 to 1960, Weatherford seeks the answers to four questions: (1) Was the working class hurt more than the middle class by the recession of the late 1950s? (2) Was this effect accurately perceived? (3) Are there class differences in perceptions of the parties in terms of domestic economic policies? and (4) Does an individual's class position influence the strength of his voting reaction to the economy?

In contrast to Klorman, Weatherford concludes that voters do respond to economic conditions as reflected in their personal financial situation and that of their families.

The political response to these economic situations is a function of the magnitude of economic change and is mediated by class status at a number of stages. Working-class families are more likely to respond politically to macroeconomic cycles, Weatherford concludes, since they are more adversely affected by worsening economic conditions.

Recent work by Weatherford (1982 and 1983) expands his work on class and points out a critical aspect of any class analysis within the American context: the U.S. and advanced industrialized societies in general are characterized by two distinct stratification systems. These differing stratification systems can be categorized, for simplicity's sake, into the Marxist-Dahrendorf emphasis on political and social relations of production, emphasizing discontinuous patterns of inequality (1982, 26) versus the status tradition of the Blau-Duncan paradigm stressing a more continuous approach to social inequality. While it is clear that inequality affects political opinions, the precise measurement of inequality chosen by the analyst will produce divergent findings concerning these political opinions. Analysts concerned with public opinion, or with the economy's impact on political support expressed through public opinion polls, thus must be wary of using "class" as a term that does not distinguish between these two concepts.

Many of the microlevel works, both because of the sociological orientation of their authors and because questions on socioeconomic status can be readily obtained from microsurvey data, move back into the noneconomic orientation toward understanding the relationship between presidential voting and popularity and the state of the economy. A microlevel analysis by Kinder and Abelson (1981), which grows out of an earlier survey of the literature on voting and political behavior, proposes that political behavior does not depend on an ideological struggle between the major parties on the voters' assessment of an administration's past performance, but rather on public perception of the candidates' personalities. In other words, the voters choose between two people, not two economic policies. Earlier work by Stokes (1966) and by Kagan and Caldeira (1975) argues that much of the change in party fortunes results from the turnover of candidates rather than from real shifts in party alignment. Kelley and Mirer (1974) also contend that people vote for the candidate whose personality they prefer, with party identification determining their choice only when they have no personal favorite. Markus and Converse capture this view of the central role played by candidates in the vote choice:

Candidate evaluations have shown to be primary determinants of the vote, with policy considerations and even partisan orientations affecting the vote either exclusively or largely through the way they help to shape feelings toward the presidential rivals. . . . In the American system of elections, the choice is ultimately between competing candidates.[59]

A recent work by Kinder and Abelson (1981) concludes that in the 1980 presidential election people's judgment of the candidates' competence, the integrity of the positive and negative feelings they have elicited, were more important factors than party identification, policy positions, or assessments of national economic conditions, all of which had primarily indirect effects. Although national economic conditions did hurt Carter, for example, they did not seem to affect Reagan's support, which was based less on his policy initiatives than on a general feeling that he would do better.[60]

These findings from microlevel analyses are useful, but their methodological generalizability has begun to evoke some serious questioning. A recent methodological analysis by Sears and Lau (1981) suggests some of the microlevel findings concerning the close association between respondents' personal economic situations and their political attitudes may be an artifact of the questionnaire construction.[61] The authors find that presidential job approval and policy preferences are significantly related to respondents' personal economic conditions only when the questions on personal economic situation are asked immediately preceding or following the questions on relevant political attitudes. This discovery is related to the theory of cognitive dissonance and the desire of people to find or present consistent views. Questions about political attitudes are "personalized" when they are asked directly after questions about the respondents' own economic situation, and questions about personal economic situations are "politicized" when they are asked immediately after respondents have indicated their political preferences.[62] The authors conclude that simple contextual factors—in other words, methodological artifacts—may be contributing to the close relationship seen between personal economic situation and political preference. Although Sears and Lau do not argue that there are no genuine linkages between personal economic situation and political attitude, their questions on methodological bias question findings of such linkages based on microlevel survey data.

The Sociotropic Voter Challenges the Pocketbook
Voter as the Concept of the Public Interest Reappears

Most of the works discussed above are based on rational decision-making theories that stress the cognitive, calculating, and utility-maximizing facets of human behavior. Encouraged by Key's (1966) claim that "voters are not fools," analysts like Downs (1957) and Riker and Ordeshook (1973) developed theories of electoral behavior that emphasize the issue proximity of voters and candidates. Fiorina (1978) and Tufte (1978) assume a looser relationship, arguing that voters make more general retrospective judgments of the incumbents' performance, and then give or withhold their political support on the basis of that judgment. The question of what constitutes a politically relevant issue is usually answered by analysts in this area in tangible economic terms of self-interest; usually these interests are those directly affecting the individuals' financial state, health, or family well-being. These analysts largely exclude nonmaterial goals or interests of voters.

Recent work begun by David Sears and expanded by Donald Kinder and several joint authors questions the wisdom of this economic emphasis. Sears provides a theoretical basis for a reformulation of political behavior by arguing that economic self-interest is too narrow a conceptualization to account for voting preferences. In particular, Sears et al. (1980) argue that self-interest, while important, has a limited utility in explaining voting behavior and that political attitudes "are formed mainly in congruence with long-standing values about society and the polity, rather than short-term instrumentalities for satisfaction of one's current private needs" (Sears et al. 1980, 671). The crucial empirical base here comes from Kinder's finding that even in the area of the economy's political impact on political support, the traditional concept of a pocketbook voter who maximizes his own self-interest has limited utility. Instead, Kinder submits that many voters act on the basis of their assessment of national economic well-being. Eventually, this empirical finding reintroduces the concept of the public interest into political behavior. Work in this area draws on the literature of symbiotic politics, which finds immediate self-interest is a weak predictor of political attitudes. The theoretical work by Sears, on which most of the studies by Kinder and his colleagues seem to be based, highlights the problem of analyzing political behavior strictly in rational terms, and suggests the beginnings of another debate in political science over the proper theoretical orientation to politics.

At the empirical level, Kinder's work, individually and with other authors, should be noted in some detail.[63] Kinder (1981) and Kinder and Kiewiet (1979) provide a sophisticated and thorough analysis of SRC data on congressional elections from 1956 to 1976. They distinguish between personal and collective economic concerns, and find that congressional voting is influenced not by a respondent's own economic situation but rather by his judgment of the collective economic situation. The specific factors Kinder and Kiewiet consider are the individual's unemployment status and his financial situation; they find no relationship between these and voting. The individual's assessment of general business trends, however, does have an impact on his voting. And the individual's assessment of the relative competence of the two political parties to manage the economy has an even stronger political impact. These findings seem particularly important in light of comments by Stigler and by Campbell et al. that the critical variable is the voter's perception that the two parties do actually differ in their ability to deal with a particular issue. Other work by Kiewiet and Kinder (1978) reaffirms their conclusion that "collective economic judgments had little to do with privately experienced economic discontents. Rather they stemmed from voters' conditions."[64] This work agrees with Fiorina's analysis of CPS data, although Fiorina uses only the subjective financial well-being item as an indication of personal economic hardship. Later work by Kiewiet (1983) provides further confirmation of this finding, as does work by Kinder and Mebane (1983) and by Kinder (forthcoming). Lau and Sears's (1981) study of the cognitive links between economic grievances and political responses also confirms the original Kinder and Kiewiet finding that collective judgments about the overall health of the economy are more important influences on political response than the individual's personal economic situation. (This was based on a 1979 CPS study in which President Carter's support was only rarely related to personal economic hardships.)

Brody and Sniderman (1977), Schlozman and Verba (1979), and Feldman (1982) offer an explanation of this lack of political response to an individual's personal economic situation that stresses the way people perceive the nature of responsibility for economic well-being. Scholzman and Verba emphasize the American dream of economic individualism as preventing the translation of personal experience with unemployment into political behavior. Feldman expands this work to suggest that Americans' belief in economic individualism "leads people to accept personal responsibility for their economic conditions, which in turn eliminates any connection between personal well-being and political evaluation."[65] In particular, Feldman's data suggest, though they do not explicitly test, that an American propensity to take responsibility for economic improvement may account for the asymmetrical relationship between economic conditions and voting noted by Bloom and Price (1975) and Mueller (1973).

As with the other microlevel analyses, several recent methodological works are relevant. Weatherford's analysis examines 1972–1974–1976 Survey Research Center data on the importance of personal and national economic situations for voting.[66] He disagrees with Kinder and Kiewiet on the classification of responses to particular questions as indicative of national economic well-being, or symbiotic or collective concerns. Kinder and Kiewiet put voters' evaluations of government economic policy and their party preferences on economic policy into the collective or symbiotic category. Weatherford argues that this classification confuses knowledge of economic events with the evaluation of them. The problem is essentially one of translating economic variables into political response. Weatherford uses an alternate coding scheme and finds no difference between symbiotic and personal economic conditions.[67]

Other methodological questions arise here. For example, most studies omit underemployment and sporadic or long-term unemployment. Lau and Sears (1981) also raise the question of a distinction between collective economic judgments, which indicate sociotropic beliefs about the economy as a whole, and policy evaluations of the government's or president's economic performance.[68] They warn that a key factor is the attribution of blame or reward, which depends on the assignment of economic responsibility to an incumbent. Their analysis uses a 1979 panel study to determine why it is so difficult to find a link between personal economic conditions at the microlevel but not at the aggregate level. First, they ask whether the measures of personal economic conditions are insufficient to detect an influence; they decide this is not the case. Then they ask whether people believe the president is not responsible for the economy, as Brody and Sniderman (1977) conclude. They find some evidence for this, but nothing definitive. Finally, they explore the sociotropic voter hypothesis advanced by Kinder and Kiewiet and find evidence to substantiate it. Still, their conclusion—that voters' political responses to the economy are based on collective judgments and have little or no personal relevance—makes no reference to their

TABLE 1-6. The Economy and Political Support: Microlevel Responses

Author	Date	Main Variables Used in Analysis	Findings	General Conclusion: Does Economy Affect Support?
Wides	1976	Presidential voting, individual's economic perceptions of personal finances.	Economic perceptions affect voting strongly, especially when controlling for party identification.	yes
Brody and Sniderman	1977	Unemployment, presidential support.	Working class blame selves for unemployment, middle class blames government, assignment of blame key.	yes
Fiorina	1978	Presidential and congressional voting, individual perceptions of personal and collective well-being.	Mixed feelings. Economy affects presidential voting (less after 1960); impact on congressional voting less certain.	yes, but evidence not definitive
Klorman	1978	Voting at all levels, perceived trend in family finances.	Economic perceptions affect voting for president and governor, less for others. Economy's impact not a major role though.	yes, somewhat
Weatherford	1978	Presidential voting, individual financial situation, controlling for class.	Individual financial situation affects voting, especially among working class.	yes

Author	Date	Main Variables Used in Analysis	Conclusions	
Schlozman and Verba	1979	Unemployment, voting.	Translation of personal experience with unemployment into political behavior is key. Class effects important.	yes
Kinder	1979	CPS data on estimation of government performance and of party competence; on family situation, family expectations, family unemployment experience, family impact of recession; and on presidential popularity for Nixon, Ford, and Carter.	The economy affects public support for the president. Presidential popularity is more affected by the public perception of the president's success in coping with the nation's economic problems (sociotropic voter hypothesis) than by individuals blaming the president for their own personal hardship (egocentric voter). Confirms sociotropic voter hypothesis over egocentric voter hypothesis.	
Kiewiet	1980/ 1981, 1983	CPS data: change in financial situation; voting for Congress, president; party identification, dummy variable for personal economic problems.	The unemployed turn to Democrats. Public sees inflation as a major problem the government should address, sees no party differences in handling the inflation problem. The costs of unemployment are substantial, objective, and concentrated among certain sectors of the labor force, while the costs of inflation are shared by all and center on psychological difficulties in coping with uncertainty.	
Kinder and Kiewiet	1979, 1981	Inflation, unemployment, and income, congressional voting,	American voters resemble more closely the sociotropic ideal (responds to change in general economic conditions)	

Table 1-6. Continued

Author	Date	Main Variables Used in Analysis	Conclusions
		individual unemployment and financial situation, national business trend.	than to the egocentric ideal. Political preferences to be shaped by the citizen's conception of national economic conditions.
Miller and Wattemberg	1981	CPS data: 1980 presidential vote; assessment of candidate performance, indices of economic issues, foreign policy, minority rights, and social issues; party identification and ideology.	Ratification model of politics supported, i.e., presidential performance and expected performance of challenger lead to vote. "Democratic theory" model, i.e., correspondence of candidate and voter issue positions yield vote, provides less adequate explanation. Partisan vote advantage associated with economic policy is partly a reflection of long-standing beliefs concerning party differences.
Hibbing and Alford	1981	Individual and aggregate data on voting, changes in real disposable personal income, voter's subjective evaluation of individual finances.	Income and subjective well being affect congressional voting only for incumbents of president's party. Assignment of responsibility for economic welfare is key in political response.
Kinder and Abelson	1981	1980 congressional voting, views of candidate competence, party ties, policy positions and assessments of national economic conditions.	Economy only indirect influence. Public views of candidates' competence more important.

Author	Year		
Weatherford	1981, 1982, 1983	Duncan socioeconomic index (averaging group income and education); income change (1974-76) and an omnibus index of impact of 1974-76 recession's impact on respondent and family. Inflation, unemployment, general economic policy. Marx-Dahrendorf class categories, perceived national business conditions, personal financial situation, and party affiliation.	Individual position within the class structure mediates both the personal impact from macroeconomic economic fluctuations and the way an individual responds politically.
Kuklinski and West	1981	Congressional voting. Economic well being, economic expectations.	Senate voting more responsive to economic conditions than House voting. Prospective not retrospective voting is key, with economic expectations central. Public debate of economy sensitizes voter to his own situation.
Sears and Lau	1981, 1982	Personal economic situations, national economic conditions, presidential job approval and policy preferences.	Contextual factors on survey may contribute to close association found between personal economic situation and political preference.
Kramer	1983	Methodological analysis of cross-sectional and aggregate data. Ecological fallacy as it may relate to sociotropic voter.	Cross-sectional analyses may yield misleading findings because of methodology. Questions conclusiveness of empirical demonstrations of sociotropic voting theory. Does not examine theory per se.

71

methodological work on questionnaire construction. This is somewhat surprising since presumably their own study suffers from the same methodological difficulties that plague the other microlevel surveys.

Finally, there is Kramer's (1983) mathematical inquiry on the differing results obtained from cross-sectional and aggregate time-series analyses of influences on political support. Kramer concludes that the findings using micro-analysis could easily be the result of mere white-noise effects from the data. Therefore he argues that conclusions based on these data may be accurate but are not definitive. Since aggregate data findings do not suffer from this possible white-noise problem, the examination of the sociotropic voter concept presented in Chapter 4 will be particularly important, although Norpoth and Yantek (1981) advance a similar methodological criticism of works using aggregate analysis, suggesting that earlier findings of an economic effect on the popularity of the West German chancellor and the French and American presidents are mere statistical artifacts.

The most serious challenges to the theoretical concept of a sociotropic voter comes from the Kramer (1983) and the Sears and Lau (1983) articles discussed above, both of which call into question the reliability of findings based on microlevel cross-sectional survey analyses. This criticism is particularly ironic in the case of Sears, who helped create the basic theoretical framework for the sociotropic voter and now asks the extent to which its empirical confirmation is the result of question placement.

CONCLUSION

This chapter's survey of the scholarly works on the economy's political impact demonstrates the long-accorded importance of the topic. Work in this area begins with very simple early studies of voting and ends with sophisticated econometric models of both voting and public opinion indicators of the mass political response to the economy. Much work has been done on the economy's impact on individuals and, in particular, on the political importance of economic perceptions. There is, however, a major gap in our knowledge of the economy's impact on key groups to the president, the politician who is assigned primary responsibility for the country. Chapter 2 will fill this gap by summarizing what is known about the economic influence on presidential popularity and outlining the major theoretical and empirical controversies in the area.

NOTES

1. Barnhart 1925, 540.

2. This is not very successful, however, and Tibbitts never clearly specifies the exact method of the weighting.

3. The index of per capita realized national income is adjusted by the cost of living and averaged over the years preceding the election and the election year. The political impact of this predictor is low ($r = 0.19$ for the period 1897 to 1940). The cost of living predictor is never defined more precisely, although Kerr does say it is corrected for century trend and averaged similarly to the income predictor. The political impact from this second cost of living predictor is also low ($r = 0.17$ from 1837 to 1936). The wholesale price index has a slightly higher political impact ($r = 0.29$ from 1861 to 1940). Kerr never provides data sources for his economic predictors and fails to give precise definitions of his variables or to explain why he analyzes different years for each predictor.

4. The number of cases is 189 of 289 from 1946 to 1952 and 162 of 236 from 1948 to 1958.

5. Illinois, $r = -0.15$; Indiana, $r = -0.23$; Iowa, $r = +0.01$; Ohio, $r = -0.03$; Pennsylvania, $r = -0.04$; Kansas, $r = +0.39$; Nebraska, $r = +0.32$; and California, $r = +0.24$.

6. Business activity is measured by the Cleveland Trust Company and the American Telephone and Telegraph indices of economic conditions between October of the election year and October two years earlier.

7. Bean, *How to Predict Elections*, 1948, 51.

8. It is defined at one point as one compiled by the Cleveland Trust and at another point as "Ayer's" index of economic well-being.

9. Key, with Cummings, 1966, 35.

10. Riker 1973; Fiorina 1978.

11. See Kramer (Bobbs Merrill Reprint), PS-498.

12. Kramer 1971, 134.

13. Kramer here ignores the limitations on the incumbent's control of the economy and the voter's realization and allowance for this fact.

14. All of these assumptions will be discussed more fully below.

15. Therefore Democratic vote refers to the share of vote received by the Democrats when they are the incumbent party and to the Democrats' share plus the minor-party share of the vote when the Republicans are the incumbent party. (A similar reverse definition holds for the operationalization of the Republican vote.)

16. Aside from the blame/reward effect that Kramer tests with this variable, Kramer sees incumbency as carrying both institutional advantages and disadvantages since voters may have high expectations with respect to economic improvements. This is the closest Kramer comes to measuring voters' expectations of economic conditions rather than actual conditions themselves.

17. Kramer 1971, 140–41.

18. Kramer 1971, 141.

19. Stigler 1973, 163.

20. The Beta = 0.47 and t = 3.12 with 1942 to 1944 omitted; Beta = 0.10 and t = 0.58 with 1944 to 1946 omitted.

21. These are unidentified by the authors. Arcelus and Meltzer 1975a, 1238.

22. Arcelus and Meltzer 1975a, 1238.

23. Goodman and Kramer 1975, 1255.

24. Goodman and Kramer 1975, 1264.

25. Arcelus 1978, 19.

26. Rosenstone 1982, 25.

27. See, for example, the arguments on statistical inference on 1259.

28. Because of the small number of observations (N = 8) on which this conclusion is based, Tufte undertakes several tests of his conclusion. First, he compares his results with Kramer's and finds congruence. Then he checks his model by excluding one election at a time from his computations and finds the R^2 never drops below 0.89 (1975, 818–19). Finally, he compares his model's predictors with actual votes and uses his model to predict the 1970 election. Again, the model performs well. Tufte therefore submits that his results are quite secure despite the small number of observations on which they are based (1975, 822). Since he finds that voting does not translate into House seats, however, he surmises that voters' attempts to use the midterm congressional elections as referenda on the president's economic policies are limited by the institutional structure of the electoral system.

29. Wright 1974, 37.

30. Unemployment is omitted since unemployment data are not readily available by counties.

31. See, for example, Frey and Schneider (1978b).

32. Their analysis of the United States examines only the government function and not the popularity function.

33. Lewis-Beck 1980, 82.

34. Frey and Schneider 1980, 81.

35. Frey and Schneider 1980, 82.

36. Hibbs and Madsen 1981, 35.

37. Results are incomplete at the time of press.

38. Schneider 1978, 53.
39. Schneider 1978, 64.
40. Schneider 1978, 64.
41. Schneider 1978, 65.
42. Schneider 1978, 56.
43. Jonung and Wadensjo 1981, 6.
44. Hibbs 1978, 261.
45. Hibbs 1978, 261.
46. See Hibbs 1982, 263–64, for details of the model.
47. Butler and Stokes 1969, 203–5.
48. Crewe, Sarlvik and Alt 1977, 168–83.
49. Hibbs ignores the kind of critique of party Weatherford suggests necessary, particularly for Britain.
50. Hibbs 1982, 286.
51. Hibbs 1982a, 1982b.
52. Hibbs 1982, 271.
53. Hibbs 1982, 274.
54. Hibbs 1982, 330.
55. Hibbs 1982, 262.
56. See Monroe 1981 for a discussion of the applications of such models to political science.
57. Arcelus and Meltzer 1975a, 1235.
58. Stigler 1973,165.
59. As quoted in Kinder and Abelson 1981, 2.
60. Kinder and Abelson 1981, 24.
61. The analysis used a three-pronged technique: a field experiment conducted on a number of economic issues, a study of the media, and academic research on the 1976 and 1980 elections.
62. Sears and Lau 1981, 2.
63. Kinder and Kiewiet 1976; Kinder 1981; Kinder and Mebane 1983.
64. Kinder and Kiewiet 1977, abstract.
65. Feldman 1982, 446.
66. Weatherford 1977, 917–38; 1978; 1983.
67. See Weatherford 1982, 20–21.
68. Lau and Sears 1981, 296.

2

The Enigma
of Presidential
Popularity

What determines a president's popularity? Despite the
importance of this question, gaps in our knowledge still
remain. What are the different levels at which the economy
enters an individual's political calculus? What role is played
by political parties? How are public policy perceptions and
preferences formulated and articulated? Does the public
attempt to maximize self-interest at the individual or at the
group level? If there is a long-term and a short-term
component to this maximization, when does each affect the
vote choice? What is the relative importance of subjective
versus objective perceptions of economic reality? What is
the role of economic expectations? Who is held responsible
for the economy: the president? the Congress? What role
does the media play in filtering this information? And how
does this affect voting? While exhaustive and definitive
answers on all of these questions cannot be provided here,
the integrated rational framework presented below will yield
insight on many of the questions. Let me consider each
general question in turn and then present such a framework.

MAJOR CONTROVERSIES

Levels of Analysis Problems

When do economic considerations enter a voter's political
calculus? The usual answer is: immediately. Thus, ana-

lysts expect contemporaneous economic conditions will explain political reactions; few then test for political influence from economic events occurring more than two years in the past. Yet the critical elections literature makes clear that there is a lasting impact from traumatic economic events. Ignoring such events will involve a level of analysis problem.

To avoid this, we must distinguish between three levels at which the economy influences electoral behavior. The most fundamental level is the one discussed by critical election theorists.[1] This work suggests the underlying predispositions towards politics, candidates, and policies are determined by dramatic events, such as the Depression. These events wrench the voter from his inherited voting patterns and cause him to reassess his political loyalties. An event dramatic enough to cause many individuals to shift political allegiances causes a critical realignment. The Depression was such an event, with present political orientations among the current voting population being inherited and shaped by this critical event.[2]

At a second level are theorists who stress party cleavages as key to electoral behavior.[3] An individual who believes one party represents his individual or group economic interests better than the other will have an underlying predisposition, changing little from election to election, that determines his response to a party and its candidates.

At the third level, we find short-term economic influences on popularity.[4] This literature assumes existing economic conditions and policies determine voting and incumbent support. Popularity is expected to follow—and to follow quite closely—even small changes in the economy as the public utilizes the political system both to send a message to incumbents concerning their political preferences on economic policies and to express anger and pleasure towards incumbents, depending on their success in achieving economic well-being. At this level, analysts ignore underlying economic orientations and cataclysmic critical events stressed by other theorists in favor of short-term economic predictors such as unemployment, inflation, and income.[5]

Further work needs to clarify the relationship among these three levels at which the economy affects political behavior. In addition to delaying the move to a more sophisticated theory, this conceptual confusion has led to the indiscriminate use of proxy variables. Party identification is often used to detect underlying economic predispositions, but there is seldom adequate control for the relationship of party identification or partisan loyalties either to the individual voter's economic issue positions or to his perception of aggregate economic conditions.

The Role of Political Parties

How do political parties affect public response to the economy? Their importance is well noted, with party serving as a perceptual screen and as an economizing device to decrease information costs for busy voters.[6] While the importance of party loyalties is widely accepted, however, the exact role played by parties is not. The evidence here is contradictory. Do voter's ignore party and respond politically to the candidate as an individual? Or do they respond to candidates primarily as party representatives? Does this suggest individual candidates are unimportant, with only party identification mattering to the voter? If a party does matter, what aspect of it is critical: mere ties of affection or past memory? Or is there a conscious assessment of the party's past performance, as Fiorina's work on retrospective voting suggests? How much of voter response is motivated by each of these?

There is much literature that emphasizes the importance of voting for a particular individual rather than a party. The rational choice literature assumes that voters use politics to maximize their financial interests rather than ties of party sentiment.[7] This unimportance of party is also emphasized by the extensive literature documenting the lack of discipline in American parties.[8] Recent survey work at the microlevel further confirms the importance of individual candidates, suggesting that personality is the key factor in voting.[9] Finally, the spatial modeling literature, measuring the distance between voters' and candidates' preferred issue positions, again stresses the importance of the individual candidate rather than the party.[10]

In contrast, the literature on critical elections and political socialization suggest voter's loyalties work through party ties inherited from parents and inculcated and reinforced by early schooling and peer pressure.[11] The origins and shifts in party loyalties come from historical events traumatic enough to roust people out of their original inherited views and to reorient or realign them. Political sociologists also argue that these shifts can occur when anxiety about one's personal status leads to recruitment to political movements. All of these works, however, stress the importance of party rather than candidate.

Hence, there is much contradictory evidence over whether votes are cast over individual candidates or party choice.

How are parties related to certain constituences? A long tradition of work on partisan loyalties finds certain religious, ethnic, or socioeconomic groups support one particular party.[12] Some empirical work has also examined parties primarily in relation to particular economic constituencies.[13] Related to this issue, of course, is the degree to which either of the parties consistently—or even for an extended period of time—will favor one group or a set of constituencies.[14] Some analysts focus on the party differences in terms of the policies pursued,[15] while others focus not on party intentions so much as on policy outcomes, with Democratic and Republican administrations producing different policy outputs.[16] All of these questions have important implications for a thorough analysis of economic influences on popularity.

Perceptions of Policy
Preferences

These questions also raise a related question: How correctly does the public perceive actual party differences on economic policies? Several important questions need to be considered here. Do the parties differ on macroeconomic policies? Does the public accurately perceive these differences? What are the voters' policy preferences and how are they communicated to the politicians? And finally, how central are economic policy issues to political behavior?

Consider first actual party differences in economic policies. While Marxists claim the two parties are virtually identical in their organization of the economic system and income distribution, this is a minor view; most non-Marxist group analysts suggest parties do differ over economic policies and that these policies systematically favor different interest groups.[17] These analysts stress Republican ties to business and Democratic ties to labor and minority groups.[18] Recent technical works suggest important macroeconomic differences between the parties center on trade-offs between unemployment and inflation.[19]

A strong dissent concerning macroeconomic party differences comes from Nobel laureate George Stigler, who argues that because there are no party differences in the intellectual, political, or ideological resources to deal with the kind of macroeconomic policies, such as unemployment, inflation, or income usually considered politically relevant, it is necessary to look at redistributive policies to detect party differences.[20]

Difficult as it may be to disentangle actual party differences on economic policy, it is even more important to understand public perceptions of party differences.[21] Current public perceptions of party differences stem from the Depression period, reinforced by experience with the Great Society and the War on Poverty programs of the 1960s. Traditional wisdom holds that the Democratic Party favors the working class, minorities, and lower economic groups and will work to decrease unemployment. And it holds that the Republican Party favors business, follows conservative economic policies favoring business and upper-class groups, and will try to decrease inflation rather than unemployment.[22]

If parties favor certain groups in their policy choices, how does the individual fit his policy preferences into those of a party?[23] The most common assumption—found in the spatial modeling literature—holds that the voter compares and selects his issue position with that of the candidate or political party closest to his own issue position. This ignores certain complexities. It makes insufficient allowances for trade-offs between economic policies. It ignores how the individual voter chooses his key issues or resolves potential conflict within his own issue space. Recent work does suggest, however, how an issue becomes politicized. Brody and Sniderman (1977) suggests that a critical factor is whether a voter conceives of an issue as a personal problem or as a public issue for which the government may require assistance.[24] They find low-income respondents tend to cast their economic situation in personal terms; because they blame themselves, they remain politically inert. The middle-income groups, however, externalize their economic problems and conclude that the government should aid in the solution.[25] An alternate explanation for such political inertia by low-income groups stresses the role of elites and political culture, and suggests the assignment of political blame for individual economic situation requires socialization into the habit of political efficacy.[26]

The last question is how important are economic issues for voting? Voting is often perceived as a choice between two alternate sets of economic policies, although the importance of other influences is always noted.[27] The central question is how much of the fluctuations in popularity are attributable to the economy? What will be the variance in the range of economic influence, given the importance of noneconomic factors, such as wars or other international crisis? How much of popularity is random or cyclical?

Policy Preferences and Individual Interest:
The Sociotropic and the Pocketbook Voter

A consideration of interests raises three questions. Do individuals, parties, and the government adopt maximizing or satisficing behavior? Are the interests that are furthered primarily those of the individual, of a particular group, or of the collectivity? Are they immediate or long-term interests?

Two alternate forms of behavior are maximizing and satisficing. Maximizing behavior occurs when the voter chooses the best of his options. Satisficing occurs when the voter is indifferent among any alternative that meets certain minimum requirements. The question of maximizing versus satisficing as a general model of economic behavior is widely discussed by economists; yet most empirical work on the economy and voting ignores this question.[28]

We have firmer knowledge about whether individuals pursue long-term or immediate interests. Most of the literature on political support assumes implicitly that individuals maximize short-term interests. Determining when individuals pursue short-term interests and when they pursue long-term interests is a critical one. A sharp disjuncture between the two will produce a highly unsteady equilibrium; if individual voters and candidates follow immediate interests and if a healthy economy depends on policies that necessitate short-term hardships for long-run good (even for the same individual), then there are serious problems in store for the economic health of the country.[29]

What happens when an individual's long-term interests conflict with his shorter ones? For the individual, these cross-cutting issue preferences cause cognitive dissonance and uncertainty; for the collectivity they will produce shifts in popularity and electoral outcomes and manipulation of the economy for political advantage.[30]

How does the government deal with the tension between immediate and long-term interests? The political business-cycle literature suggests governments emphasize immediate goals even at the expense of long-term interests.[31] Work on economic influences on voting also suggest that if there is a divergence between the two, then the immediate interests are pursued. Arguments that first-term presidential behavior differs significantly from second-term behavior exemplify this.[32]

The literature on party behavior differs sharply with this view, suggesting that parties stress the interests of long-term constituencies more than the immediate chance of gaining votes by appealing to a new or swing group of

voters.[33] Further specification of voter, party, or governmental maximization of immediate versus long-term interests
will be an important part of any empirical analysis of the
economy and voting and incumbent popularity.[34]

Interests: Individual, Group, or Collective

When are the politically relevant economic interests individual, group, or collective? The rational choice literature
emphasizes the individual. Sociological analyses of voting
emphasize the group. The sociotropic voting theory emphasizes the interests of the collectivity. There has been too
little integrated work on this topic. The individual's
self-interest, his various group interests, and his collective
interest may correspond; but it is not clear precisely when
they will coincide or for whom. There may be times when
virtually everyone—and certainly some individuals—may
prefer to stress the interests of the collectivity or a particular group rather than their own individual interests. This
may be out of duty, civic consciousness, guilt, peer pressure, or habit.[35] The problem is to specify more clearly
the circumstances when the collective rather than the
individual good is maximized and to determine whether there
is a typical individual or group that consistently behaves in
such altruistic behavior.

Acquisition of Information

How do voters obtain information about the economy? About
politics? At what cost is this information acquired? How
much does media control of information affect political
popularity?[36]

Analyses of the economy's influence on voting and popularity theoretically solve the problem of information acquisition by assuming that economic conditions in existence
during time in office will be accepted as the relevant measure of the incumbent party's abilities and preferences on
specific economic policies. Thus the individual citizen need
not invest the time to discover the party's or candidate's
economic issue positions. Each individual voter knows his
own economic situation and approves or disapproves of
incumbents depending on how well he has fared under the
incumbent. While this solves the problem of how information is gathered, it omits several important considerations.
One concerns the media filtering of information.

At one extreme, the individual voter has been concep-
tualized as an information processor, with the political
reactions to the economy seen primarily as reflections of

the sources of information on which individuals rely in forming their economic judgments. While this view seems a bit overstated, the media's role certainly is important, particularly if there is a distinction made by the individual between his own economic situation and that of the country as a whole. If assessments of overall well-being are more important politically than are assessments of individual economic well-being, then the source of an individual's perceptions of national condition is critical.

The media also determine whether personal economic situations become politicized in the first place; Brody and Sniderman discovered that working-class voters are less likely to view their economic situation as the result of general governmental policies than are middle-class voters.[37] Such a perception is crucial before either political blame or reward will be assigned for an individual economic situation. This suggests the economy usually should be a more important factor politically for upper middle-class voters and that the media's role in politicizing economic issues is critical.[38]

For most voters the media present both general images and specific information on the economy. The media interpret the causes of economic downturn, attributing it to poor presidential leadership or exogenous forces, such as greedy oil sheiks. The media are also the source of information on the president's economic positions and on the policies advocated by the two main political parties.[39] While both the president and the media can manipulate economic statistics as they please, the media enjoy the advantage of supposed objectivity.

Governmental Responsibility, Expectations, Perceptions, and Objective Economic Reality

Who is held responsible for economic conditions in our system? For what kind of economic conditions is the government held responsible? Is Congress held responsible for presidential policies? Are the differences between Congressional and Presidential parties relevant? Does the bifurcated aspect of legislative power in the United States make the American experience an abberant system, not one on which extensive theoretical work should be based?

A few authors suggest the public assigns little responsibility to the government for individual economic situations.[40] If so, this decreased responsibility means incumbents will receive little reward or blame from the economy. For the most part, however, analysis of the economy and popularity have not adopted this view. Rather, they have found a strong relationship between economic well-being and political support. Given this, the lack of agreement on the economy's exact political influence is startling.

Even more surprising is the extent to which analysts have failed to develop the logic behind key empirical hypotheses. Why exactly should unemployment be expected to influence popularity? The political power of the unemployed, whether expressed through public opinion surveys or voting, is considerably less than their numbers in the country. What conditions must arise before the unemployed will mobilize and exert political influence commensurate with their numbers? Do the unemployed hold the government responsible for their unemployment?[41] Do they hold the government responsible for voluntary and short-term unemployment? Will this temporary unemployment have political repercussions? And how will the employed respond politically to unemployment? Will it frighten them, raising doubts about their own job security or mobility? Or may some employed people look at increasing unemployment and be grateful to the government for protecting their jobs, as Stigler suggests? These questions await empirical answers.

What do particular economic conditions indicate about economic progress? Does inflation indicate economic distress or merely a growing economy? Both increases and decreases in prices have been found to have unsettling political effects. Uncertainty over future inflation has been found to be more important politically than high inflation.[42] Is it possible that people view inflation as part of an expanding, healthy economy and therefore partially discount its otherwise negative aspects?[43] Most analyists assume this is not the case. Much poll data suggest the public is troubled by inflation and responds politically simply to the rapid increase of prices. But economists working on the money illusion stress the importance of comparing the increase in income with the general increase in prices.

More detailed theoretical work is also needed on the relative importance of different economic predictors. Is income a better measure of economic health than the stock market? Than the balance of payments? Until recently, empirical work has focused primarily on unemployment, inflation, and income. Other economic indicators should also be considered. Explicit theoretical arguments need to be constructed concerning an economic predictor's political relevance. In addition to such general theory, theoretical justifications for measurement choices are essential since the measurements of economic variables can critically affect economic findings, as demonstrated by the substantive differences found in Stigler's reanalysis of Kramer's data.[44]

Finally, consider the political importance of economic expectations, economic perceptions, and objective economic reality, a substantive issue related to measurement decisions. How much correspondence is there among the objective economic indicators of economic conditions usually considered in political analysis, and the public's view of this reality? If there are critical differences between public perceptions and more objective measures of economic well-being, which phenomenon is more important politically? If there are differences, how do we compare survey analyses of responses to explicit questions on the individual's perception of economic reality with aggregate time series based on government economic statistics?

What about economic expectations? Work on violent political responses to economic discontent has noted the importance of rising economic expectations and relative deprivation. Recent work on less dramatic fluctuations in incumbent support suggests economic expectations are critical here, too.[45] How do we allow for voters who expect Republican presidents to lower inflation but are angered when inflation is not lowered rapidly enough? A paradoxical situation may develop where unrealistically high expectations of presidential performance lead voters to punish presidents who try—but fail—to provide the desired economic policy, whereas presidents from whom the voter expects and receives nothing in policy terms is not punished at all.

Other paradoxical situations might occur because of the importance of perceptions and expectations. There is much evidence suggesting voters believe the Democratic Party will lower unemployment. This suggests high employment helps the Democrats. Does it follow, then, that it is in the Democratic Party's interest to increase unemployment before an election? No, because in the long-run such a policy will change the party's image. Yet the fact that the Democratic presidents do not behave thusly suggests parties and politicians pursue more than short-term electoral gains.

Conclusion

The theoretical considerations raised above are too extensive to be resolved in any one work. Several important questions, however, can be addressed, and addressed particularly well by an analysis of presidential popularity among key groups. The first question is whether all groups respond uniformly to the president. If there are differences, what exactly are they? Do men or women, blacks or whites, young or old, have higher or lower levels of support for a president? Do existing differences in group popularity levels hold true for all presidents? Are the distinctive group patterns affected by the incumbent president's party affiliation? Are the patterns of group popularity regular? Are they attributable to some rational explanation, be it economic or noneconomic? Or are they merely predictable cycles of honeymoon and then gradual disillusionment, as Stimson suggests? What is the group variation in any such cycles of initial enthusiasm and gradual disillusionment? These are initial questions to be answered below.

The second topic concerns the economy's impact on group support for the president. When discernible differences in a group's political response to presidents do exist, are they related to the economy? If so, how varied is the response to the economy among different groups? Whose political support is influenced by unemployment? Whose is more affected by inflation? Are some groups more responsive to general macroeconomic conditions while others respond more to economic redistribution? Some initial determination can be made here. It is more difficult to use group data to discover whether the politically relevant economic considerations are collective, group, or individual. Some tentative indications can be gained, however, by comparing presidential support among the young, women, and nonwhites with unemployment among these groups.

Finally, a group analysis can provide insight on the public's expectations concerning party economic priorities. Is popularity for Democratic presidents more responsive to economic conditions than popularity for Republicans? If so, which economic conditions cause Democrats to rise or fall? Which are the Republican issues? Are Democratic presidents blamed more for unemployment and Republicans more for inflation? And do these patterns vary among different groups? These are important questions to be answered, both for political economists and for the public and politicians concerned with sound, democratic economic policies. These are the questions which will be addressed using the integrated rational model presented below.

A FRAMEWORK FOR ANALYSIS

The integrated rational model presented here incorporates critical nonrational factors in an analytical framework essentially rational in orientation. It assumes the public's political response to the economy is a rational calculation of perceived self-interest, with the individual, group, and national well-being constituting the primary economic considerations. The president is assumed to be the main incumbent held responsible for economic well-being, with a close connection made between the president's economic program, final government policy, and actual economic conditions.

What key nonrational factors need to be incorporated into this framework? The most important is partisan affiliation. Partisan feeling affects both individual policy preferences and assessment and expectations of presidential performance. While many partisan attachments clearly originate in economic concerns, it is nevertheless difficult to detect such attachments using traditional econometric models because of the time between the initial formation of such attachments and their political manifestation. (The working-class attachment to the Democratic party long after the Depression is an obvious example.) Despite difficulties in integrating these events into a rational framework, this must be done to avoid the controversy existing between advocates of ideological and cultural explanations of political behavior and those who stress more easily discernible rational responses. What are these nonrational factors and how can we best integrate them into our approach? A beginning framework for this purpose is presented below.

Economic Well-Being and the Responsibility for Domestic Economic Conditions

The framework sketched in Figure 2–1 includes the critical factors influencing public political response to the president. It sketches the links between public perception of the government's ability to influence economic conditions and each citizen's assessment of his individual, group, or national economic well-being. Figure 2–1 begins by assuming actual domestic economic conditions result from both domestic macroeconomic policies and exogenous economic events and influences.[46] This is a crucial assumption. Do individuals who believe the government can or should control the economy blame or reward the president for economic conditions more than those who do not?[47] Do those who advocate more limited government intervention in the economy blame the government less for economic deterioration than those who believe economic well-being is a major responsibility of the government? If external factors seriously constrain domestic policy makers from achieving

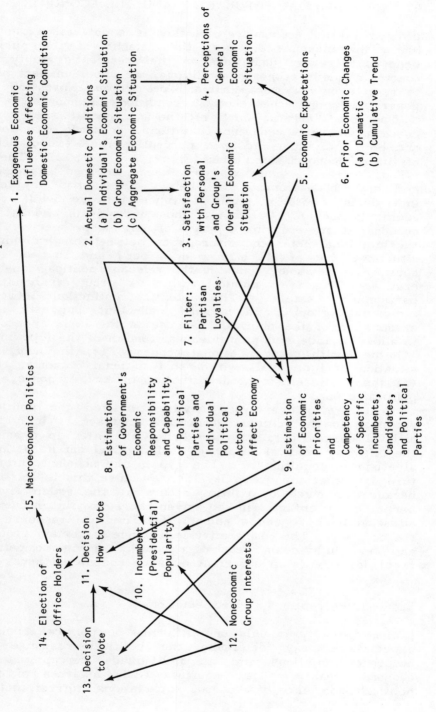

Figure 2-1. Short-term Political-Economic Interactions: A Conceptual Framework

1. Exogenous Economic Influences Affecting Domestic Economic Conditions

2. Actual Domestic Conditions
   (a) Individual's Economic Situation
   (b) Group Economic Situation
   (c) Aggregate Economic Situation

3. Satisfaction with Personal and Group's Overall Economic Situation

4. Perceptions of General Economic Situation

5. Economic Expectations

6. Prior Economic Changes
   (a) Dramatic
   (b) Cumulative Trend

7. Filter: Partisan Loyalties

8. Estimation of Government's Economic Responsibility and Capability of Political Parties and Individual Political Actors to Affect Economy

9. Estimation of Economic Priorities and Competency of Specific Incumbents, Candidates, and Political Parties

10. Incumbent (Presidential) Popularity

11. Decision How to Vote

12. Noneconomic Group Interests

13. Decision to Vote

14. Election of Office Holders

15. Macroeconomic Politics

89

desired internal economic goals, then it is not reasonable to blame the incumbents.[48] If the majority of the public believes there are limitations on the president's ability to control domestic economic conditions, we should expect him to receive only a more limited blame as an expression of generalized anger when economic conditions deteriorate.

The next critical part of the conceptual framework concerns national economic conditions, economic situation, and both individual and mass perceptions and expectations of future economic conditions (Figure 2–1, Step 2). There is, of course, a close correspondence between aggregate and individual economic well-being. But what of those individuals whose economic fortunes improve while the country's decline? Or what of those individuals who suffer economic distress during a period of national prosperity? If the individual notes the discrepancy between his individual situation, that of his main peer group, and that of the country as a whole, which is the relevant political consideration? This is a point at which a group analysis is particularly useful.[49] The potential distinction between individual, group, and national well-being suggests any examination of the political response to the economy needs to allow for independent influences from all of the following: (1) the health of the national economy, (2) the economic situation of individuals within that national economy, and (3) the particular economic situation of key economic and political groups.

Most previous analyses have emphasized the political response to the national economy. Analyses of individual-level survey data are now being presented to measure the differing political responses to individual versus national economic conditions.[50] The gap in the scholarly literature occurs at the group level.[51] Because this is so, and because so much of politics occurs at the group level, particular attention will be given here to the economic situation of key groups and to their political response to the economy. The comparative importance of certain groups and how individuals resolve a conflict among competing group loyalties is an important question considered here.

Economic Perceptions and Expectations

Economic reality is only one influence on politics. Public expectations may determine the political response to economic conditions and an individual's perceptions of economic reality. The important early analyses of the political importance of economic expectations suggest that it is not so much higher or even improving levels of economic well-being that are politically relevant as it is the gap between actual economic conditions and what people expect economic conditions to be.

The general theory of a revolution of rising expectations can explain seemingly anomalous situations such as the following. People expect economic downturn and it occurs. But since the downturn is not as bad as expected, people are relieved and reward the incumbent for minimizing an economic deterioration that they thought was inevitable. Conversely, an economy actually could improve during a president's term, but if the improvement is not as great as had been expected, the president could be punished politically. The validity of this theory can easily be seen simply by recalling that FDR, the only president to be reelected to four terms, was the president who held office during the worst economic depression the country has known. The fact that the voters continued to support him, even during the prewar years when economic conditions showed little improvement, suggests the pocketbook theory of voting needs some modification to allow for other psychological factors in voter response to the economy.

The political importance of economic expectations may be even greater in the Vietnam and post-Vietnam period in the United States. This was a period of both dramatic economic changes—as the country experienced high inflation and high unemployment—and of increasing public awareness that the archetypal strong president, modeled after Franklin Roosevelt, no longer could perform the miracles we had come to expect. During this period, the traditional party lines in this country shifted for several reasons. First, the once-solid Democratic South realized that although Republicans had ended slavery a hundred years earlier, the Democrats were now ending segregation, thereby removing the strongly institutionalized—albeit informal—political privileges the Southern Democrats had enjoyed for so long. Second, the expectations based on an earlier historical period—the 1930s Depression—were no longer applicable either in reflecting the goals and priorities of the two political parties or the current economic situation and needs of the voter. In part, much of the liberal Democratic economic agenda had been realized for many voters. The ethnic minorities who had supported the Democrats under Roosevelt and had benefited from the New Deal social welfare legislation now became the middle class. This class was now expected to pay for expanded social welfare programs benefiting newer immigrants and other ethnic groups, groups who were now taking the jobs or places in college that had traditionally been reserved for the children of the older ethnic groups. These older ethnic groups, who no longer so desperately needed the government-sponsored programs to raise them from the marginal poverty level, resented paying so much of their tax dollars for the expanded welfare programs for others. Resentment grew and took the form of hostility toward the very liberal Democratic party and state that had once benefited them. Finally, as American economic and military preeminence declined, the country shifted its economic expectations. This process of shifting expectations began around the late 1960s. It corresponded with the end of the war in Vietnam and with Nixon's cut-back of Johnson's Great Society programs. Accompanying these domestic changes was a decline in the U.S. international economic preeminence.

The extent to which this process is still under way is unclear. It is possible, although unlikely, that Americans no longer expect their government to provide continual economic improvement, but now expect it simply to slow the rate of economic decline. Certainly the country is presently experiencing uncertainty over what it expects its presidents to do concerning the economy. This uncertainty was reflected in the 1980 election and the difficulty that analysts had in interpreting the election. Was it a rejection of the Democratic Party's liberal policy of economic intervention and a mandate for a new economic program? Or was the election a referendum on the dismal economic performance of the Carter administration? If the latter is true, then the 1980 election may reflect the very success of Democratic liberalism in achieving enough economic well-being for the public that the voters now demand such strong action on the part of the government and will reject any president who fails to provide it. This period of shifting expectations makes it particularly important to analyze the role of public expectations concerning the president and the economy.

Partisan Ties and Economic Priorities

The process through which both actual economic change and the expectations and perceptions of this economic change are internalized by the voter and then translated into a political response is critical. This process does not occur in a political vacuum. It is molded through a partisan filter consisting of an individual's prior partisan attachments and feelings that have much to do with the way he interprets and responds politically to current economic conditions.[52]

The impact of partisan loyalties, however, may also occur at an even more fundamental level. Earlier economic changes may shape an individual's underlying economic priorities, his later political reaction to economic change, and his fundamental political loyalties. These earlier economic changes may be dramatic changes, such as the 1930s Depression, or gradual trends that slowly shift economic expectations, perceptions, and loyalties. These earlier economic experiences may shape voter reactions to later economic events.[53]

In addition to these prior economic events, there are other attachments, often noneconomic in origin, that enter a voter's conscious thinking or preconscious cognitive map. These attachments act as important components in the construction of a partisan filter through which the voter responds politically to both the economy and the president. This partisan filter, omitted in most earlier empirical work, clearly exists and should be provided for in an empirical analysis of how the economy influences presidential popularity. It will be included here by focusing on political responses to the economy among key partisan groups and by examining separate responses to the presidents of each political party.

The next part of the conceptual framework concerns assessment of economic priorities and capabilities (Figure 2–1, Steps 8 and 9). An individual's economic situation, his assessment of group and national well-being, and his personal expectations are filtered through his partisan loyalties to produce his estimate of the economic competence and priorities of a president, presidential candidates, and the major political parties. Prior feelings about a president and his party provide either a charitable or a negative predisposition in this evaluation. Favorable predisposition to a president may mitigate political reaction to economic downturn or heighten the voter's favorable political response to economic improvements. Beyond a certain point, however, a reverse phenomenon may occur. The feeling of special attachment to a president and/or his party, of having given support and trust to this president, may foster a negative reaction to economic deterioration. This reaction may be unusually intense precisely because the voter feels earlier trust has been broken. The disappointment and sense of betrayal may add extra retribution to the normal desire to punish a president for not ensuring economic well-being.

Public beliefs about economic priorities of presidents are critical here. Most voters believe Democratic presidents place higher priorities on decreasing unemployment and on helping the poor and the working class, while Republican presidents follow more conservative social welfare policies and encourage an economic climate conducive to business expansion. This partisan differential in perceived economic priorities may affect the public's political response to economic conditions in several ways.[54]

How can we best allow for this partisan filter? Several ways are useful. One is to control for the individual's political affiliation and noted partisan loyalties through an analysis of microlevel survey data. Another way is to examine Democratic, Republican, and Independent voters as separate response groups to determine how their party affiliations and partisan attachments affect their political responses to the economy. A third way is to analyze as separate units the terms of Democratic and Republican presidents to determine whether general public responses to the economy differ according to the political affiliation of the incumbent president. The last two approaches are adopted in this book.

After Popularity: The Vote and Macroeconomic Policies

Simply to complete the circular process by which the economy and popular support intertwine in this country, consider voting and economic policy outcomes. The same forces that determine popularity also affect the decision on whether and how to vote. The spatial modeling literature suggests that, contrary to myth, voting is not always the product of careful consideration of the candidate's position and a selection of the candidate whose critical positions most closely correspond to the voter's. Rather, this literature suggests the voter's partisan filter, group influences, nonpolitical preferences, and even whimsey, all may combine to give the voter a favorable predisposition or a selective perception of the candidates and their issue positions. The voter then may align his own issue positions so that they correspond with those of the candidate he already prefers for reasons totally unrelated to preferred positions on key policy issues. Or the voter may have such divergent or inconsistent issue positions that no simple matching of candidate and voter issue positions is possible.

Most work on voting has focused on the vote choice rather than on voter turnout. Is a decision not to vote related to dissatisfaction with the economy? The evidence on this is contradictory, with the most recent work suggesting economic adversity decreases voter turnout.[55]

Does voting result in important differences in the macro-economic policies pursued by two main political parties?[56] Does it affect actual policy outcomes? While both Democratic and Republican parties advocate both lower unemployment and lower inflation, they make different comparative commitments on the trade-off aspect of these policies. In doing so, perhaps the parties' economic performance should be judged not as indicative of their ability to direct the economy, so much as indicative of their relative redistributive economic priorities.[57] It is particularly important to ask how key political and socioeconomic groups are affected differentially by governmental policies. This differential will lead to quite varied political responses to the same governmental policies. By emphasizing a group analysis, by looking at the political consequences of unemployment among different groups, and by constructing variables to measure the political importance of taxation and social welfare policies in particular, the following analysis will provide for the political response to governmental redistributive economic policies, even when such redistributive policies may be taken under the guise of general macroeconomic policies.

Conclusion

The above provides a conceptual framework for an integrated rational analysis of the economy's influence on presidential popularity. It assumes a pluralist political system and voters who, while essentially rational in their political reaction to changing economic conditions, still filter economic and political perceptions through partisan attachments. It focuses on the previously undetected group political responses to the economy, and it assumes that macroeconomic policies that redistribute economic goods and services in a zero-sum fashion will be the areas of greatest political controversy.[58] It builds on the advances made by Kramer's satisficing model of political behavior. Emphasizing Fiorina's retrospective voter in its construction of public views of party economic policies and priorities, it also provides for explicit testing of the sociotropic voter theory developed by Kinder and his colleagues and for the importance of economic expectations noted by Alt, Hibbs, and Monroe and Levi.

NOTES

1. See, for example, Key 1955 or Burnham 1970.
2. See Weatherford 1978.

3. For example, *The American Voter,* as well as later work by Hibbs (1976, 1977), Tufte (1978) and Peretz (1978), all find politically relevant differences in the economic orientation of the two parties, both in actual policy terms and in terms of the public's perception of the two parties' outlook on economic policies.

4. The majority of the literature is of this kind.

5. There has been virtually no rigorous empirical econometric work that integrates all three levels at which the economy may influence popularity. Nor has there been any rigorous work that tests for the kind of economic influence on popularity discussed by the critical election theorists. There has been some work on the underlying economic orientations of class.

6. Early work by Campbell et al. (1960, Chapter 7) stresses the importance of party identification. This emphasis has been underlined by other more recent works. Fiorina refers to party identification as "an enduring, affective affiliation . . . not only the single most important influence on voting . . . but . . . a 'perceptual screen' through which individuals evaluate politically relevant events and conditions, such as an administration's economic performance" (Fiorina 1978, 9) Rivers (1980) finds that nothing else in the political environment, including the candidate, specific issues, or the party's relative performance in office, counts as much for voters as their party identification. Rivers finds, however, that party identification has shifted as a concept as voters cross party lines more often. He adopts a Downsian view of party membership as an economizing device to decrease information costs for those who do not closely follow elections.

7. Downs 1957; Davis et al. 1970; Riker and Ordeshook 1973.

8. James MacGregor Burns's distinction between presidential and Congressional parties is a prime example of this work.

9. Kinder and Abelson 1981.

10. See Hinich 1979 or Brody 1978 for references.

11. Bell 1963.

12. *The American Voter* and its intellectual heirs are the prime advocates of this view.

13. The early simple models of political reaction to the economy assumed macroeconomic conditions affected candidate choice. These models were criticized by one group of scholars because of their treatment of party differences on macroeconomic policies and because they assumed governments do control the economy. Another group of analysts accepted the view that the public response to the economy,

based on public evaluation of governmental economic performance, is a natural part of the democratic process. Hibbs's (1977) analysis of parties and macroeconomic policies, Weatherford's (1978) work on class differences, or Pomper's (1975) work on governmental policies that favor different interest groups are all early examples of this. Later work by Weatherford juxtaposes works in this area, comparing those that see vote shifts as a result of the response to economic recession with those that see voting as a class-based demand, especially for alternate trade-offs in the Phillips curve. For Weatherford, the aggregate analysis by Kramer (1971) and Fair (1978) and micro level analysis by Fiorina (1978) and by Kinder and Kiewiet (1979) exemplify the first kind of work, while aggregate analyses by Hibbs (1977) and by Frey and Schneider (1978) and individual level analyses by Weatherford (1978) and Campbell et al. (1960, 401) exemplify the latter.

14. Weatherford 1978, 920; Hibbs 1977; and Lekachman 1966 argue that this is the case.

15. Ladd and Hadley 1978; Petrocik 1981.

16. Hibbs 1977; Hibbs and Vasilatos 1982a; Frey and Schneider 1978.

17. See Roelofs 1976.

18. See Pomper 1975.

19. See Hibbs, Weatherford, and Lekachman.

20. Most empirical analysis of economic influences on both voting and popularity have begun by assuming implicitly that there are policy differences between the parties, precisely on the important inflation or income policies that Stigler argues are too general to be the area where differences will occur. They then test whether people respond on the basis of fluctuations in the economic conditions that reflect these differences in policy or competence. While the consistency with which some kind of differences are found to occur suggests Stigler's arguments about no party differences is overstated, the degree to which the actual findings fail to agree on the specific party differences indicate Stigler's suggestion to examine other policy areas, particularly the redistributive policies, is well taken.

21. Theoretically, there should be a close relation between the public perceptions and the actual differences. The authors of *The American Voter* found that a belief that there are actual party differences is crucial before a voter will switch his vote. This literature, as well as the theoretical rational choice literature, suggests that differences of perception may be crucial in the vote choice.

22. See Hibbs 1978; Weatherford 1977; Frey and Schneider 1978; or Kiewiet (1983).

23. The empirical literature analyzing the economic influences on voting and popularity assumes the voter wants more economic well-being, operationalized for the most part as lower unemployment and inflation and higher income. Very little of the literature considers the question of trade-offs within the voter's preference for certain policies, although works that consider class effects do get into some of this. Recent work on political business cycles focuses on another dimension of this question.

24. Their 1980 work found that "those who describe their economic plight as the 'cost of living' are three times as likely to look to government for aid as those who describe their problem as being unable to 'make ends meet'" (1980, 22).

25. Low-income respondents were those earning less than $8,000 a year.

26. This probability modification is found in some of the rational choice literature at the theoretical level. It is not common in the spatial modeling literature. And there is no explicit empirical work that tests this.

27. These have been included in models through proxy variables or through more systematic, noneconomics predictors, such as time in office or wars. See Tufte 1973; Mueller 1970; Kernell 1977, 1978.

28. Kramer (1971) says that he accepts a satisficing model but never elaborates on this and does not say how it is distinguished from one that accepts maximizing behavior. Barry (1970) argues that satisficing is a more reasonable behavior pattern, although his argument deals primarily with the party's behavior rather than the individual's. There has been no empirical work that makes an explicit test of this question, although some of the work on preference selection does raise the issue. The work on correspondence of voter and candidate issue position suggests that voters choose the best of the alternatives available to them. This suggests maximization as the more plausible behavior model. To the extent that the distinction is relevant for issue preference, however, this is something that should be tested directly.

29. See Keech (1980) and Keech and Simon (1983) for a review of this literature.

30. See Hibbs 1982.

31. Tufte 1978; Frey 1978; MacRae 1977; Nordhaus 1975; Wright 1974.

31. The arguments concerning first-term presidential behavior as differing from second-term behavior exemplify this.

32. See Keech and Simon (1983) for a discussion of how

such cycles might be related to the question of term length.

33. It would be interesting to examine instances when a party may deviate from this behavior. It is important to consider how a party makes trade-offs between long-term and short-term interests, when such conflicts arise. Discussion of the grass roots versus national parties or of the conservative versus liberal wings of the parties are relevant in this regard.

So far, however, Frey and Schneider are the only authors to build this juxtaposition into their model.

34. See Downs 1957; Riker and Ordeshook 1973; or Brody 1978, 306–15, for a summary.

35. Downs (1957, 270) talks of voters who vote even at short-term cost to themselves in order to do their share to provide long-term benefits both for themselves and for the system. Certainly such behavior occurs.

36. Economists focus their analysis on information costs, taken to refer to the opportunity costs involved in any action. As applied to voting, this builds on the important and basic economic concept that a person will vote if his expected benefit from voting is greater than his economic cost. The cost includes the time and effort spent in obtaining the information, including the opportunity costs in the transaction. Social psychologists view the key as the schematic frame work individuals have and how this affects their expectations. See Nesbit and Ross (1980) or Kahneman and Tversky (1973) for reviews of the rational aspect of this and Higgins (1981) on the cognitive happenings. Recent important work on the sociotropic voter has suggested that individual evaluations of the overall economic situation are more important politically than are individual evaluations of their own economic situation. See Kinder and Kiewiet (1977), Kiewiet and Kinder (1978), Kinder and Mebane (1983), and Sears and Lau (1981).

37. Brody 1980, 22–23 and Brody and Sniderman 1977.

38. There has been some work, relevant for consideration of economic influences on political support, that allows for this (see Brody, 1980; Brody and Page 1973, 1975; Brody and Sniderman, 1977a, 1977b; Kernell 1978). For the most part, however, the main interest has been in explaining the general media influences on voting, rather than on the way the media may filter or distort the basic information concerning the state of the economy.

39. Brody's work (1980) suggests these perceptions are strongly influenced by media presentations. Other work has expanded this. Mackuen (1980) focuses attention on citizen response to media content, particularly the cognitive capacities, personal motivations, and socially induced incen-

tives. Weatherford (1981) develops a model of political translation that makes explicit the key sources of economic information. In all these works, the media is central.

40. Brody and Sniderman find Americans believe their economic situation is their own responsibility, not that of the government. Their work (1977) considers the broad question of which problems become political and to whom an individual looks to solve his problem.

41. See Lewis-Beck 1980, 321 and Brody and Sniderman 1977a, 1977b.

42. See Monroe and Levi 1983.

43. See Lepper 1974.

44. Minor modifications in Kramer's data series led to dramatic shifts in findings. For example, Stigler shifted the analysis from one- to two-year changes in economic conditions so they corresponded to Congressional terms. This alteration caused unemployment and real income to lose statistical significance (Stigler 1973, 163). This may be an atypical example. But if substantive findings are going to be mere artifacts of measurement, then the empirical work in this area is of little value.

45. Work by Alt, Hibbs, and Kuklinski and West stresses the importance of expectations. Monroe and Levi find expectations of economic growth more important for the president than the actual levels or rates of growth. With the exception of these and Katona's (1963) pathbreaking work on this subject, however, there has been little attempt to measure the existence and political impact of economic expectations.

46. These are the linkages between Steps 1, 2 and 15 in Figure 2-1.

47. Earlier analysts have assumed the public views actual domestic economic conditions as the results of government policies. Few analysts have allowed for public beliefs that the government has a more limited control over the economy. See Keech 1980; MacRae 1977; Monroe 1978.

48. Economic or political constraints, such as the institutionalized division of legislative responsibility in the U.S. federal system, limits the presidential ability to control and shape the economy as he wishes. Responsibility for economic events should be even more limited. A first question, then, is whether such limitations on the president's ability to control economic conditions do exist. A second question is whether these constraints are noted by the American public.

Works on the political business cycle suggest the capacity for such manipulation is limited both by external economic and political factors and by counter forces within the domestic political arena. The extent to which the public recognizes these constraints is crucial in determining the degree of economic responsibility assigned to the incumbent president. Here there is no direct empirical evidence. This is regrettable since the question is central to the assignment of political punishment and reward for the economy. See Nordhaus (1975) and Tufte (1975) on attempts to manipulate the economy for political advantage.

49. Miller, Gurin, and Gurin (1979) argue that the key stages in the development of group consciousness include (1) a feeling of belonging to a group, (2) positive attitudes to one's group and a dislike of nongroup members, (3) a level of discontent that group members feel about both their own group's influence in society compared to others, and (4) the accepted bases for the group's position in the hierarchy.

50. Philosophical works on the public interest raise questions posed in recent empirical work on the sociotropic voter. (See Fiorina 1978; Kinder and Kiewiet 1978, 1979; Kinder and Mebane 1983; D. Roderick Kiewiet 1978, 1979, and 1983.) This theory suggests an individual's assessment of national well-being may be politically more important than his assessment of his own individual economic situation. While the definitive nature of these findings has been questioned by Kramer and by Lau and Sears, the substantive question concerning the relative importance of individual versus group or national economic situation for the voter's political calculus remains.

51. The gap that occurs in the literature exists at the level of group analysis. This is particularly unfortunate since so much of politics is organized at the group level. Those who perceive common interests and organize to achieve shared goals are those who do well in our pluralist political system. Those who, for whatever the reason, are unable to work together to express their needs and to fight to achieve their demands, seldom see their interests advanced. As in most political systems, the American political system ignores those without power.

52. A strong Democrat, for example, may respond differently to economic deterioration occurring under a Democratic president than he would to deterioration under a Republican president.

53. The important early analyses of the political importance of economic expectations suggest that it is not so much high or even improving levels of economic well-being that are politically relevant as it is the gap between actual economic conditions and what people expect economic conditions to be. See De Tocqueville (1840) or Davies

(1969) on the general theory of rising expectations. See
Alt (1979), Monroe and Levi (1983), or Frey and Schneider
(1980, 77) on the impact of expectations on incumbent
popularity. See Brody (1980, 25) on the link between
public expectations, the president's expressed policy goals,
and the media's reporting of presidential actions.

54. Southern attachment to the Democratic Party because
of the Civil War is one obvious example. The extreme fear
of inflation that still marks the German voter and shapes
his economic priorities is but one dramatic example of this.

55. Arcelus and Meltzer (1975a, 1975b) find the economy's political influence worked directly on the decision to
vote rather than on the vote choice itself. This finding
was strongly disputed by Goodman and Kramer (1975) and
modifications in the basic theory were suggested by Bloom
and Price (1975), who found there is an asymmetrical
effect, with economic downturn hurting incumbents but
economic improvement providing little significant support for
the incumbent. Later work by Arcelus confirmed this
asymmetrical effect of the economy in voting. But recent
work by Rosenstone (1982), analyzing both cross-sectional
CPS data from November 1974 and a longer aggregate time
series from presidential and midterm elections from 1896,
concludes that economic adversity increases the opportunity
costs of political involvement and thus will decrease voter
turnout. Until this debate is resolved, it seems reasonable
to build into our conceptual framework those group memberships and group loyalties that may enter into the voter's
decision on whether or not to vote. Again, it is important
to remember that those most in need of help from the
government economically—the poor—are those least likely to
vote. A failure to look closely at voter participation rates
among the disadvantaged and to concentrate instead on
aggregate statistics may have distorted earlier findings
about the economy's actual impact on voting, although the
overall impact may not have been distorted. Therefore,
this is another area where a group analysis would prove
helpful in determining whether certain groups respond
differently to the economy, although it is a question that
lies outside the scope of the present empirical analysis.

56. Some analysts (Ladd and Hadley 1978; Petrocik 1981)
suggest actual party differences are more in policies pursued rather than conditions achieved. Others (e.g., Hibbs
1977; Frey and Schneider 1981; Hibbs and Vasilatos 1982a)
suggest there are actual differences in economic outcome.
(See Weatherford 1983.) Kernell takes issue with both of
these views and suggests a strategic party theme. He
suggests that left- and right-wing governments "adapt their

economic policies to the preferred unemployment/inflation mix of the public" (1980, 3). Testing this for the industrialized democracies, he finds that "only for the United States do the economic determinants of presidential support vary significantly with party control." This is a minor view, however. The majority of analysts continue to find important differences in party priorities concerning changes in prices and unemployment, with alleviating unemployment a higher priority for Democratic presidents and inflation for Republicans, and with the public accurately perceiving these differences.

57. Stigler (1973) argues that the two parties do not differ in either their intellectual or political resources available to deal with the general macroeconomic phenomena. This is particularly true, he argues, for party policies concerning inflation and unemployment, the economic predictors most often considered critical politically. Stigler argues further that party priorities on these macroeconomic questions are essentially the same, with both parties seeking to decrease unemployment and lower the inflation rate. Hibbs (1977, 1978) suggests the parties do differ, however, in their relative emphasis of unemployment versus inflation. Even more importantly, Hibbs argues that the public correctly perceives these differences. Stigler's response is that the area to examine closely for party differences is the area of redistributive economics, such as taxation or social welfare policies. On the whole, Stigler's theoretical arguments about party differences seem convincing for general macroeconomic phenomena. The problem overlooked by Stigler, and the reason that Hibbs is more likely right in this argument, is that many of these so-called macroeconomic phenomena have important redistributive consequences. (See Bach and Stephenson's [1974] work on the redistributive aspects of inflation.) For example, if the classic Phillips curve still exists, then administrations do have to choose between lowering inflation or lowering unemployment.

58. See Thurow 1980.

3

Fluctuations
in Presidential
Popularity
1965–1980

How can we best explain fluctuations in presidential popularity? Two of the most frequent explanations come from the cycle theory and from rational choice theory. The cycle theory, which reflects the view of mass action as nonrational, argues that shifts in presidential popularity result from recurring patterns in public opinion that are unrelated to specific presidential actions or events. In contrast, the rational choice theory explains these shifts through specific presidential acts and events. Neither theory is entirely sufficient. To demonstrate the need to integrate these two approaches, the analysis presented in this chapter charts public support for the last four presidents among key political and socioeconomic groups. The highs, lows, and crucial shifts in this support are marked on each time chart and are elaborated in separate tables for each president. The analysis demonstrates that while there are indeed cycles in presidential popularity, they are neither as uniform nor as unresponsive to presidential actions as the cycle theorists claim. And they by no means provide sufficient explanation for the fluctuations in presidential popularity. For this, we must include specific presidential acts and key events in the analysis. Thus, a full consideration of presidential popularity must encompass both the rational and the cyclical components of political life.

Beyond establishing this, the analysis serves an additional function: It provides specific political information on the less theoretical and more factually substantive questions about presidential popularity and the economy. What has been the public's general response to presidents since 1965? Are there important differences in group responses? Have all presidents enjoyed roughly equal levels of political support? Have all been equally loved and respected by different groups in society? If not, are all new presidents given equal chances to prove themselves? Did Johnson and Ford enjoy a longer honeymoon period because of the traumatic and tragic circumstances under which they took office? Did Nixon, who was disliked by so many people throughout his long political career, enjoy the same grace period as the relatively unknown Carter? Is there a trend in the years since Vietnam and Watergate toward a more cynical or critical evaluation of incumbents? Are we now in for a period of one-term presidents whom we expect to perform miracles and then repudiate when they fail to do the impossible?[1] If angry disappointment is the recent pattern of public response, is it caused by the presidential candidates themselves in raising unrealistic public expectations during the campaign?

To answer the above, my analysis will focus on these central questions: Do all presidents enjoy a brief honeymoon period followed by declines in their public support? Is such a decline inevitable, or does the pattern and extent of the decline vary from president to president, depending on his specific policies or personality? If actions do matter, what kind of actions or events are most critical politically? In the process of answering these questions, I shall make some further observations about the popularity levels of different presidents among key socioeconomic groups in this country, paying special reference to these groups' voting behavior.

RECENT TRENDS IN PRESIDENTIAL POPULARITY

In statistical terms, the trends and seasonal variations in the data series must be considered before we can answer the more interesting question of whether specific actions or events cause changes in presidential popularity. Seasonal variations are peaks or declines in time-series data that tend to occur at a particular time every year. Given the nature of American politics, seasonal variations are not usually a problem when analyzing political variables over time. The political affections of Americans are not influenced by the weather or by Christmas cheer—or even by the April 15 income tax deadline. Economic variables, on the other hand, are so routinely affected by the weather (e.g., employment in housing construction declines in the winter) and other seasonal factors (e.g., the June graduates' search for jobs affects unemployment rates) that the government automatically adjusts all economic series to allow for seasonal variation. Therefore, seasonal variation is a minimal complication in analyzing either the economic or the political data discussed here.

Trends are potentially more serious complications. Trends exist in many data series, both political and economic; they represent the long-term tendency or direction evident in the series. Income, for example, has steadily increased during the postwar period, although its real increases may have been eroded by inflation.[2] To begin the examination of trends in popularity, special attention must be paid to analysts who suggest the American public is becoming more critical of its presidents.[3]

When this is done we find that popularity has not followed any particular trend in recent years, even though every president has lost popularity over time (Figure 3-1). Contrary to what some scholars hypothesize, the average popularity of individual presidents is not declining.[4] Table 3-1 lists the national figures for each president's average popularity, as well as his inaugural, end-of-term, and overall highest and lowest approval ratings. Close analysis

TABLE 3-1. Presidential Popularity: A 43 Year Review

President	Inaugural Popularity	End of Term Popularity	High Popularity	Low Popularity	Average Popularity
Carter	66.0%	34.0%	75.0%	21.0%	47.0%
Ford	71.0	53.0	71.0	37.0	46.0
Nixon	59.0	24.0	67.0	24.0	49.0
Johnson	78.0	49.0	80.0*	35.0	55.0
Kennedy	72.0	58.0	83.0	56.0	70.0
Eisenhower	68.0	59.0	79.0	48.0	64.0
Truman	87.0	31.0	87.0	23.0	41.0
Roosevelt	60.0	66.0	84.0	54.0	75.0

*Data from pre-1965, before group level data collected regularly.
Source: Gallup Handbook, October-November 1980.
Note: Data presented in Table 3-1 come only from published estimates of national approval ratings. Data from Tables 3-2 through 3-5 and Figure 3-1 include nonpublished data provided by Gallup. Slight discrepancies will occur as a result.

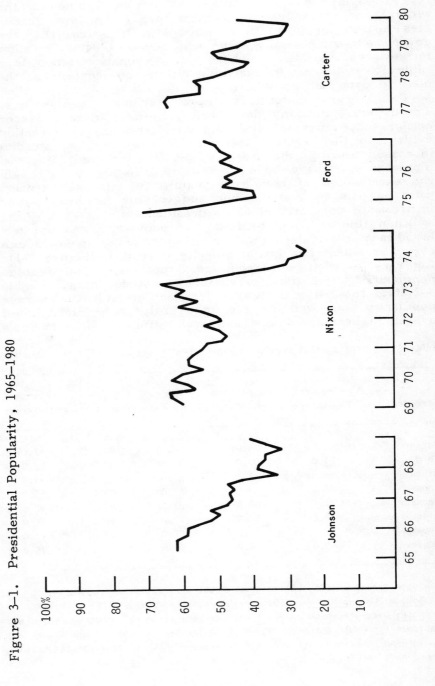

Figure 3-1. Presidential Popularity, 1965-1980

108

of Tables 3–2 through 3–5 and of Figure 3–1 shows that three of the four presidents between 1965 and 1980 had an average popularity of 48 percent. The exception was Nixon, whose average was 51.65 percent.

What about inaugural and end-of-term popularity? According to the data, a president's popularity does decrease during his term of office, but there is only a slight pattern of decreased inaugural popularity over time. Johnson enjoyed the highest inaugural popularity of the four presidents, with a 78 percent approval rating in January 1964. Nixon, who had a long and controversial prior political career, apparently retained enough of his political enemies to enter the presidency with only a 59 percent national approval, the lowest for any incoming president during this period. Ford's initial rating was 71 percent and Carter's was 66 percent—both respectable, but significantly lower than Johnson's.

The end-of-term popularity figures show a similar pattern: a general decline in the average over time, with Nixon's end-of-term rating being the extreme deviation. Johnson and Ford were the only presidents to leave office with anything approaching the veneration in which Americans are supposed to hold their former presidents. Johnson left the White House with a 49 percent approval rating, a surprisingly high figure given the contemporary impression that he was hounded from office because of his Vietnam policies. Ford, who had an end-of-term approval rating of 53 percent, was the only recent president to leave office with the support of more than half of his countrymen. Nixon and Carter did not fare so well: Nixon left with only 24 percent approval and Carter with only 34 percent.

Have the highest and lowest approval ratings for the last four presidents been declining because the public has grown increasingly critical? Although this is a common perception, the evidence suggests otherwise. The highest approval ratings are remarkably similar: 67 percent for Johnson, 66 percent for Nixon, 71 percent for Ford, and 64.9 percent for Carter. Clearly there is no downward time trend here. The lowest ratings are erratic. Johnson's lowest rating was 37.5 percent, while Nixon's was 24 percent. Ford's lowest was 38 percent and Carter's was 29 percent. Like the figures for inaugural and end-of-term popularity, the highest and lowest approval ratings for the last four presidents show no downward trend over time.

How do these figures pertain to the theory that the American people have become more critical of their presidents in recent years, particularly since the Vietnam War and the Watergate scandal eroded the prestige of the so-called "imperial presidency?" Although one must be cautious about drawing conclusions based on a sample of only four presidents, the data analyzed here do not reveal a trend towards increased public criticism of presidents. A more fruitful explanation of the variation in presidential popularity over time would be based on specific actions or personality.

RECENT CYCLES IN PRESIDENTIAL POPULARITY:
INDIVIDUAL PRESIDENCIES, 1965–1980

A consideration of cyclical fluctuations in popularity focuses on the main theoretical concern of this chapter, the examination of the cyclical and the rational choice theories of presidential popularity. Cyclical fluctuations are variations in the ups and downs of popularity that recur periodically over the time span studied, but with less regularity than the seasonal variations. The chief proponent of the cycle theory, James Stimson, has argued that variations in presidential popularity are more a reflection of "expectation/disillusionment among the less well-informed segments of the public" than the result of any particular actions or policies followed by the president.[5] When Stimson looks at the gradual decline in popularity that occurs for each president, he see not just a trend but a cycle. He argues that all presidents begin their terms with high popularity; thereafter, their popularity declines in a parabolic fashion. According to Stimson, the decrease in popularity continues for three years. Then, as the president's term nears an end, he enjoys a slight surge in popularity either because the public is comparing him with an all-too-human alternative or because of a nostalgia effect, a reluctance to make the break from the familiar to the unknown.

Despite its widespread acceptance, Stimson's cycle theory has been seriously criticized by Kernell (1977) and Monroe (1978).[6] These critics argue that more rational factors can explain the beginning and end-of-term shifts in popularity noted by the cycle theorists. While Stimson's argument that "presidential approval may be almost wholly independent of the president's behavior in office" and is instead "a function largely of inevitable forces associated with time" (1976, 1) seems greatly overstated, it does alert us to potential cyclical aspects to popularity that have to be allowed for in the analysis and that should be examined in more detail at this point. In particular, we should focus on the honeymoon period, during which a new president is given a chance to learn his job, and the nostalgia period, which occurs as the president's term ends.

My examination of the cyclical aspect of presidential popularity begins with a close consideration of the graphs of presidential popularity from 1965 to 1980. After looking at the trends over time, I then consider popularity at the two key dates in the cycle theory: the inauguration and the end of the term. Such an analysis will determine whether every president loses popularity, what the average loss is, and whether public disillusionment with presidents is increasing. The date when each president experienced his highest and lowest popularity ratings will then be pinpointed to discover whether these extremes are associated with specific events or are merely random. Finally, these cyclical patterns for different groups in American society will be compared.

When one looks at the graph of presidential popularity from 1965 to 1980, it is easy to understand why the cycle theory is so popular. Figure 3–1 depicts the overall national response to Presidents Johnson, Nixon, Ford, and Carter in one graph, with the end-of-term popularity for each president marked by a slash. The pattern of overall national popularity illustrated in Figure 3–1 is generally indicative of the political response to presidents among all groups, with a few notable exceptions.[7] Tables 3–2, 3–3, 3–4, and 3–6 present group data on each president from 1965 to 1980, with special reference paid to (1) the inaugural and end-of-term popularity of each president, (2) the date and level of each president's nadir in popularity, and (3) the average popularity enjoyed by each president while in office. For Ford and Carter, additional data are presented in Tables 3–5 and 3–7. For Ford, the prepardon and postpardon approval ratings are noted. For Carter, approval ratings are given just before the Iranian seizure of American hostages, after the hostages were seized but before the invasion of Afghanistan, and then after the Russian invasion of Afghanistan.

Johnson: Vietnam and the Vocally Disaffected

The first Gallup Poll on Johnson's popularity as president was taken in December 1963. His 78 percent national approval rating reflected the public's rallying around him following the national trauma of the Kennedy assassination the previous month. As demonstrated in Table 3–2, Johnson experienced a marked decline in public popularity after 1965. By the time he left office in January 1969, his national approval had dropped by almost 30 percentage points. It hovered around 40 percent to 45 percent, and

TABLE 3-2. Presidential Popularity by Groups: Johnson

Group	Inaugural Popularity [a]	End of Term Popularity [b]	Difference	Level and Date of High Popularity	Level and Date of Low Popularity	Difference	Average Popularity During Term [c]	Points lower or higher than the average popularity all presidents, 1965-1980 (49.70%)
National	78.00	49.00	-29.00	67.00 (8/65)	37.50 (8/68)	-29.50	48.53	-1.17
Age								
< 30	75.00	48.00	-27.00	75.00 (4/65)	33.00 (8/68)	-42.00	51.43	+1.73
30-49	68.00	49.00	-19.00	68.00 (4/65,8/65)	37.00 (10/67)	-31.00	50.88	+1.18
50+	63.00	49.00	-14.00	66.00 (6/65)	36.00 (10/68)	-30.00	48.80	-0.90
Income [d]								
$< 3	69.00	54.00	-15.00	69.00 (4/65)	38.00 (10/67)	-31.00	50.33	+0.63
$3-5	64.00	49.00	-15.00	68.00 (6/65)	36.50 (10/67)	-31.50	50.98	+1.28

112

$5-7	72.00	53.00	-19.00	72.00 (4/65)	36.50 (8/68)	-35.50	51.92	+2.22
$7-10	64.00	45.00	-19.00	66.00 (6/65)	34.50 (8/68)	-31.50	49.04	+0.66
$10+	--	41.00	--	47.50 (6/67)	33.00 (8/68)	-44.50	40.44	-9.26
Party Identification								
Republican	51.00	32.00	-19.00	51.00 (4/65)	22.00 (10/67)	-29.00	32.90	-16.80
Democrat	77.00	63.00	-14.00	80.50 (6/65)	51.00 (8/68)	-29.50	64.86	+15.16
Independent	62.00	42.00	-20.00	62.00 (4/65)	30.00 (4/68)	-32.00	43.32	-6.38
Occupation								
Professional	67.00	40.00	-27.00	67.00 (4/65)	34.50 (10/67)	45.03	-4.67	
White Collar	64.00	45.00	-19.00	66.30 (12/65)	36.00 (8/68)	-30.30	49.58	-0.12
Blue Collar	69.00	54.00	-15.00	72.50 (6/65)	37.50 (8/68)	-35.00	50.67	+0.97
Religion								
Protestant	60.00	45.00	-15.00	63.00 (8/65)	33.50 (10/67)	-25.50	45.45	-4.25
Catholic	81.00	59.00	-22.00	81.50 (6/65)	44.00 (8/68)	-37.50	61.59	+11.89

TABLE 3-2. Continued

Group	Inaugural Popularity[a]	End of Term Popularity[b]	Difference	Level and Date of High Popularity	Level and Date of Low Popularity	Difference	Average Popularity During Term[c]	Points lower or higher than the average popularity all Presidents, 1965-1980 (49.70%)
Sex								
Male	67.00	47.00	-20.00	69.50 (6/65)	38.00 (8/68)	-31.50	51.41	+1.71
Female	66.00	49.00	-17.00	66.00 (4/65)	36.00 (8/68)	-30.00	48.85	-0.85
Region								
East	79.00	54.00	-25.00	79.00 (4/65)	42.50 (8/68)	-36.50	58.56	+8.86
Midwest	70.00	54.00	-16.00	70.00 (4/65)	35.50 (10/67)	-34.50	50.39	+0.69
South	52.00	40.00	-12.00	60.00 (8/65)	32.00 (8/68)	-28.00	41.30	-8.40
West	63.00	44.00	-19.00	71.00 (6/65)	33.00 (6/68)	-38.00	49.62	+0.08

Race								
White	64.00	47.00	-20.00	64.00 (4/65,8/65)	35.00 (10/68)	-29.00	47.89	+1.81
Nonwhite	--	--	--	--	--	--	--	--

[a] First poll ratings for Johnson were in December 1963. This poll gives no group data. The group data begin in April 1965. National popularity at this time was 67.00%.

[b] January 1969

[c] Calculated from April 1965 to January 1969

[d] Income in thousands of dollars

ended with a slight surge to 49 percent at the end of his term.

How did Johnson fare among the major groups in American society? Did he experience a honeymoon period, a decline, and then an end-of-term nostalgic surge among any or all groups? The data in Table 3-2 are useful. Since the December 1963 Gallup study was not conducted on group lines, Johnson's initial popularity among different groups can be examined only by looking at his inaugural popularity at the beginning of his second term in 1965. The first Gallup Poll taken after Johnson's inauguration was in March 1965. These popularity figures, presented in the first column of Table 3-2, are slightly lower than the national figure for December 1963, but they are nevertheless quite high and indicate Johnson's great popularity after his stunning 1964 electoral victory over Goldwater. And they are quite interesting when compared to Johnson's end-of-term popularity among the same groups.

We have seen that Johnson's popularity dropped 30 percentage points nationally between December 1963 and January 1969, but how did he fare among separate groups from March 1965 to January 1969? Johnson lost a great amount of popularity among young people, the under-30s who originated the phrase "never trust anyone over 30" partly in response to Johnson's hated Vietnam policy. However, the March 1965 figures indicate the strong support Johnson initially enjoyed among the young because of his progressive civil rights stance and his contrast with Goldwater. Johnson began his second term in office with a 75 percent approval rating among those under 30, 68 percent among those between 30 and 49, and 63 percent among those over 50. Clearly Johnson's strongest supporters were the young. By the time he left office, he had lost his youthful supporters, but he still registered approval levels of 48 percent to 49 percent among all age groups. Johnson's great loss in popularity among the young, then, is more indicative of a decline in early enthusiasm than any eventual extreme disaffection. These data show that many young people did not like Johnson when he left office, but they were not atypical among Americans, only more vocal.

The figures on popularity according to income are less surprising, but must be considered tentative because of data limitations.[8] Johnson lost support among all income groups in approximately equal amounts: 15 percent to 19 percent. He began his second term with his highest support among those earning $5,000-7,000 a year. These people initially gave Johnson a 72 percent approval rating. They were closely followed by those earning less than

$3,000 a year, who approved of Johnson by a rate of 69 percent. Johnson retained his strongest support among these two groups, ending his term with 54 percent approval among the poorest members of society (those earning less than $3,000 a year) and 53 percent approval among those earning $5,000–7,000 a year. On the whole, though, these differences in popularity among income groups are not striking and do not suggest a strong variation in public response to Johnson according to income categories.

The reason for this may lie in the data classifications used by Gallup at the time. Having the top income category range from $7,000–10,000 hardly makes it easy to detect any upper-class antagonism to the New Society programs. Even so, the figures on Johnson's end-of-term popularity do show a slightly lower approval rating as income increases. For example, Johnson ended his term with approval ratings of 54 percent from respondents earning less than $3,000 a year and 41 percent from those earning above $10,000. Because the Gallup's highest income category for 1969 was $10,000 a year and above, it is difficult to differentiate between the responses of the middle- and the upper middle-income classes. Moreover, since this top category was not used at all in 1965, only a rough insight into the importance of income groupings on Johnson's popularity and decline can be gained.

Given that Gallup did not poll an income group high enough to be labeled upper class, the occupation categories may be more useful in detecting socioeconomic class response to Johnson. Johnson began with roughly equivalent support among all occupation groups and then lost support among all groups, but lost it most dramatically among the upper professional class. This corresponds to the crude impression gained from analysis of the income data.

The figures on occupation are more interesting for their differential decline than for the difference in initial approval ratings. This is in marked contrast to the patterns for other groups, such as age, where the differential comes from the variations in initial appraisal. Professional and blue-collar people gave Johnson slightly higher initial support than other income groups: He received 67 percent approval from the professionals and 69 percent from blue-collar workers compared to 64 percent from white-collar workers. However, Johnson's biggest loss of support came from professional people, among whom his popularity decreased by 27 percent.

Turning next to religious groups, we find a striking difference between the support levels Johnson enjoyed among Protestants and Catholics. His decline among both groups was comparable: 15 percent among Protestants and 22 percent among Catholics. However, the initial difference in approval ratings was 21 percent. The Catholics' initial approval of 81 percent was the highest of any group, including Democrats, for the man who ran and was elected vice president on a ticket with the first Catholic president. This differential along religious lines occurs only for Johnson among the four presidents under study.

Johnson's popularity among Catholics corresponds to the traditional wisdom that says Catholics tend to vote Democratic rather than Republican. Since Carter, the other Democratic president during this period, did not enjoy this strong Catholic support, however, it is necessary to ask why Catholics differed in their approval of the two presidents. The following explanations may account for the difference: (1) this period may be one of a shift in Catholic voting patterns, (2) Carter's membership in a fundamentalist Baptist religion may have offended Catholics, or (3) Johnson's association with Kennedy in a period when anti-Catholic feeling was still extant may have endeared him to Catholic supporters and strengthened their Democratic bias. The last explanation seems the most likely, but it can only be considered speculative, given the limitation of time-series data.

The figures on popularity among men and women reveal little difference on the basis of sex. Both groups gave Johnson strong and roughly equivalent initial approval (67 percent among men, 66 percent among women). Johnson also lost support in approximately equivalent amounts among both groups: 20 percent among men and 17 percent among women. There has traditionally been little difference in vote choice according to sex, and these patterns correspond to that tradition.

The figures on regional support patterns are more surprising. Both Johnson's greatest initial support and his greatest loss of support came from the East, where his initial popularity was 79 percent but dropped 25 percentage points to 54 percent. In the Midwest, Johnson's initial support was 70 percent, while in the West it was 63 percent. By the time he left office, Johnson's popularity had decreased in the Midwest by 16 percentage points to 54 percent and in the West by 19 percentage points to 44 percent. The South gave him the lowest approval ratings. His 1965 approval in that region was only 52 percent, a full 27 percentage points lower than his initial support in the East, suggesting that his civil rights stance had already cost him dearly in the South by the time of his second inauguration. By the end of his second term, Johnson's popularity had dropped 12 percentage points in the South. Although this was his smallest regional decrease, it reflects his initially low approval level rather than any unusual staying power, since the South's 40 percent approval rating for Johnson when he left office was his lowest in the country.

As expected, Johnson had higher levels of initial support among Democrats (77 percent) than among Independents (62 percent) or Republicans (51 percent). His decline was also somewhat less precipitous among Democrats (14 percent) than among Republicans or Independents. Given the tensions in the Democratic party at the time—the McCarthy and Kennedy challenges, the internal dissension, and the near riot at the 1968 Democratic convention—the size of Johnson's decline among members of his own party is amazingly small. Certainly the decline seems large when it is contrasted with Ford's 3 percent gain in popularity among Republicans while in office. But Ford was an unusually popular president among the Republican rank and file and was considered a good party man by the party hierarchy. When Johnson's 14 percent loss in popularity among his party members is compared with Nixon's 30 percent drop and Carter's 28 percent decline among members of their own parties, Johnson's loss seems relatively small. Though these figures highlight the roller-coaster aspect of presidential fortunes over the last 15 years, they do not support the popular idea—expressed by political columnists such as Anthony Lewis (1981)—that Americans are becoming more cynical about their presidents. These data on party support for presidents suggest, rather, that the harsher tone we hear in evaluating presidents is less reflective of widespread public sentiment than of extremely vocal and pressworthy political groups.

Johnson lost support, then, among every single group, with his largest declines among the young, professionals, and Easterners, all groups who initially supported his civil rights program but who became disenchanted with him because of the Vietnam War. The figures presented here reveal Johnson as the classic New Deal liberal who disaffected his critical voting groups and left office because of that.[9]

Nixon: Watergate Turned Nostalgia to Relief

How did Nixon fare? Figure 3–1 shows that during Nixon's first term his overall national popularity declined remarkably little from his inaugural high. In fact, Nixon's levels of public popularity remained fairly constant throughout his first term. Although his first term shows little of the inevitable decline predicted by the cycle theorists, it does end with an extremely small surge in popularity, as predicted by the theory. The only group to deviate noticeably from this overall national pattern is blue-collar workers, whose level of support declined drastically during Nixon's first term and failed to increase at the end of the term. During Nixon's second term, of course, his popularity declined precipitously among all groups, and he never recovered among any group, not even Republicans.

Table 3–3, which notes the crucial dates in Nixon's popularity, is striking because it shows how much lower Nixon's initial popularity was compared to that of other presidents. Nixon enjoyed little of the traditional honeymoon period. At 59 percent, his initial popularity is 19 percent lower than Johnson's. Nixon's relative unpopularity when he took office may be the result of his controversial prepresidential political career; his many political detractors simply did not give him the kind of initial trust presidents usually enjoy. It also may be explained by the fact that when Johnson and Ford took office, the country was in a state of shock and turned to its new presidents for unity, leadership, and reassurance. But when we contrast Nixon's initial popularity with that of Carter, who took office under normal conditions, we still find a difference of 7 percent. This difference is significant, but not dramatic, and is probably accounted for by the intense dislike certain groups felt for Nixon.[10] Nixon left office with a national approval level of merely 24 percent, the lowest overall approval rating of any president during this period. His overall national loss of popularity while in office, however, is 35 percent, a decline again comparable to Carter's overall loss of 32 percent. Both presidents took office under normal circumstances, but both left in disgrace: Nixon because of Watergate, Carter because of the deterioration of the economy and the Iranian hostage crisis.

Who were the groups that so disliked Nixon they deprived him of the usual grace period enjoyed by presidents? The figures in Table 3–3 generally correspond to the voting literature's conclusions about traditional Republican supporters. The most striking differentials appear in the income and occupation categories, as well as along traditional political party lines. There is some indication that religion, region, and age also affected the initial support given Nixon, although the differences here are not so dramatic. Sex was the only category in which there was no differential. (Separate figures on Nixon's support among nonwhites are not available until later in his term.)

The groups who withheld support from Nixon were, for the most part, the expected ones. Democrats were unenthusiastic about their new president, giving him only a 45 percent approval rating, 14 percentage points less than his initial national approval. This partisan pattern is common, however. Upon taking office, Carter received an initial Republican approval rating of 49 percent, 17 percentage points lower than his initial national approval rate. Ford was the exception, receiving widespread support of 68 percent among Democrats compared to 71 percent national approval. But it is interesting to note that among Republican voters, Nixon initially was better liked than Ford, with 80 percent Republican approval compared to Ford's 77 percent. (Comparable group data on Johnson's inaugural support ratings are not available.)

The more interesting differentials in initial support fall along socioeconomic class lines in the income and occupation categories. As income levels increase, so does Nixon's initial support. His ratings begin at 52 percent among those earning less than $3,000 a year and gradually increase until they reach 70 percent among those earning more than $10,000 a year, the highest income category Gallup used in 1969. This typical socioeconomic class pattern also holds for occupation groups, where the traditional voting patterns are again replicated. Professionals gave Nixon his strongest initial support (68 percent), while white-collar (62 percent) and blue-collar (53 percent) respondents were less enthusiastic.

There were less dramatic differences in Nixon's initial approval ratings according to age, religion, and geographic region. Support for Nixon increased slightly as we examine older voters. Nixon initially had only 58 percent approval among those under 30, compared to 62 percent from those over 50. This is not what would be expected if the assumption is that the people who opposed Nixon were those who remembered his earlier political record, e.g., his campaign against Helen Gahagan Douglas in California or his actions during the Alger Hiss case. Instead, we find older voters slightly more sympathetic to Nixon. This bears out the traditional wisdom that the old tend to favor the Republican party more than the young. These findings are interesting given the discussions of the impact of the lowered voting age discussed during the 1968 campaign. The expected differential did not show up in the subse-

TABLE 3-3. Presidential Popularity by Groups: Nixon

Group	Inaugural Popularity[a]	End of Term Popularity[b]	Difference	Level and Date of High Popularity	Level and Date of Low Popularity	Difference	Average Popularity During Term	Points lower or higher than the average popularity all presidents, 1965-1980 (49.70%)
National	59.00	24.00	-35.00	66.00 (2/73)	24.00 (8/74)	-42.00	51.65	+1.95
Age								
< 30	58.00	19.00	-39.00	62.50 (4/73)	19.00 (8/74)	-43.50	48.98	-0.72
30-49	57.00	20.00	-37.00	69.20 (2/73)	23.00 (8/74)	-46.20	51.91	+2.21
50+	62.00	27.00	-35.00	71.00 (2/73)	27.00 (8/74)	-44.00	53.83	+4.13
Income[c]								
$< 3	52.00	19.00	-33.00	65.00 (12/69)	19.00 (8/74)	-46.00	45.90	-3.80
$3-5	55.00	26.00	-29.00	63.50 (4/69)	26.00 (8/74)	-37.50	48.45	-1.25

$5-10	57.70	24.50	-33.20	69.50 (2/73)	22.00 (6/74)	-47.50	51.06	+1.36
$10-15	70.00[d]	21.00	-49.00	71.00 (2/73)	25.80 (2/74)	-45.20	55.11	+5.41
$15+	--	27.50	--	73.00 (4/73)	26.50 (2/74)	-46.50	43.07	-6.63
Party								
Identification								
Republican	80.00	50.00	-30.00	91.00 (4/73)	50.00 (8/74)	-41.00	77.35	+27.65
Democrat	45.00	13.00	-32.00	54.00 (2/69)	12.30 (2/74)	-42.30	37.17	-12.53
Independent	59.00	22.00	-37.00	71.00 (2/73)	22.00 (8/74)	-49.00	52.08	+2.38
Occupation								
Professional	68.00	24.00	-44.00	69.50 (4/69,2/70)	24.00 (8/74)	-45.50	56.44	+6.74
White Collar	62.00	24.00	-38.00	73.00 (12/69)	24.00 (8/74)	-49.00	53.68	+3.98
Blue Collar	53.00	18.00	-35.00	66.00 (2/73)	20.50 (4/74)	-45.50	48.40	-1.30
Religion								
Protestant	63.00	28.00	-35.00	71.00 (12/69)	30.00 (4/74)	-41.00	54.68	+4.98
Catholic	57.00	18.00	-39.00	68.00 (2/73)	18.00 (8/74)	-50.00	48.36	-1.34

TABLE 3-3. Continued

Group	Inaugural Popularity[a]	End of Term Popularity[b]	Difference	Level and Date of High Popularity	Level and Date of Low Popularity	Difference	Average Popularity During Term	Points lower or higher than the average popularity all Presidents, 1965-1980 (49.70%)
Sex								
Male	60.00	23.00	-37.00	71.00 (12/69)	23.00 (8/74)	-48.00	54.53	+4.83
Female	59.00	24.00	-35.00	65.00 (2/73)	24.00 (4/74)	-41.00	50.75	+1.05
Region								
East	51.00	20.00	-31.00	66.00 (4/69)	20.00 (8/74)	-46.00	49.12	-0.58
Midwest	65.00	21.00	-44.00	71.00 (12/69)	21.00 (8/74)	-50.00	50.20	+0.50
South	60.00	30.00	-30.00	71.50 (2/73)	23.00 (4/74)	-44.00	55.20	+5.50
West	62.00	25.00	-37.00	67.00 (6/69)	23.00 (4/74)	-44.00	48.43	-1.27

124

Race							
White	61.00	26.00	-35.00	69.50 (2/73)	26.00 (8/74)	-43.50	52.96	+3.26
Nonwhite	--	10.00	--	44.00 (12/69)	9.50 (8/74)	-34.50	24.50	-25.2

[a] January 1969
[b] August 2-5, 1974
[c] Income in thousands of dollars
[d] $10,000+

125

quent 1972 vote, but the lower Republican support among those under 30 does show up in the public opinion data on Nixon's initial support.

Protestants gave Nixon higher initial approval ratings (63 percent) than did Catholics (57 percent). This finding agrees with the traditional voting patterns, although the differences are not striking and certainly do not compare to Johnson's 60/81 percent Protestant/Catholic differential.

The figures on regional approval reveal a significant differential in initial approval, with the East giving Nixon his lowest initial approval. Easterners liked Nixon less (51 percent) than Midwesterners (65 percent) or Westerners (62 percent). Nixon's initial Southern approval rating of 60 percent suggests that the South had not yet broken with its Democratic past. It is during Nixon's term in office that we see the beginning of the political shift in the Sunbelt, a shift that burst forth most dramatically only in the 1980 election.

In sum, then, Nixon's support pattern during his first term fits the traditional stereotype of Republican voting patterns. The older, Protestant, upper-income and higher occupational-status groups gave their strongest support to the Republican president. There are some less dramatic differences according to age and geographic regions, with the traditional regional support patterns just beginning to shift.

How did Nixon's popularity hold up among these groups? Figure 3–1 suggests that he maintained national popularity fairly well during his first term, with his inaugural rate of 59 percent followed by fluctuations that stayed mostly in the 50 percent to 60 percent rage. A decline, but not a marked one, shows up during Nixon's first term. The interesting pattern appears in his second term, when Watergate contributed to the largest drops in popularity of any of the four presidents considered here. Although this logically raises the question of what causes high and low points in popularity, let us postpone the discussion of that issue until we complete the consideration of end-of-term surges in presidential popularity. From the data in Table 3–3, it appears that Nixon enjoyed a slight but not striking surge of popularity at the end of his first term, and that there was no surge at all at the end of his second term. Indeed, Nixon's low point for all groups except the two upper-income groups and Democrats comes within the last four months of his second term. (See Table 3–3 for the dates of Nixon's lowest popularity for each group.) Thus Nixon's end-of-term pattern of popularity does not reveal strong public support or affection for an outgoing leader.

However, his exit from office was hardly typical. And the general pattern for his first term suggests a brief upturn at the end. All of these figures, as I shall later demonstrate in detail, fit in better with a rational theory stressing the rebuilding of a national coalition as a campaign for reelection looms than with a cyclical theory of presidential popularity.

Ford: The Pardon Ended the Honeymoon

What about Ford's pattern? Did any group withhold initial support from Ford? Did his popularity throughout his term follow the pattern predicted by the cycle theory? The evidence in Tables 3–4 and 3–5 and Figure 3–1 suggests that nonwhites were the only group who denied Ford a honeymoon period and that Ford took office with high levels of popularity among most groups. But did these initial high ratings last the standard period and then decline gradually, as the cycle theory predicts? Here the evidence is strongly at variance with the theory.

Table 3–4 shows that Ford began his presidency with fairly high popularity among the elderly and the upper-income and upper-occupation groups, as might be expected for a Republican, and much lower popularity among non-whites. The regional patterns are not striking, with Ford being only slightly more popular among his fellow Midwest-erners. There are no differences according to religion or sex. As expected, Republicans are more enthusiastic about Ford than Democrats (77 percent versus 68 percent), although both groups give fairly high initial approval ratings.

When the cycle theory is applied to Ford, three problems appear. First, Ford's honeymoon ended almost before it began, since he lost popularity among all groups when he pardoned Nixon shortly after taking office. Second, following this initial decline, Ford's popularity remained relatively constant among all groups. Third, Ford did not experience any marked end-of-term surge of popularity, although there may have been a very slight increase in support among Southern and Midwestern voters.

The validity of the cycle theory can be examined more thoroughly at the group level by looking at Ford's initial and end-of-term popularity. Table 3–4 provides summary information on how Ford fared among different groups and shows whether the predicted honeymoon and decline periods did occur among any of these groups. The table suggests Ford did, in fact, lose popularity among all groups except

TABLE 3-4. Presidential Popularity by Groups: Ford

Group	Inaugural Popularity[a]	End of Term Popularity[b]	Difference	Level and Date of High Popularity	Level and Date of Low Popularity	Difference	Average Popularity During Term	Points lower or higher than the average popularity all presidents, 1965-1980 (49.70%)
National	71.00	53.00	-18.00	71.00 (8/74)	38.00 (2/75)	-33.00	48.50	-1.20
Age								
< 30	69.00	56.00	-13.00	69.00 (8/74)	39.50 (2/75)	-27.50	50.37	+0.67
30-49	69.00	47.00	-22.00	69.00 (8/74)	38.00 (2/75)	-31.00	47.57	-2.13
50+	74.00	56.00	-18.00	74.00 (8/74)	36.00 (12/75)	-38.00	46.67	-3.03
Income[c]								
$3-5	64.00	47.00	-17.00	64.00 (8/74)	28.00 (10/75)	-36.00	40.30	-9.40
$5-10	65.00	46.00	-18.00	65.00 (8/74)	33.50	-31.50	43.87	-5.83

$10-15	77.00	53.00	-24.00	77.00 (8/74)	37.00 (2/75)	-40.00	49.31	-0.39
$15+	75.50	59.00	-16.50	75.40 (8/74)	41.70 (12/75)	-33.80	53.11	+3.41
Party Identification								
Republican	77.00	80.00	+3.00	80.00 (12/76)	59.50 (12/75)	-20.50	68.60	+18.90
Democrat	68.00	40.00	-28.00	68.00 (8/74)	28.00 (2/75)	-40.00	37.77	-11.93
Independent	70.00	54.00	-16.00	70.00 (8/74)	38.00 (2/75)	-32.00	49.20	-0.50
Occupation								
Professional	78.00	60.00	-18.00	78.00 (8/74)	43.00 (2/75)	-35.00	55.93	+6.23
White Collar	72.00	49.00	-23.00	72.00 (8/74)	43.00 (2/75)	-29.00	38.43	-11.27
Blue Collar	65.00	49.00	-16.00	65.00 (8/74)	36.00 (2/75)	-29.00	44.73	-4.97
Religion								
Protestant	71.00	54.00	-17.00	71.00 (8/74)	41.00 (2/75)	-30.00	48.79	-0.91
Catholic	73.00	56.00	-17.00	73.00 (8/74)	36.50 (4/75)	-37.00	46.04	-3.66

TABLE 3-4. Continued

Group	Inaugural Popularity[a]	End of Term Popularity[b]	Difference	Level and Date of High Popularity	Level and Date of Low Popularity	Difference	Average Popularity During Term	Points lower or higher than the average popularity all Presidents, 1965-1980 (49.70%)
Sex								
Male	70.00	53.00	-17.00	70.00 (8/74)	37.00 (2/75,4/75)	-33.00	47.20	-2.50
Female	71.00	54.00	-17.00	71.00 (8/74)	39.00 (2/75)	-32.00	48.37	-1.33
Region								
East	67.00	49.00	-18.00	67.00 (8/74)	28.00 (8/76)	-39.00	43.13	-6.57
Midwest	76.00	58.00	-18.00	76.00 (8/74)	34.00 (8/76)	-42.00	48.23	-1.47
South	68.00	54.00	-14.00	68.00 (8/74)	30.00 (8/76)	-38.00	45.33	-4.37
West	72.00	51.00	-21.00	72.00 (8/74)	37.00 (8/76)	-35.00	47.17	-2.53

Race							
White	74.00	58.00	-16.00	74.00 (8/74)	41.00 (2/75)	-33.00	50.80	+1.10
Nonwhite	51.00	27.00	-24.00	51.00 (8/74)	21.00 (12/74)	-30.00	29.60	-20.10

[a] August 16-19, 1974
[b] December 10-13, 1976
[c] Income in thousands of dollars

the Republicans, among whom he actually gained 3 percentage points. Among all other groups, however, Ford's popularity dropped 13 to 28 percentage points below the rates recorded in the August 16–19, 1974 Gallup Poll. There are no major distinctive group deviations from this overall pattern, i.e., Ford did not lose more popularity among certain occupation or income groups.

Returning to the pattern of popularity for Ford depicted in Figure 3–1, however, we are alerted to an early point in Ford's term that is atypical of the overall pattern. Perusal of Ford's popularity immediately after taking office reveals that his initial approval ratings dropped drastically among all groups immediately after he pardoned Nixon. (See Table 3–5.) The only exception here occurs among Republicans, whose support declined only 4 percentage points, from 77 percent to 73 percent. Among all other groups, however, Ford lost great support immediately after the pardon. The losses ranged from 13 percent among Protestants, those under 30, and nonwhites, to 22 percent among those earning between $10,000–15,000 a year, and 24 percent among Democrats. When we compare Ford's postpardon popularity, as indicated by the Gallup Poll of October 18–21, 1974, with his end-of-term approval ratings, his ratings remained remarkably constant for most groups. Once the decline caused by the Nixon pardon is allowed for, then, Ford's first and last popularity ratings are identical (53 percent) at the national level. In eight out of the twenty-four groups, Ford actually gained popularity between October 1974 and December 1976, the last poll taken during his presidency. His popularity increased among those under 30 and over 50, Republicans, Catholics, Midwesterners, Southerners, men, and whites. His popularity remained constant among those earning under $3,000 a year, women, and professionals. It declined among the other thirteen groups: those 30–49 years old, voters earning over $5,000 a year, Democrats, Independents, white-collar and blue-collar workers, Protestants, Easterners, Westerners, and nonwhites.

In summation, Ford's popularity ratings do not support the cycle theory of presidential popularity. Although there was an overall decline in his support, the pattern of decline is strongly at variance with that predicted by the cycle theory. Instead of the predicted honeymoon, gradual decline, and end-of-term surge, Ford experienced an immediate and substantial drop in popularity followed by a relatively constant level of public approval. Moreover, there is a rational explanation for the decline: the Nixon pardon. After this drop is accounted for, Ford's popu-

TABLE 3-5. Effect of Pardoning Nixon on Ford's Popularity

Group	Pre-Pardon Popularity[a]	Post-Pardon Popularity[b]	Difference
National	71.00	53.00	-18.00
Age			
< 30	67.00	54.00	-13.00
30-49	69.00	54.00	-15.00
50+	74.00	53.00	-21.00
Income[c]			
$3-5	64.50	47.50	-17.00
$5-10	65.00	49.50	-15.50
$10-15	77.00	55.00	-22.00
$15+	75.50	60.50	-15.00
Party Identification			
Republican	77.00	73.00	-4.00
Democrat	68.00	44.00	-24.00
Independent	70.00	56.00	-14.00
Occupation			
Professional	78.00	60.00	-18.00
White Collar	72.00	52.00	-20.00
Blue Collar	65.00	52.00	-13.00
Religion			
Protestant	71.00	58.00	-13.00
Catholic	73.00	52.00	-21.00
Sex			
Male	70.00	52.00	-18.00
Female	71.00	54.00	-17.00
Region			
East	67.00	52.00	-15.00
Midwest	76.00	55.00	-21.00
South	68.00	53.00	-15.00
West	72.00	54.00	-18.00
Race			
White	74.00	56.00	-18.00
Nonwhite	56.00	38.00	-13.00

[a] August 16-19, 1974
[b] October 18-21, 1974
[c] Income in thousands of dollars

larity remains remarkably constant and does not conform to the cycle theory of presidential popularity in any way.

Carter: The Rally Effect Turned Sour

How does Carter's record correspond to the cycle theory of presidential popularity? On first examination, Figure 3–1 yields a pattern that corresponds closely to that predicted by the cycle theory. Carter's popularity shows a marked decline among all groups, followed by an end-of-term surge after the taking of the American hostages in Iran. This pattern occurred among all groups, as summarized in Table 3–6. Carter's decline in popularity is extreme. He lost approximately 30 points in approval ratings among most groups except nonwhites, with the smallest loss (a 21 percent drop) coming from Westerners and the lowest income earners and the greatest loss (a 42 percent drop) from white-collar workers.[11] Nonwhites are the only group among whom Carter maintained popularity throughout his term, dropping only 7 percentage points, from 62 percent to 55 percent. His decline among Democrats was slightly less than his overall decline, but at 28 percent was nonetheless striking and much greater than Johnson's 14 percent drop.

On first consideration, the patterns of popularity for Carter and Johnson seem closest to the predictions of the cycle theorists. A logical question arises, however: Were these declines caused by the vagaries of public opinion or by specific presidential actions? The first explanation would support Stimson's theory that declines in presidential popularity are caused by the disillusionment that results from unrealistic public expectations of a new president. The second explanation would support Mueller's theory that declines are caused by a president's antagonism of key groups who eventually form a coalition of disaffected minorities to work against him.

To complete the examination of the cycle theory and to test it against Mueller's coalition-of-minorities theory, the specific high and low points for each president must be considered. Do these high and low points correspond to specific dates when crucial presidential actions were taken? And do they occur simultaneously for all groups, particularly those that later formed coalitions either for or against the president?

The Highs and Lows of Popularity:
Do They Reflect Random Cycles or Presidential Actions?

The evidence strongly suggests that cycles in presidential popularity are better explained by specific events than by the vagaries of public opinion. Johnson's decline corresponds to the growing public discontent with the Vietnam War. Nixon's first term was marked by foreign policy successes that kept his popularity high. His second term was ended by the Watergate scandal, which produced the single lowest group approval rating of any president: 9.5 percent among nonwhites. Ford's only real loss of support followed the Nixon pardon. Carter's decline corresponded to economic deterioration, while his end-of-term surge was the result of the public's rallying around him as national leader after Americans were taken prisoner in Iran. Let us now consider how closely the highs and lows in popularity can be matched with specific events and whether these peaks and troughs in popularity correspond for groups that later worked together for or against a president.

First consider Table 3–2, which depicts Johnson's group popularity from 1965 on. Johnson's highest popularity ratings occurred between April and August of 1965 for all groups except white-collar workers and top-income earners, whose support peaked in December 1965 and June 1967, respectively. The year 1965 was the period of civil rights legislation, culminating in the passage of the Voting Rights Act on August 6 and the National Housing Act on August 10. The Los Angeles race riots erupted on August 11, 1965. So all but two groups responded most favorably to Johnson during the period when his activities on behalf of civil rights were greatest, but before a backlash had had time to develop.

Johnson's lowest popularity occurred in October 1967 or between April and October of 1968, depending on the group examined. The Newark and Detroit riots occurred in July 1967. The strong McCarthy showing in the New Hampshire primary, Johnson's March announcement that he would not seek renomination, the slow deterioration of U.S. strength in Vietnam, and the growing antiwar feeling all occurred during the spring and summer of 1968, when Johnson's popularity ratings were at their lowest. The antiwar sentiment remained focused on Johnson even after he decided not to run, since Humphrey was viewed by many as Johnson's proxy. The antiwar anger culminated in college demonstrations in the spring of 1968 and the Democratic convention in Chicago in August 1968. Thus, matching Johnson's popularity ratings with specific events further supports a rational explanation of presidential popularity, since Johnson's highest and lowest popularity, and most of his decline, are attributable to specific significant events.

What about Nixon? The dates of his lowest popularity should be obvious to anyone who lived through the Water-

TABLE 3-6. Presidential Popularity by Groups: Carter

Group	Inaugural Popularity[a]	End of Term Popularity[b]	Difference	Level and Date of High Popularity	Level and Date of Low Popularity	Difference	Average Popularity During Term	Points lower or higher than the average popularity all presidents, 1965-1980 (49.70%)
National	66.00	34.00	-32.00	69.40 (4/77)	29.00 (10/79)	-40.40	48.68	-1.02
Age								
30	70.70	43.00	-27.70	77.00 (4/77)	33.50 (8/79)	-43.50	53.11	+3.41
30-49	64.70	29.00	-35.70	71.00 (4/77)	24.00 (6/79)	-47.00	48.13	-1.57
50+	62.90	32.00	-30.90	68.00 (4/77)	28.00 (6/79)	-40.00	46.80	-2.90
Income[c]								
$< 5	64.10	43.00	-21.10	66.00 (4/77)	43.00 (2/81)	-23.00	51.03	+1.33
$5-10	65.90	42.00	-23.90	72.00 (4/77)	32.00 (6/79)	-40.00	49.89	-0.17

136

$10-15	66.70	31.00	-35.70	73.00 (4/77)	30.00 (12/79)	-43.00	50.02	+0.32
$15-20	67.00	31.00	-36.00	72.00 (4/77)	30.00 (8/79)	-42.00	49.49	-0.21
$20+	64.30	32.50	-31.80	74.00 (4/77)	21.00 (6/79)	-53.00	46.32	-3.38
Party Identification								
Republican	49.00	14.00	-35.00	56.00 (4/77)	14.00 (2/80)	-40.00	33.33	-16.37
Democrat	77.00	49.00	-28.00	81.00 (4/77)	34.00 (6/79)	-47.00	60.71	+11.01
Independent	60.00	30.00	-30.00	70.00 (4/77)	28.00 (6/79)	-42.00	47.55	-2.15
Occupation								
Professional	64.00	31.00	-33.00	76.00 (4/77)	24.00 (6/79)	-52.00	48.47	-1.23
White Collar	70.00	28.00	-42.00	78.00 (4/77)	28.00 (8/79,2/80)	-50.00	49.70	0.00
Blue Collar	67.00	35.00	-32.00	73.00 (4/77)	30.00 (6/79)	-43.00	51.47	+1.77
Religion								
Protestant	67.00	36.00	-31.00	71.00 (4/77,8/77)	29.00 (6/79)	-42.00	51.35	+1.65
Catholic	63.00	34.00	-29.00	74.00 (4/77)	28.00 (6/79)	-46.00	52.76	-3.06

TABLE 3-6. Continued

Group	Inaugural Popularity[a]	End of Term Popularity[b]	Difference	Level and Date of High Popularity	Level and Date of Low Popularity	Difference	Average Popularity During Term	Points lower or higher than the average popularity all Presidents, 1965-1980 (49.70%)
Sex								
Male	67.00	30.00	-37.00	71.00 (4/77)	28.00 (6/79)	-43.00	48.82	-0.88
Female	64.00	38.00	-26.00	72.00 (4/77)	28.00 (6/79)	-44.00	48.86	-0.84
Region								
East	63.20	28.00	-35.20	72.00 (4/77)	25.00 (6/79)	-47.00	49.27	-0.43
Midwest	65.60	35.00	-30.60	74.00 (4/77)	25.00 (6/79)	-49.00	51.45	+1.75
South	73.70	38.00	-35.70	73.70 (2/77)	32.00 (6/79)	-41.70	52.67	+2.97
West	57.10	36.00	-21.10	71.00 (4/77)	31.00 (8/79)	-40.00	48.39	-1.31

138

Race								
White	66.00	31.00	-35.00	78.00 (4/77)	26.00 (6/79)	75.00	48.16	-1.54
Nonwhite	62.00	55.00	-7.00	72.00 (4/77)	36.00 (12/79)	-42.00	57.89	+8.19

[a] February 4-7, 1977
[b] January 1981
[c] Income in thousands of dollars

gate period: all are in 1974 and most occurred in August, just before he resigned. The Watergate break-in and coverup is the obvious explanation. This cost Nixon between 34.5–50 percentage points in popularity, a drop much greater than the decline of 29.5 percent suffered by Johnson between August 1965 and August 1968. Nixon's popularity declined by at least 41 percent among all groups except two: those earning incomes of $3,000–5,000 and nonwhites. Although Nixon did not lose as much popularity among nonwhites as among other groups, this was because he never had had much to lose. His highest rating among nonwhites was only 44 percent. When he left office, only 9.5 percent of nonwhites supported him, the lowest group approval rating recorded for any president in recent history.

We saw earlier that Ford's popularity was relatively constant except for the steep drop after the Nixon pardon. How much did the pardon cost Ford? The data in Table 3–5 suggest that, except among Republicans, the pardon cost Ford from 13 to 24 percentage points. At the national level, his prepardon popularity on August 16–19, 1974 was 71 percent. After the pardon, his national popularity dropped to 53 percent, a loss of 18 percentage points. Old people seemed to react more strongly to the pardon than young people, but this difference appears to result from the higher level of initial enthusiasm for Ford, since the postpardon approval levels are approximately the same for all three age groups. Ford's varying declines among different income groups appear to have been similarly affected by differing initial approval levels rather than by discrepancies in the actual level of approval to which he fell among these different income groups. His initial approval ratings among higher-income groups— $10,000–15,000 and over $15,000—were approximately 10 percent higher than his ratings by people earning under $10,000 a year. After the pardon, however, Ford's approval ratings among each group dropped over 15 percent, with the decline being slightly greater in the $10,000–15,000 income group.

The pattern of reaction to the pardon among occupation groups corresponds to the pattern for the various income groups. Ford had higher initial support among professionals than among white-collar workers, who in turn gave Ford greater support than blue-collar workers. Ford retained his support among professionals better than he did among white-collar workers, but not as well as among blue-collar workers. The differences here, as with the income groups, are not great: 18 percent, 20 percent, and 13 percent drops among professional, white-collar, and blue-collar workers, respectively.

As might be expected, partisan groups varied greatly in their response to the Nixon pardon. Republican approval of Ford dropped only 4 percent. Among Independents, Ford's approval fell by a moderate 14 percentage points. But for Democrats, the honeymoon was definitely over. Their support declined by 24 percent, a loss from which Ford never recovered. The partisan nature of this drop in popularity conforms closely to the pattern of support for Nixon when he left office, with only 13 percent of the Democrats supporting him, compared to 22 percent of the Independents and 50 percent of the Republicans.

The Nixon pardon had a slightly greater effect on Catholics than on Protestants. Catholic support of Ford was 2 percent higher than Protestant support before the pardon. After the pardon, Ford's rating dropped 21 percent among Catholics, from 73 percent to 52 percent, but only 13 percent among Protestants, from 71 percent to 58 percent. Again, Ford seemed to have maintained his strength better among the traditionally Republican Protestants, who may have been less critical of Nixon.

The pardon cost Ford a loss in popularity of 17 percent to 18 percent among men and women, with both initial male and female approval ratings (70 percent and 71 percent) and postpardon declines (18 percent and 17 percent) being almost identical. The regional differences are slight, but follow the patterns for income and occupational groups. The regions that gave Ford his highest initial support, the Midwest and the West, were the ones where the pardon cost him dearly: 21 percent in the Midwest and 18 percent in the West. In absolute terms, however, Ford's postpardon support in these regions remained higher than in the East or the South. The pardon ended the honeymoon permanently in the East and West, where Ford left office with a support level 3 percent lower than his postpardon level. He managed to recover somewhat among Midwesterners, ending his term with a popularity level of 58 percent, 3 percentage points higher than his postpardon level. Ford's popularity remained about the same among Southerners.

Ford's ratings among both whites and nonwhites declined after the pardon. The greater drop among whites—18 percent versus 13 percent for nonwhites—was only partly a reflection of the higher response they gave Ford initially: 74 percent for whites versus 56 percent for nonwhites. The level of nonwhite approval sank to 38 percent after the pardon, compared to a decrease to 56 percent among whites. Ford recovered a fraction (2 percent) of his lost popularity among whites but continued to lose favor among nonwhites.

Ford's overall pattern, then, strongly fits a rational explanation of popularity fluctuations. He took office with high approval ratings reflecting the American public's collective relief at the ending of the Watergate trauma. This feeling was widespread among all groups except nonwhites, with Ford's popularity ratings ranging from 64 percent to 78 percent. The first poll taken after the Nixon pardon, however, shows how drastically the pardon affected his public support: It abruptly ended the public's honeymoon with an otherwise popular president. Although Ford was able to maintain his postpardon popularity fairly consistently, he could never repair the damage done by this act among most key groups. While it is impossible to say exactly how great an impact the pardon had on voter calculus in the 1976 election, the evidence here strongly suggest that the pardon of Richard Nixon cost Ford that margin of popular support he needed to win the election.[12]

An examination of Carter's popularity again reveals how strongly public attitudes to a president are affected by specific events. Carter's highest popularity occurred in April 1977 for all groups except Southerners, whose approval ratings peaked in February 1977. These high ratings early in the term correspond to the honeymoon period of the cycle theory. Carter's popularity was lowest with most groups in the second half of 1979, then gradually increased at the end of that year. This, too, seems to bear out the cycle theory. But Carter's period of decline also corresponds with the deterioration of the economy and the worsening of his relations with Congress. Moreover, the public reaction to the seizure of the American hostages and the Russian invasion of Afghanistan dramatically highlights how the cycle theory's predicted period of honeymoon and decline are often derailed by sudden and traumatic political events.

Tables 3–6 and 3–7 present the relevant data here. The months preceding the seizure of the hostages were characterized by both the worsening of the U.S. economy and the decline of Carter's popularity. Carter's approval ratings dropped to levels approaching those of Richard Nixon during his last days in office, with Carter's national low point of 29 percent occurring in October 1979. This figure is only slightly higher than Nixon's national low of 24 percent. Carter's national rating in the Gallup Poll just before the Iranian seizure of the American diplomats was 32 percent. Among Republicans, his popularity had dropped to 18 percent. Democrats gave him a 40 percent approval

TABLE 3-7. Effect of Iranian Hostage Crisis and Afghanistan Invasion on Carter's Popularity

Group	Pre-Iran Hostages[a]	Post-Hostages/ Pre-Afghanistan Invasion[b]	Post-Afghanistan Invasion[c]	Total Increase
National	32.00	51.00	55.00	23.00
Age				
< 30	36.00	56.00	54.00	18.00
30-49	27.00	48.00	56.00	29.00
50+	35.00	52.00	56.00	21.00
Income[d]				
$< 5	34.00	59.00	56.00	22.00
$5-10	37.00	53.00	57.00	20.00
$10-15	30.00	52.00	53.00	23.00
$15-20	33.00	49.00	57.00	24.00
$20+	28.00	50.00	55.00	27.00
Party Identification				
Republican	18.00	39.00	43.00	25.00
Democrat	40.00	62.00	65.00	25.00
Independent	31.00	48.00	48.00	12.00
Occupation				
Professional	24.00	47.00	53.00	29.00
White Collar	35.00	54.00	63.00	28.00
Blue Collar	36.00	51.00	53.00	17.00
Religion				
Protestant	34.00	52.00	56.00	22.00
Catholic	29.00	53.00	55.00	26.00
Sex				
Male	30.00	49.00	53.00	23.00
Female	34.00	54.00	57.00	23.00
Region				
East	25.00	48.00	54.00	29.00
Midwest	33.00	55.00	55.00	22.00
South	38.00	58.00	64.00	26.00
West	30.00	43.00	44.00	14.00
Race				
White	31.00	51.00	55.00	24.00
Nonwhite	36.00	53.00	60.00	24.00

[a] November 2, 1979
[b] November/December 1979
[c] Early January 1980
[d] Income in thousands of dollars

rating, up 6 points from June 1979 but still 11 points lower than Johnson's lowest Democratic rating. Among other groups, Carter's prehostage popularity ranged from 24 percent among professionals to 38 percent among Southerners. For most groups, his prehostage percentage ratings ranged from the upper 20s to the low 30s.

On November 4, 1979, militant Iranian students seized the U.S. embassy in Tehran and took the staff hostage. Carter's national popularity jumped to 51 percent in the Gallup Poll of late November/early December 1979. He gained 21 percentage points among Republicans and 22 points among Democrats. Among other groups, he showed similarly large gains: 20 percent among the youth, 21 percent among those between 30 and 50, 17 percent among those over 50. Though greatest among the lowest-income groups, his gains were substantial for all income groups. They were up 25 percent (from 34 percent to 59 percent) among those earning under $5,000 a year, up 16 percent (from 37 percent to 53 percent) among the $5,000–10,000 group, up 22 percent (from 30 percent to 52 percent) among the $10,000–15,000 group, up 16 percent (from 33 percent to 49 percent) in the $15,000–20,000 category, and up 22 percent (from 28 percent to 50 percent) among those earning over $20,000 a year. The pattern is similar for all other groups. Thus the taking of the American hostages reversed the slide in popularity of an unpopular president, as the American public rallied behind its leader in a time of national crisis.

The Afghanistan invasion accelerated this rally process, pushing up Carter's poll ratings in early January 1980 to 55 percent nationally, 57 percent among some income groups, 60 percent among nonwhites, 64 percent among Southerners, and 65 percent among Democrats. Carter capitalized on this public support during the crucial early primary campaigns. Unfortunately for his reelection prospects, however, this strategy could not work indefinitely. An event that began as a rally event, and that Carter successfully exploited for the greatest political advantage, gradually shifted to become a leadership event, that is, an event on which the president's judgment is assessed. The continuation of the hostage crisis—perhaps precisely because it had been so highly politicized by Carter himself—eventually cost him dearly.[13] By March or April 1980, the rally effect of the hostage issue had peaked. More importantly for Carter, its positive impact on his popularity had totally dissipated. By the time of the November election, Carter's popularity had sunk dangerously close to his all-time lows of early 1979. By the end of his term in office, the hostage issue had become a major political liability and was viewed as reflecting badly on his leadership ability. Carter's last popularity rating on January 16, 1981 showed him with the approval of only 34 percent of the American public. He maintained his support best among young people (43 percent approval), low-income voters (42–43 percent among those earning no more than $10,000 a year), nonwhites (55 percent), and Democrats (49 percent).

CONCLUSION

Do the highs and lows of presidential popularity reflect random cycles or presidential actions? What does this examination of the recent trends and cycles in presidential popularity suggest?

In more theoretical terms, the evidence suggests that public cynicism towards presidents has not been growing since 1965; it may only be expressed more vocally within the parties. There are important group responses towards presidents, with popular support heavily dependent on a president's ability to keep close ties with his traditional constituent groups. Johnson and Ford enjoyed strong honeymoon periods because of public reaction to the tragic circumstances under which each took office. Johnson, however, was a classic New Deal liberal who had to leave office because he alienated his critical voting groups. Nixon's first-term support remained high but plummeted precipitously among all groups after Watergate. And Carter, neither a charismatic president nor well-loved by any group, was hoisted on his own political petard as his own exploitation of the Iranian hostage issue to rally public support behind him as president soured, causing many to view him as an ineffectual leader.

Although presidents do experience a decline in popularity while in office, the pattern of a honeymoon followed by slow decline and a brief end-of-term surge described by the cycle theory of presidential popularity is only partly accurate. Not all presidents fit this general pattern. And even for those presidents whose popularity does follow this general pattern, rational causes can usually better explain the fluctuations in popularity. Close examination of key events during a president's term in office shows how closely presidential popularity is tied to important political events, such as the Watergate breakin, the Nixon pardon, or the Iranian seizure of American hostages. This again suggests that the underlying basis of American public support for presidents is rational, with the polls providing useful ongoing information on the desires and mood of the American people for policy makers and politicians.

The evidence presented here supports what common sense suggests: Economic and political events do affect a president's popularity. Therefore, while the cyclical aspect of popularity noted by the cycle theorists should certainly be included in any systematic analysis of popularity, the emphasis should be on incorporating the cycles in presidential popularity into an integrated rational model.

NOTES

1. In "The King Must Die" (*St. Louis, Post-Dispatch,* January 13, 1981, 11a), Anthony Lewis compares the current behavior of the American public toward their presidents with that of the people in Mary Renault's mythical Naxos where a king was elected to rule for one year and then was condemned to death to make way for a successor.

2. It may be useful to study the trend of a variable simply in order to describe the progression of values or to compare the trended variable with another similarly trended variable. However, if the main interest is in determining which other factors influence the series, as our interest here is in determining the influences on popularity, then it is necessary to isolate and eliminate any trend in all of the variables. This is done in the more systematic empirical analysis of the economic influences on popularity presented in Chapter 4.

3. See Lewis 1981.

4. The estimate of average presidential popularity is the arithmetic mean of all observations for presidential popularity during 1965–1980. Using all available observations to calculate the mean seemed the most accurate way to measure average presidential popularity during this period, although it naturally includes more observations for presidents, such as Nixon, who were in office longer than for those, like Ford, who had short incumbencies. An alternate way of calculating average popularity during this period would be to calculate the average popularity of each president, add these four values together, and divide by four. This will produce slightly different findings because of the disparities in lengths of incumbencies. For example, the 49.41 percent national approval ratings using this second method was 0.29 points less than the average national approval calculated using all of the available observations—a difference that is small and that reflects the

many high ratings given Richard Nixon during his first term.

5. See Stimson 1976, 1.

6. See Chapter 1 for a review.

7. For reasons of space, the graphs of presidential popularity among each of the 24 groups analyzed are not presented here; the main information is summarized in Tables 3–2, 3–3, 3–4, and 3–6, and analysis of special circumstances during the Ford and Carter administrations presented in Tables 3–5 and 3–7, respectively. Any other striking variations in group responses to presidents are noted in the text. Complete graphs are available from the author upon request.

8. Perhaps the largest surprise is the dollar amount of the categories used by Gallup, with annual income of $7,000–10,000 the top category in 1965. In 1969 Gallup made income above $10,000 the highest classification.

9. It is unfortunate that figures on presidential popularity among nonwhites were not collected separately until after Johnson left office, since that group benefited most from the Great Society programs.

10. It is interesting to note that the initial public response to President Reagan reflected rather definite public views of him early in his presidency. At 59 percent approval, Reagan was as low as Nixon. The low percentage of those responding "don't know" or "ambivalent" about Reagan suggests that the early honeymoon period depends on people whose support is soft and could easily shift from the charitable favorable column to the "don't know" category or from the "don't know" to the dislike category.

11. Data for these charts come from examination of all the polls conducted by the Gallup organization during this period and included polls that are among several occurring in the same month. The empirical analysis in Chapter 4 is a more technical analysis requiring regular data series. Replication of the tables in Chapter 3 from the data presented in the appendix may have slight discrepancies because of this.

12. The closeness of the election and Ford's end-of-term popularity, slightly over 50 percent, underline the close correspondence of the poll and the voting indications of public support, the importance of the Electoral College, and the possible importance of the nostalgia effect at the margin.

13. It is interesting to see how Truman handled a similar situation in 1948, when the Chinese Communists took American hostages in Mukden. Truman kept a low profile, avoiding discussion of the hostages, who were released in

1949. Probably because of this, and the resultant difference in media coverage of the event, the Mukden hostages never became the political issue that the U.S. hostages in Iran became.

4

Understanding Changes
in Presidential
Popularity

To fully understand changes in presidential popularity, we need to develop systematic predictors to measure the relative importance of different kinds of influences on presidential popularity.[1] In this chapter, I consider both cyclical and political determinants of popularity and compare their impact with that of economic predictors. I then determine whether the major shifts in popularity correspond more closely to particular political events or to general economic conditions. To do this, a multivariate statistical model is developed to provide a more systematic explanation of presidential popularity in terms of redistributive and macroeconomic predictors, political influences, and cyclical phenomena.

A PARADIGM FOR UNDERSTANDING CHANGES IN PRESIDENTIAL POPULARITY

The most important influences on presidential popularity can be grouped into four different categories: cyclical, political, general macroeconomic conditions, and redistributive economic policies.

Economic Variables: Macroeconomic and Redistributive Economic Policies

Macroeconomic predictors include aggregate government data on inflation (INF), changes in real personal income (YRPI),

149

the Standard and Poor stock market index (SP), and unemployment at both the aggregate and the group level. To measure the differential group response to unemployment, the unemployment rate is broken down into the rates for the following groups, which are included in separate tests of the model: overall unemployment (UNEMP), unemployment among married men (UNMMEN), men (UNMEN), women (UNWOM), youth (UNYUTH), blacks (UNBLK), whites (UNWHT), white-collar (UNWHCL), and blue-collar (UNBLCL) employees.[2]

This model builds on earlier works in this area and assumes rationality on the part of the public. That is, it assumes a voter's dislike of conditions and events that harm his individual economic well-being, that of his primary group or his nation, will have negative political consequences for the incumbent president. If this is true, inflation and unemployment should have a negative effect on popularity. Changes in income and the stock market should be positively related to popularity, since both of these predictors indicate economic growth or improvement. Similarly, unemployment should have a stronger political impact among lower socioeconomic groups, while inflation should have a stronger political impact among the higher-income and higher occupational-status groups.

These basic assumptions accept the traditional view of the voter as rational. Other arguments that suggest alternative but equally rational reactions to the economy are also considered. Stigler (1973), for example, argues that unemployment should have negative political consequences only among those who actually lose or cannot find jobs. The actual number of people thus affected, he argues, is quite small compared to the total population. Furthermore, according to Stigler, the unemployed are not well represented in the voting population, and they are even more underrepresented in the population polled by public opinion researchers. Therefore a strong negative political response to aggregate unemployment, at least at the rates seen between 1965 and 1980, might not occur because unemployment's direct effect falls primarily on those outside the political establishment.[3]

Stigler also raises the question of the relative political importance of general macroeconomic conditions and redistributive policies. It is reasonable to expect strong political reactions to economic conditions resulting from government policies that take wealth from one group in order to redistribute it to another. Groups that lose in this process quite naturally might wish to punish the government by withdrawing their approval. Groups that benefit from the

policies should reward the government. There are, however, two difficulties here. First, before a voter blames
the government for either macroeconomic or redistributive
policies, he might need to consider whether the other party
will follow the same policy or will substitute one that is
more favorable to his interests. Some voters, of course,
may not do this. Their desire to punish a president who
has hurt them may blind them to the need to consider
whether the other party offers any improvement. Simple
revenge may motivate behavior. Although most of the
works in this area do not assume such motivation, there is
some indirect evidence that this is precisely the way voters
behave. Mueller, for instance, suggests that while voters
blame the president for economic downturn, they do not
give him credit for economic improvement. Bloom and
Price, who note a similar asymmetrical economic effect on
voting, support this portrait of the vindictive voter. This
question of the public's political response to redistributive
economic policies remains open and is an important issue on
which to focus analysis.

A second difficulty concerning the political consequences
of redistributive policies arises in deciding which economic
conditions reflect general macroeconomic policies and which
ones reflect redistributive policies.[4] The overall political
consequences from both unemployment and inflation are
assumed here to be negative, although both will cause
redistribution of economic goods. Some of the redistributive aspects of unemployment can be detected by looking
closely at those groups for whom separate unemployment
figures are calculated: blacks, whites, men, women,
youths, married men, white-collar workers, and blue-collar
workers. If, on the one hand, unemployment's political
impact arises from its effects on individuals, then we should
find a stronger and more differentiated political impact on
presidential popularity among members of groups whose
unemployment rate is high. If, on the other hand, its
political importance derives from the public's equating it
with governmental inability to manage the economy, then we
should find little difference in the political importance of
varying group unemployment rates. This method of analysis will provide a test of the sociotropic voter's claim that
the critical economic predictor is the voter's concern for
national well being, a claim contrasted with the more traditional, rational Downsian view of the pocketbook voter who
cares only how he has fared economically during a president's tenure. Beyond this, such a group analysis corrects
some of the problems that arise from looking only at aggregate unemployment figures. And it certainly provides more

fully for the detection of a direct political response from unemployment by focusing on the political reactions of groups with unusually high unemployment rates.

Other economic predictors seem more obviously redistributive in their impact. Under the category of redistributive economic predictors, I therefore included aggregate data on government expenditures for social welfare (YGOVEXP) and a variable on government redistributive policies (TAX), measured by legislative and executive action on taxation policy and the voted increases in social security and public aid. The taxation series come from the *Congressional Quarterly* notations identifying changes in all major tax legislation, public aid, and disaster relief. The tax variable was constructed by making TAX equal to zero at all times but the following: (1) any time the *Congressional Quarterly* noted a significant tax increase, a -1 was given to the tax variable; a tax decrease or rebate was coded +1; and (2) when the passage of a bill opened up significant new government funding to a substantial group of people, as occurred most frequently during the Johnson years, this variable was coded as +1. The basic logic followed here was that people dislike tax increases unless they benefit from the newly created tax revenues in some obvious way.

There are further refinements to be made here. Such obvious tax benefits might well antagonize groups who resent paying for a government subsidy to another group or who feel they are unjustly being made to pay for a welfare state. On the whole, however, it seemed more reasonable to assume that the greater political effect would arise among people actually benefiting from, if not lobbying for, passage of such increased aid, since they would gain tangible benefits from the decision to grant aid and would offset those relatively few who noticed the tax increases and grumbled about someone other than themselves benefiting from a government policy. The group benefited would have a strong specific reason to like the incumbent, whereas the resentment of the groups who are paying indirectly for new programs would have a more diffuse political reaction. Ford's reluctant approval of aid to New York City, Johnson's model cities program, and periodic increases in social security payments are all examples of presidential actions that probably have diffuse negative consequences but specific positive ones.[5]

The last acts that were coded to construct the tax variable are government decisions, ranging from votes in Congress to executive actions by the president or his cabinet, to provide disaster relief to areas hit by natural or manmade catastrophes. Since such public aid is usually viewed in humanitarian rather than zero-sum terms, it is presumed to have predominately positive political consequences. Such aid is accordingly coded +1. Any of the above-described events give the tax variable a value other than zero. If more than one such event occurred during the same bimonthly period, the codings were added together and the cumulative score was entered.

The variable on government expenditures for social welfare is the actual dollar amount spent on social welfare programs rather than the decision to change the policy. This variable will always tend to increase. Furthermore, since it is pegged to other economic conditions—just as social security payments rise with the rate of inflation—it produces a multicollinear series if it is entered into the model simply as its dollar value. In order to avoid the problems of time trend and multicollinearity, therefore, this variable was entered as the change in government expenditures. Presumably, this method of entering the variable will more accurately detect the political response to shifts in these expenditures that might benefit or damage a president's popularity.

It is important to include in the model both the variable on taxation and the variable on government social welfare expenditures because they measure different aspects of redistributive actions. The taxation variable should be important for detecting public response to specific actions that the government, especially the president, has taken to redistribute economic goods. The social welfare expenditures variable will detect public reactions to the release of money. By pegging one variable to the date of the policy decisions and the other to the date at which funds are released, I can test for political responses to separate and distinct phenomena. If the politically significant variable is the government's decision to transfer money to a particular group or to tax a certain group, then the tax variable should be significant. But if the politically important variable is the actual release of the money, then the social welfare variable, noting the time when the money is actually awarded, should be more significant.[6]

Cyclical and Political Events

How do cyclical and political events affect presidential popularity? Work here must be somewhat exploratory since, despite the importance of such events, it is more difficult to operationalize the cyclical and political influences on presidential popularity than the economic influences. In particular, it is necessary to systematize these events and fit them into a framework describing short-term influences on presidential popularity. How much of a president's popularity originates in political considerations and how much in economic? How do the two intertwine? What are the politically relevant cyclical factors and where do they enter the equation? These are the important questions to be answered.

The difficulty lies in allowing for political events and cyclical influences on popularity in a rigorous analysis. How can such events be operationalized and coded so their political impact can be analyzed systematically and then measured in comparison with the key economic indicators? Earlier analysts relied heavily on the two variables used by Mueller in his analysis of popularity and wars: (1) the coalition-of-minorities and (2) the "rally-round-the-flag" variable.

The coalition-of-minorities variable allows for inevitable presidential actions that alienate or disillusion at least small groups within society. The opposition may form a coalition of these minorities, and then have enough votes to oust the incumbent. Mueller operationalizes this variable as "the length of time, in years, since the incumbent was inaugurated (for first terms) or reelected (for second terms)" (1973, 206). The second term signals a new start for this variable, since Mueller argues that the president will use the campaign to rebuild his coalition. Mueller has a honeymoon variant of this variable in which popularity shows an exponential decline. He also has a second variant that uses a logarithmic transformation to measure a slowing rate of decline. Mueller finds that neither of these variants is as important as the simple linear coalition-of-minorities variable. Later analyses, experimenting with even more complex variations on this honeymoon-and-decline phenomenon, generally support Mueller's conclusions on the linear form of this variable.[7]

Mueller's second variable attempts to measure the swelling in public support for a president that follows immediately upon a specific dramatic international event directly involving the United States and particularly the president. He lists thirty-four such events during the Truman-Johnson period.[8] Mueller operationalizes this "rally-round-the-flag" variable by measuring the "length of time, in years, since the last rally point" (1973, 212). He experiments with a variant of this variable, which tests for "good" rally points (e.g., the Cuban missile crisis) and for "bad" rally points (e.g., the Bay of Pigs Invasion). He finds the differences small and inconsistent, and concludes that "the public seems to react to 'good' and 'bad' international events in about the same way" (1973, 212).

Clearly, Mueller and the other analysts, such as Kenski, who have followed his lead, are on to something here. It does seem sensible to allow for key political events that affect both popularity and the economy. It also seems sensible to allow for any erosion in presidential popularity over time that originates either because of disillusioned or alienated minorities, as Mueller suggests, or because of apolitical cyclical fluctuations in popularity, as Stimson argues. Since the analysis presented in Chapter 3 suggested that shifts in popularity can be explained more fully by events than by cycles, I have followed Mueller's basic approach.

Even this approach seemed too narrow, however, so I combined the approach used by Mueller with an attempt to include the key political events of the period as indicated by a careful reading of the important political memoirs and histories of the 1965–1980 period. On this basis, the events listed in Appendix C were selected as the ones most likely to have affected presidential popularity from 1965 to 1980. These events fell into four categories useful for classification in four systematic variables: a variable measuring the party affiliation of the incumbent president (IDEO), and three variables measuring the important political events that occur with some regularity and that fall into three separate categories—rally, leadership, and corruption.

Rally events are defined as events indicating extreme domestic unrest or external threats to the United States that produce internal solidarity and a rallying around the president as national leader. Leadership events are those that call for a response by the president, which may be seen by the public as confirming the president's competence and leadership ability or as casting doubt on his judgment. Corruption is indicated, first, by events that suggest or confirm the presence of corruption or extralegal activities in the White House or among the president's close advisers, and, second, by events that indicate positive attempts by the president to alleviate corruption.

The first category of event corresponds to the rally event developed by Mueller (1973) and later used by Kenski (1977). There is substantial theoretical literature outlining the psychology of the rally phenomenon.[9] The seizure of the *USS Pueblo* in January 1968 and the Iranian capture of American hostages in November 1979 are two clear examples of external events that caused the public to feel the nation was being threatened and to respond by rallying around the president as national leader. On rare occasions, internal domestic unrest has a similar effect. The assassination of John Kennedy shocked the nation and made Americans feel vulnerable as a people. It resulted in a rallying around the new president as national leader in time of crisis. The Bicentennial celebration and the moon landing in July 1969 might have had a similar rallying effect. The psychology for these events was different, however, because the impetus to rally behind the president as national leader came from a sense of pride or accomplishment as a people. Still, this kind of event is classified as a rally event because it causes people to stand behind the president not as an individual but as the holder of the nation's highest office.

The political importance of leadership or competence is underlined by all those scholarly works that discuss the presidency in terms of the president's actions.[10] Despite its obvious importance, however, this phenomena has not been widely used in earlier systematic analyses on the economy and presidential popularity. Events indicating leadership competence are events that present the president with opportunities to demonstrate his leadership ability and good judgment by acting or not acting in certain situations. These events could include a president's response to a prolonged crisis, such as the holding of the American hostages by Iran. While this situation initially had the effect of rallying public support behind President Carter, it later shifted and became interpreted as a situation calling for presidential response and leadership, a leadership the electorate found Carter sadly lacking.[11] Presidential restraint during the 1979 Nicaraguan revolution demonstrates leadership through nonaction. The defeat or passage of legislative programs can also measure leadership. The Andrew Young resignation, major cabinet changes, and passage of the Panama Canal Treaty are examples of events that indicate competence or leadership.

There is no major theoretical work on the political effect of corruption, but none seems necessary to justify inclusion of this variable, particularly after the Watergate scandal and the Nixon resignation. The corruption variable measures shifts in presidential popularity occurring as a result of activities, disclosures, investigations, or rulings by official government tribunals on possible violations of law or unethical conduct by the president or any other high government official whose behavior reflects on him, either directly or on his judgment in choosing his close associates. The most obvious examples come from the Watergate period, e.g., Dean's implication of Nixon in the coverup of the

Watergate break-in and Nixon's firing of Cox and Richardson during the so-called Saturday Night Massacre. The fine against the Carter Campaign Committee for illegal use of the Bank of Georgia's airplane and the Burt Lance resignation amid charges of impropriety are less dramatic examples whose effects were more contained. The investigation of Korean influence peddling and bribery is an example of a government responding positively to allegations of corruption by trying to eliminate corruption or punish wrongdoers.

VARIABLES, MODEL CONSTRUCTION, AND DATA

Variables and Data

The events listed in Appendix C were judged to be the most important noneconomic ones affecting presidential popularity in the postwar period. Each event is listed by date and described briefly. Each is then assigned an R, L, or C, indicating classification as a rally, leadership, or corruption variable.[12] Events that reflect well on a president's leadership are coded +1. Those that reflect poorly on his leadership or competence are coded -1. The leadership variable should be positively associated with presidential popularity. Events indicating corruption are coded -1. Those events indicating an attempt to alleviate corruption are coded +1. The corruption variable thus should have a positive correlation with popularity, with popularity increasing as corruption decreases. All rally events are coded +1 since the rally effect, by definition, should have only a positive effect on popularity. Presumably there are some events that cause a feeling of national shame, which would reflect on the president's popularity. Since the fall of South Vietnam was the only event that truly seemed to belong to this category more than to the leadership classification, I did not add a new code but classified it under the rally variable.[13]

The final political influence to measure is the prior partisan feeling that may affect an individual's assessment of the president's actions or policies. These earlier partisan loyalties may act as a filter during several stages in the process by which the economy affects popularity. They may affect the voter's response to the president, his evaluation of the president's actions on the economy, his perception of the gravity of the economic situation, and the extent and nature of the economic responsibility he assigns to the president or different political parties. To measure the political importance of these partisan loyalties, I include a variable called partisan loyalties or ideology of the president and code it +1 for Democratic presidents and -1 for Republicans. This will detect any variation in the political response to the economy that is strongly affected by party identification and will be an important aid in avoiding specification error when analyzing a time series covering presidents of both parties.

This leaves only cyclical influence to build into the model. Cyclical patterns in presidential popularity have nothing to do with specific presidential actions or economic or noneconomic conditions. Rather, they simply reflect the vagaries of public opinion toward any president. These patterns are indicated by a honeymoon variable and a preelection nostalgia variable. These two variables measure the regular variations that recur periodically in all presidents' popularity but cannot be classified as seasonal variations. As noted in Chapters 1 and 3, these cyclical influences have been expanded into a theory of presidential popularity by several analysts, who argue that presidential popularity is more the reflection of "expectation/disillusionment among the less well-informed segments of the public" (Stimson 1976, 1) than a judgment on any particular presidential actions or policies. In particular, the cycle theorists argue that all presidents start their term of office with great popularity, but thereafter, their popularity declines in a parabolic fashion. According to Stimson, the decrease in popularity continues for three years. Then, as the president's term nears an end, he enjoys a slight surge in popularity.

The cycle theory has received serious criticism from Kernell (1977), Monroe (1978), and Lee (1979). The impressionistic analysis presented in Chapter 3 showed that cycles of presidential popularity are not as uniform as the theorists have claimed. This analysis was able to explain many of the highs and lows in popularity since 1965 in terms of specific events. The gist of the rebuttal of the cycle theorists is essentially the rational explanation characterized by the coalition-of-minorities theory advanced by Mueller in 1973; i.e., it is not simply the passage of time that damages presidents politically, but rather the fact that as time passes, presidential actions and events alienate different groups in society, groups that eventually join forces to form a coalition against the president. Like Stimson's, this explanation allows for a deterioration of presidential popularity over time, but it attributes the decline to rational explanations rather than the mere fickleness of voters.

While the cyclical argument is surely overstated, the analysis in Chapter 3 alerts us to potential cyclical aspects of popularity that should be allowed for in the econometric models. In particular, the honeymoon period during which a new president is given a chance to learn his job and the nostalgia effect as his term nears an end are two factors that should be considered. They are combined here into one variable called honeymoon-nostalgia (HONNOS). This variable is coded zero except for the six months before and after a presidential inauguration. It is then set equal to 6 for the first two months of the new presidency, 4 for the third and fourth months, and 2 for the fifth and sixth months. As the term draws to an end, this variable is coded as 2 for the fifth and sixth months before it ends, 4 for the third and fourth months, and 6 for the last two months. These times were the ones that contained the bulk of the honeymoon and nostalgia periods according to earlier work.[14] Other variations of this decline were also analyzed. The substantive findings remain the same.[15] This variable should have a positive relationship with presidential popularity, since it measures the early public enthusiasm for a president, the gradual diminution of this honeymoon affection, and then the resurgence of public support for the incumbent as his term ends, either because of whimsical cyclical reasons, because the president rebuilds his coalition for the approaching campaign, or because people now compare him to a real rather than a hypothetical alternative.

Model and Hypotheses

These variables are combined in a model that can be represented as follows:

$$POP = a + INF + UNEMP + YRPI + SP + YGOVEXP + TAX + RALLY + LDRSHP + CORRUPT + HONNOS + e, \text{ where}$$

POP = popularity
INF = inflation
UNEMP = unemployment (either aggregate or group)
YRPI = change in real disposable income
SP = stock market index
YGOVEXP = change in government expenditures on
     social welfare
TAX = tax and public aid policies
IDEO = partisan affiliation of the incumbent president
RALLY = a rally variable

LDRSHP = a leadership variable
CORRUPT = a corruption variable
HONNOS = honeymoon and nostalgia phenomena
a = a constant
e = an error term

Let us consider the precise impact of these predictors on popularity by generating general hypotheses to test. These hypotheses will yield insight concerning the relative importance of rational versus nonrational influences on presidential popularity and will definitely resolve three important substantive controversies in the literature. The first concerns the cyclical patterns of popularity. The second involves the relative political importance of economic and noneconomic factors. And the third question concerns the importance of party affiliation and party loyalty in the process by which the economy influences presidential popularity. Let me consider each question in detail and express the essence of each in the form of a general hypothesis to be tested.

Hypothesis 1

Popularity for all presidents follows a cyclical pattern of initially high support followed by gradual erosion; the pattern varies, however, for each president, with specific presidential actions or events having an impact that is more significant politically than these general cycles. Resolving the controversy about the significance of the cyclical aspects of presidential popularity is important for several reasons. First, there is a large debate in the literature on this question, with Stimson, Stimson and LeGette, and Lee claiming that popularity is merely a cyclical phenomenon reflecting predictable shifts in public opinion that are unrelated to any presidential actions or events. (Miller and Mackie advance a similar explanation for British popularity.)
Second, the resolution of this question is crucial for public policy. If presidents became convinced their actions were unrelated to their public support, public policy making would be a very different process from what it is now; presumably it would become more ideological and involve fewer electoral considerations.[16] Finally, the issue of political rationality is related to the issue of cyclical patterns in presidential popularity. If popular support for all presidents follows the same inevitable pattern—i.e., it is unrelated to individual differences on policy, party affiliation, or even personality—then the belief in public rationality has been dealt a serious blow. The systematic

analysis presented below will complete the initial, more impressionistic analysis in Chapter 3 on the importance of rational behavior in causing cyclical aspects of presidential popularity.

Hypothesis 2

Economic factors are the constant underlying determinants of a president's popularity, although the importance of their influence may be diminished or distorted temporarily by the existence of dramatic national or international crises. This hypothesis concerns the relative importance of economic, political, and cyclical influences on popularity. To test it, group support for the president must be examined to compare (1) the relative importance of political and economic predictors and (2) the relative importance of various economic predictors, such as unemployment and inflation, for the major political groups in the United States: sex, race, occupation, religion, income, geography, age, and political party. This analysis is particularly important for discovering how group ties affect the process by which popularity is influenced by the economy. It will determine whether political support among particular groups is affected by certain kinds of economic events.

Hypothesis 3

Party affiliation will strongly affect the process by which the economy influences presidential popularity. A voter's prior partisan loyalties may affect both his assessment of the economic situation and his judgment of the president's actions on the economic front. The public's expectations and assignment of economic responsibility also may vary according to both the president's and the individual voter's affiliations. Democratic presidents, for example, may be expected to give higher priority to unemployment than Republicans. As a consequence, high unemployment may be more damaging politically for Democrats than it is for Republicans. Or, in a time of stagflation, a public that believes Democrats will attack unemployment more rigorously than the Republicans may turn to Democrats even more strongly as unemployment increases. This would indicate a very long memory pattern and suggest interesting possibilities about political behavior. To consider all of these questions, public support for the Democratic and Republican presidencies will be analyzed separately, paying special attention to partisan variations in response to the economy among Democratic and Republican voters. Integrating

factors such as partisan ties into analysis will be a first
step toward the integrated rational approach I have advocated earlier.

Let us now turn to a consideration of the first of these
general hypotheses and to the presentation of the empirical
findings.

PREDICTORS OF PRESIDENTIAL
POPULARITY, 1965–1980

The empirical findings underline the importance of party
affiliation in determining the political response to the economy among respondents of all groups. The economy's political impact differs greatly according to the political party of
the incumbent president. The shift in the political importance of unemployment is the most dramatic change that
occurs when the popularity of Democratic and Republican
presidents is examined separately. But unemployment is by
no means the only determinant of popularity whose influence
changes direction when the political affiliation of the incumbent president is controlled. Nor is it the only predictor
whose overall political importance is lost or canceled out
when we analyze a time series including presidencies of
both parties. This last finding raises serious questions
about most of the earlier time-series work in this area,
which uniformly failed to allow for such shifts in party
control of the presidency.

Consider Table 4–1 through 4–4. Table 4–1 summarizes
the patterns of public support for all presidents from 1965
to 1980 among the twenty-four different groups analyzed
here. Table 4–2 summarizes the pattern of public approval
for Democratic presidents, and Table 4–3 presents the
findings for Republican presidents. Table 4–4 is a conden-
sation of these three tables. It compares the most important predictors of popularity (1) for all presidents, (2) for
Democratic presidents, and (3) for Republican presidents,
by noting the groups for which each predictor is a
significant political influence.

Taken together, the results presented in Tables 4–1
through 4–4 mark the tremendous importance of party ties
in forming the public's response to the president. Over
the entire time period (Table 4–1), the model works better
in predicting popularity among Republicans ($R^2 = 0.84$)
than among Democrats ($R^2 = 0.70$). Beyond this, the
political importance of specific predictors shifts direction
from positive to negative, or even loses significance alto-
gether, depending on the party affiliation of the incumbent
president. This suggests the public has different expec-

tations of the relative economic priorities of the two political parties, that voter calculus is more intricate than earlier works on the economic influences on popularity have assumed, and that econometric models—no matter how elegant mathematically—must build in such political factors if they hope to understand the process by which the economy influences the popularity of incumbents.

The Importance of Party Affiliation

Table 4–1 presents findings from a model that includes the popularity of all four presidents from 1965 through 1980. On first consideration, these findings correspond with both earlier conclusions in this area and with some of the initially hypothesized relationships. Inflation has a negative significance for many groups, corruption hurts presidents' popularity, and ideology is often an important factor. Unemployment has an erratic political influence, sometimes positive, sometimes negative. The rally variable has an isolated and negative impact on the political support of nonwhites. For all twenty-four groups, the percent of total explained variance, as indicated by the R-squared, ranges from 0.16 to 0.80. The two exceptions here are Republicans and Democrats: the model explains 84 percent of the variation in Republican support for all presidents and 70 percent of the variation in Democratic support.

The Durbin-Watson statistics are low, however, which suggests that something important has been omitted from the equation.[17] And indeed, a comparison of Table 4–1 with Tables 4–2 and 4–3 shows that an important factor has been overlooked: political affiliation of the incumbent president, a factor of such importance that not even the kind of political ideology variable, employed here and in earlier analyses, adequately allows for its full impact. A comparison of Tables 4–2 and 4–3 makes it clear that an aggregate analysis will lead to overlooking important relationships between the economy and popularity, relationships that differ significantly enough for Democratic and Republican presidents to cancel each other out in a longer time series. This is an important finding in light of earlier time-series analyses, most of which analyzed Republican and Democratic popularity in a single series, with only a proxy variable to gauge the importance of partisanship. Although a proxy variable (IDEO) similar to the ones used in earlier analyses was often significant here, it was still insufficient to capture the full effect of partisan feelings on public expectations or even perceptions of the economy, let alone the political assignment of blame or reward for economic conditions.

TABLE 4-1. Popularity of All Presidents, 1965-1980

	YRPI	YGOVEXP	INF	UNWHCL	SP	HONNOS	RALLY	LDRSHP	CORRUPT	TAX	IDEO	R²	D.W.	N	X̄
National	0.01	0.00	-2.62[a]	-1.37	-0.02	1.01	0.96	0.97	2.41[a]	0.47	-1.65	0.29	0.54	90	50.18
Party Identification															
Republican	0.01	0.00	-2.27	-4.06[a]	0.17	0.09	0.90	0.05	2.69[a]	1.20	-31.83[a]	0.84	0.59	90	55.24
Democrat	0.03[a]	-0.00	-1.13	-2.24	-0.10	1.21	1.54	-0.11	2.26[a]	-0.30	6.20	0.70	0.74	90	49.31
Independent	0.03	-0.00	-1.26	-4.66[a]	0.00	0.45	1.56	0.24	2.69[a]	0.38	-17.15[a]	0.31	0.74	90	48.41
Occupation															
Professional	0.04[a]	-0.00	-1.59	0.60	0.01	0.99	1.50	0.43	2.84[a]	-0.26	-4.74[a]	0.29	0.65	90	52.53
White Collar	0.03	-0.00	-0.94	-0.82	-0.06	0.82	0.45	1.16	3.54[a]	-0.50	-3.13[a]	0.23	0.77	90	51.52
Blue Collar	0.03	-0.00	-1.88	-1.25	0.03	0.94	1.76	0.12	2.02[a]	-0.05	1.71	0.23	0.54	90	49.68
Income[b]															
$5	0.02	-0.00	-1.27	-1.67	0.07	0.31	-1.40	0.14	1.46	0.21	2.35	0.21	0.62	90	47.73
$5-10	0.02	-0.00	-1.82	-1.58	0.07	0.33	-0.76	0.50	2.27[a]	-0.11	-0.21	0.16	0.61	90	49.46
$10-15	0.02	0.00	1.58	4.55[a]	0.54[a]	1.37	-0.98	-1.13	1.29	-2.97	-8.40[a]	0.41	0.52	79[c]	50.56
$15+	0.03	0.00	-4.10	20.39[a]	-0.08	0.04	-2.84	-0.39	-1.54	-1.56	0.04	0.80	0.92	63[d]	52.44
Sex															
Male	0.03[a]	-0.00	-2.62	-1.44	0.03	0.41	-0.56	0.41	2.66[a]	0.19	-1.42	0.28	0.69	90	50.81
Female	0.03[a]	-0.00	-2.13	0.14	0.00	0.87	0.02	0.23	2.24[a]	-0.15	-0.43	0.26	0.64	90	48.94

Race															
White	0.05	-0.00	-3.29^a	-3.63	0.07	2.89^a	0.55	-0.66	2.04^a	0.55	0.22	0.38	0.90	90^d	50.22
Black	0.05^a	-0.00	-1.37	0.18	-0.06	1.58	-1.67	0.02	1.22	0.73	16.96^a	0.80	1.41	63	35.71
Age															
Under 30	0.02	-0.00	0.62	11.82^a	0.33^a	0.14	-1.01	0.33	-0.15	-0.59	1.96	0.60	0.85	90	39.75
30-49	0.04	-0.00	-2.31	-0.79	0.06	-0.18	0.62	0.29	1.81	-0.73	-1.22	0.20	0.75	90	48.89
Over 50	0.03^a	-0.00	-2.25	-2.31	0.15	0.22	1.96	-0.49	0.89	-0.14	-2.73^a	0.21	0.81	90	49.41
Region															
West	0.02	-0.00	-1.63	-0.69	-0.13	0.99	0.81	0.53	2.67^a	-0.27	-0.50	0.23	0.81	90	48.43
South	0.02	0.00	0.12	0.07	0.19	-0.62	-0.07	0.60	2.32^a	0.14	-3.85^a	0.21	0.67	90	49.34
East	0.02^a	-0.00	-2.62^a	-3.25^a	-0.09	0.41	0.87	0.24	2.82^a	0.26	1.89	0.35	0.67	90	50.49
Midwest	0.03^a	-0.00	-1.68	-1.23	-0.07	0.71	2.13	0.57	2.48^a	0.13	-1.36	0.26	0.73	90	49.36
Religion															
Catholic	0.02	-0.00	-3.70	-2.27	0.00	0.97	1.57	1.09	3.77^a	0.11	3.26^a	0.40	0.78	90	52.31
Protestant	0.01	-0.00	-0.88	0.00	0.14	0.02	-1.35	1.29	2.98^a	0.14	-3.51^a	0.18	0.78	90	50.70

[a] Significant at the 95 percent confidence level
[b] Income in thousands of dollars
[c] Category does not contain beginning of Johnson administration
[d] Category does not contain the Johnson or the beginning of the Nixon administration

TABLE 4-2. Popularity of Democratic Presidents, 1965-1980

	YRPI	YGOVEXP	INF	UNMMEN	SP	HONNOS	RALLY	LDRSHP	CORRUPT	TAX	IDEO	R²	D.W.	N	X̄
National	0.01	-0.00	-2.26	8.95[a]	-0.78[a]	2.39[a]	3.89	1.04	-1.11	-0.26		0.54	0.74	42	49.62
Party Identification															
Republican	0.01	-0.00	-2.37	-9.96[a]	-0.53	2.42[a]	4.17	0.34	-1.39	1.39		0.48	0.63	42	33.10
Democrat	0.02	-0.00	-0.03	-6.92[a]	-0.86[a]	2.51[a]	3.18	-0.46	-1.93	-0.59		0.38	0.86	42	62.98
Independent	0.02	-0.00	-1.15	-12.95	-0.72	1.96	3.84	-0.08	-1.21	0.83		0.61	1.12	42	45.25
Occupation															
Professional	0.03	-0.00	-0.72	11.87[a]	-0.77[a]	2.08	3.68	-0.86	-2.62	0.81		0.49	1.16	42	48.24
White Collar	0.01	-0.00	0.27	10.63[a]	-0.95[a]	2.91[a]	2.85	0.25	-1.49	-1.13		0.49	1.09	42	49.64
Blue Collar	0.02	-0.00	-0.84	10.32[a]	-0.93[a]	2.32[a]	4.53	-0.82	-2.83[a]	0.03		0.51	0.78	42	52.46
Income[b]															
$5	0.02	-0.00	-1.11	8.95[a]	-0.52[a]	1.16	1.56	-0.68	-2.28	-0.12		0.55	0.90	42	50.82
$5-10	0.02	-0.00	-1.14	10.29[a]	-0.78[a]	1.84	1.44	0.27	-1.82	-0.18		0.54	0.74	42	50.19
$10-15	-0.02	0.00	-2.25	17.07[a]	1.31[a]	2.21	4.77	-1.83	-1.07	-5.59		0.60	0.77	31[c]	46.31
$15+	-0.02	-0.00	0.32	36.21[a,d]	0.29	1.47	3.08	-0.62	-2.33[a]	-3.45		0.92	0.80	19[d]	47.90
Sex															
Male	0.03	-0.00	-1.16	9.27[a]	-0.83[a]	2.14	1.66	-0.45	-2.47	-0.15		0.58	0.91	42	50.24
Female	0.02	-0.00	-1.78	10.79[a]	-0.61	1.79	2.47	-0.35	-1.85	-0.11		0.52	0.81	42	48.86

166

Race														
White	0.03	-0.00	-1.68	10.94[a]	-0.65[a]	2.04	2.37	-0.34	-2.14	-0.34	0.57	0.84	42	47.95
Black	0.00	-0.00	1.08	12.35	0.07	1.20	-3.40	-0.11	-0.69	-0.50	0.77	2.04	19[e]	57.84
Age														
Under 30	0.01	-0.00[a]	-0.17	26.15[a]	-0.27	1.57[a]	1.97	-0.19	-1.13	-1.65	0.94	1.15	42	37.90
30-49	0.03	-0.00[a]	-2.18	10.03[a]	-0.66[a]	1.46	2.39	-0.33	-1.94	0.23	0.48	0.90	42	49.26
Over 50	0.03	-0.00[a]	-2.76	7.71[a]	-0.38	1.20	3.89	-0.46	-1.79	1.02	0.43	1.12	42	47.10
Region														
West	0.02[a]	-0.00	-1.44[a]	10.76[a]	-0.76[a]	2.46[a]	2.63	-0.43	-1.04	1.30	0.46	0.78	42	48.98
South	0.04[a]	-0.00	0.16	14.37[a]	-0.48[a]	1.41	3.48[a]	-0.18	-2.49	-0.24	0.77	1.22	42	46.31
East	0.03	-0.00	-0.95	5.66[a]	-1.01[a]	2.52	3.72	-0.03	1.71	0.12	0.40	0.78	42	54.31
Midwest	0.02	-0.00	-0.99	9.01[a]	-0.77[a]	2.27	4.08	-0.14	-1.48	0.48	0.41	0.85	42	49.24
Religion														
Catholic	0.01[a]	-0.00	-1.04	5.97[a]	-1.27[a]	3.00[a]	3.79	1.10	-1.32	-0.95	0.50	1.15	42	57.60
Protestant	0.00[a]	-0.00	0.09	12.81[a]	-0.86[a]	2.04	2.74	1.16	-1.42	-1.47	0.61	0.89	42	48.12

[a] Significant at the 95 percent confidence level

[b] Income in thousands of dollars

[c] Category of $10,000 to $15,000 was not collected during beginning of Johnson administration

[d] Carter administration only, separate category for over $15,000 was not collected during Johnson administration

[e] Category not collected for the Johnson administration, data for Carter administration only

167

TABLE 4-3. Popularity of Republican Presidents, 1965-1980

	YRPI	YGOVEXP	INF	UNWHCL	SP	HONNOS	RALLY	LDRSHP	CORRUPT	TAX	IDEO	R²	D.W.	N	X̄
National	-0.04	0.00	-5.47[a]	-6.61[a]	0.03	1.88[a]	6.66	-0.89	2.72[a]	1.55		0.58	0.73	48	50.68
Party Identification															
Republican	-0.06[a]	0.00	6.46[a]	-7.13[a]	0.23[a]	0.98	7.21	-1.81	1.86	1.86		0.54	1.00	48	74.62
Democrat	-0.03	0.00	4.16	-5.14[a]	-0.02	1.02[a]	7.55[a]	-1.18	2.55[a]	0.99		0.56	0.95	48	37.35
Independent	-0.05	0.00	4.89	-6.02[a]	0.13	1.59	8.99	-1.19	2.37	1.04		0.43	0.78	48	51.18
Occupation															
Professional	-0.03	0.00	-4.35	-4.72[a]	0.08	1.62	8.85	-1.26	3.43[a]	0.43		0.50	0.91	48	56.28
White Collar	-0.02	0.00	-4.03	-6.98[a]	-0.00	0.50	9.99[a]	-0.65	3.83[a]	1.12		0.56	1.22	48	52.41
Blue Collar	-0.03	0.00	-4.69	-6.26[a]	0.11	1.51	6.72	-1.61	2.31[a]	0.61		0.48	0.89	48	47.26
Income[b]															
$5	-0.05	0.00	-4.33	-8.47[a]	0.09	1.02	6.37	-0.93	2.02	1.91		0.49	1.07	48	45.03
$5-10	-0.05	0.00	-4.51	-8.86[a]	0.13	1.00	10.73[a]	-1.61	2.66[a]	1.53		0.55	1.13	48	48.80
$10-15	-0.04	0.00	-4.85	-8.28[a]	0.08	0.82	12.78[a]	-1.92	2.02	1.29		0.43	0.91	48	53.30
$15+	-0.01	0.00	3.83	14.04[a]	-0.21	-0.11	1.84	-1.64	-0.42	0.06		0.66	1.05	44[c]	54.40
Sex															
Male	-0.05	0.00[a]	-8.46[a]	-8.30[a]	0.05	1.53	8.32[a]	-0.89	2.95[a]	1.74		0.64	0.84	48	51.30
Female	-0.05[a]	0.00	-6.28[a]	-5.65[a]	0.03	2.03	6.92	-1.21	2.75[a]	1.01		0.63	0.90	48	49.01

Race													
White	-0.05	0.00	-4.62	-5.81[a]	0.03	1.65	3.33	-1.66	2.83[a]	1.45	0.45	1.14	48	52.21
Black	0.02	0.00	-3.94	-1.58	-0.06	0.93	-0.13	-0.13	1.81	1.62	0.44	1.41	44[d]	26.14
Age													
Under 30	-0.03	0.00	0.68	6.49[a]	0.49[a]	1.04	9.45	-0.81	0.32	1.46	0.46	1.10	48	41.36
30-49	-0.02	0.00	-3.57	-6.59[a]	0.07	0.24	10.78[a]	-1.24	2.70[a]	0.68	0.45	0.99	48	50.44
Over 50	-0.05	0.00	-4.85	-7.79[a]	0.24	0.89	10.14	-2.60	1.41	0.85	0.43	1.01	48	51.44
Region													
West	-0.05	0.00	-7.71[a]	-7.07[a]	-0.14	1.79	8.41[a]	-0.68	2.88[a]	0.62	0.61	1.25	48	47.96
South	-0.03	0.00	-7.72[a]	-9.18[a]	0.05	0.06	9.29[a]	-1.05	2.27[a]	1.55	0.57	1.06	48	52.00
East	-0.05	0.00	-8.39[a]	-8.47[a]	-0.00	1.13	8.16[a]	-1.41	2.88[a]	1.24	0.59	1.01	48	47.15
Midwest	-0.03	0.00	-6.64[a]	-6.63[a]	-0.07[a]	1.39	8.59[a]	-0.64	2.63[a]	0.91	0.58	0.99	48	49.48
Religion													
Catholic	-0.04	0.00	-7.27[a]	-6.31[a]	0.11	2.49[a]	5.55	-0.81	3.57[a]	0.29	0.61	0.93	48	47.68
Protestant	-0.03	0.00	-6.52[a]	-7.17	0.10	1.47	4.06	-0.71	2.53[a]	0.87	0.63	0.90	48	52.96

[a] Significant at the 95 percent confidence level
[b] Income in thousands of dollars
[c] Category of over $15,000 was not collected during the beginning of the Nixon administration
[d] Category was not collected at the beginning of the Nixon administration

TABLE 4-4. Determinants of Group Support for Presidents

Presidents	Significant Predictor*	Groups for which predictor is significant
All	YRPI	Democratic, Professional, Male, Female Black, Over 50, Midwest
	INF	National, White, East
	UNWHCL	Republican, Independent, $10-15, $15+ Under 30, East
	SP	$10-15, Under 30
	HONNOS	White
	CORRUPT	National, Republican, Democratic, Independent, Professional, White Collar, Blue Collar, $5-10, Male, Female, White, West, South, East, Midwest, Catholic, Protestant
	IDEO	Republican, Independent, Professional, White Collar, $10-15, Black, Over 50, South, Catholic, Protestant
Democratic	YRPI	South, Protestant
	YGOVEXP	Under 30, 30-49, Over 50
	INF	West
	UNMMEN	National, Republican, Democratic, Independent, Professional, White Collar, Blue Collar, Under $5, $5-10, $10-15, $15+, Male, Female, White, Under 30, 30-49, Over 50, West, South, Midwest, Protestant
	SP	National, Democratic, Independent, Professional, White Collar, Blue Collar, Under $5, $5-10, $10-15, Male, Female, White, 30-49, West, South, East, Midwest, Catholic, Protestant
	HONNOS	National, Republican, Democratic, White Collar, Blue Collar, Under 30, West, Catholic
	RALLY	South
	CORRUPT	Blue Collar, $15+
Republican	YRPI	Republican, Female
	YGOVEXP	Female
	INF	National, Republican, Male, Female, West, South, East, Midwest, Catholic, Protestant
	UNWHCL	National, Republican, Democratic, Independent, Professional, White Collar, Blue Collar, Under $5, $5-10, $10-15, $15+, Male, Female, White, Under 30, 30-49, Over 50, West, South, East,

170

	Midwest, Catholic, Protestant
SP	Republican, Under 30, Midwest
HONNOS	National, Democratic, Female, Catholic
RALLY	Democratic, White Collar, $5-10, $10-15, Male, 30-49, West, South, Midwest
CORRUPT	National, Democratic, White Collar, Blue Collar, $5-10, Male, Female, White, 30-49, West, South, East, Midwest, Catholic, Protestant

*Key: YRPI = changes in real personal income; INF = inflation; UNWHCL = white collar unemployment; SP = Standard and Poor Stock Market Index; HONNOS = presidential honeymoon and nostalgia phenomenon; CORRUPT = corruption; IDEO = partisan affiliation of incumbent president; YGOVEXP = change in government expenditures; UNMMEN = unemployment among married men; RALLY = crisis rally phenomenon

When the time series is broken into separate Democratic and Republican presidencies, the direction of influence shifts strikingly (Tables 4–2 through 4–4). Unemployment is the predictor whose political influence shifts most drastically when the party affiliation of the incumbent president is thus controlled for more fully. For all presidents (Table 4–1), unemployment has an occasional and erratic influence, being a significant negative influence for Republicans, Independents, and Easterners and a significant positive influence for those under 30 and for those earning more than $10,000 a year. For none of the other twenty-four groups is unemployment a significant political influence.

The Peculiar Political Importance of Unemployment

When the series is broken into separate Democratic and Republican presidencies, however, unemployment takes on a consistent and extremely strong political influence for the vast majority of the groups. The direction of unemployment's political influence varies according to the political affiliation of the incumbent president. And although the results suggest that when unemployment among one group is statistically significant, unemployment among other groups will also be significant, the particular kind of unemployment that has the greatest political impact varies, often in a surprising manner. In general, unemployment among married men is the most important influence on the popularity of Democratic presidents, while unemployment among white-collar workers is most important for Republicans.

For Republican presidents, unemployment has a strong negative impact, as earlier works by Mueller and by Lee found, and as the traditional assumptions concerning rational citizen behavior would suggest. The political importance of white-collar unemployment was the greatest; but all other measures of unemployment also were significant for a majority of the groups. The importance of unemployment was substantial, with the unstandardized beta coefficients suggesting that a 1 percent annual increase in white-collar unemployment is associated with a decline in presidential popularity ranging from 4.72 percent among professionals to 9.18 percent among southerners. The overall national decline is 6.61 percent, and the decline among white- and blue-collar workers is 6.98 and 6.26 percent, respectively. Only for nonwhites is unemployment not relevant in determining the public's political response to Republican presidents.

Can a socioeconomic class interpretation be found here? Is unemployment more important for those with less income, lower occupational status and fewer skills? Are the poor more concerned with unemployment and the rich with inflation? Is group political support more affected by unemployment rates among group members than by aggregate unemployment? In general, no.

Consider first support for Republican presidents. Occupation groups show only weak class effects. The beta statistics suggest unemployment is more important for blue-collar workers than for professionals; the differential is not great, however, and these same statistics suggest unemployment is more important for white-collar workers than it is for blue-collar workers. An analysis of the political response to unemployment among sexual and racial groups reveals even fewer class effects. Women, who earn less and have higher unemployment rates than men, are less influenced politically by unemployment than are men. And among blacks, the group with the highest unemployment rates in this country, unemployment has no statistical significance whatsoever. The evidence thus is strikingly at variance with a class theory when we examine those groups with lower occupational status and higher unemployment rates.

The results for income and age groups are less conclusive; essentially, however, neither group offers clear confirmation of a class interpretation. For income groups, the beta statistics indicate unemployment's political influence is roughly equivalent for all income groups except those earning over $15,000 a year. Once this income level is reached, unemployment suddenly takes on a positive influence. This could be the first evidence for a class theory. If upper income groups, concerned with inflation, believe the government must make trade-offs between unemployment and inflation, then an increase in unemployment might please them, at least in so far as they interpret high unemployment rates as indicative of the government's efforts to control inflation. The fact that inflation has no political significance for upper income groups, however, undercuts the credibility of this evidence. Further skepticism concerning a class view arises when we consider unemployment's positive influence among those under thirty, a group whose support should be strongly affected by unemployment, if a class interpretation is accurate. But here we find unemployment has a greater political significance for those over 50 than it does for any other age groups, a fact strongly at variance with a class interpretation.

A word of caution is in order. Conclusions should not rest heavily on small differences between beta statistics among groups, particularly when dealing with the extensive amount of data analyzed here, since small aberrations are inevitable occurrences. (Stigler's reanalysis of Kramer's data demonstrates how susceptible findings are to minor statistical changes.) Careful analysis of support for Republican presidents, however, coupled with the close analysis of political support among groups with particularly high unemployment rates—women, blacks, and the youth—presented in Appendix D, suggests there are few class effects at work.

In general, then, unemployment follows the expected pattern for Republican presidents: It decreases presidential popularity as the rate rises and boosts a president's popularity as the rate is brought under control. The political impact of unemployment seems fairly uniform among all groups in American society, however; it does not follow a class pattern of being more important among the lower-income and lower-occupation groups or among those groups with disproportionately higher unemployment.

For Democratic presidents, the results are dramatically different and extraordinary for what they suggest about the greater importance of political affiliation than class in American politics. First, unemployment is significant, with unemployment among married men having the strongest political impact. Second, this impact is again uniform, occurring among twenty-one of the twenty-four groups analyzed here. But third, and most importantly, while unemployment's political influence is significant among all groups except blacks, Easterners, and Catholics, the direction of its influence is positive for all of these groups except the party affiliates. The strength of the influence is almost as striking as the fact that its direction is often positive. The beta coefficients in Table 4–2 suggest that a 1 percent increase in unemployment is associated with an increase in popularity of Democratic presidents of 8.95 percentage points at the national level. Among the different groups, the increase in popularity of Democratic presidents that is associated with a 1 percent rise in unemployment ranges from 7.71 percentage points among those over 50 to an incredible 26.15 points among those under 30.[18]

Economic Expectations and Unemployment Policies

How should we interpret the substantive significance of this strange finding concerning unemployment's reverse impact for Democratic and Republican presidents? First of all, it is important for what it demonstrates about the limitations of long time series and of aggregate analysis, and about the political relevance of individual versus national economic well-being. Both Stigler's (1973) theory that unemployment has no influence on voting and Schneider's (1978) work on income and occupation classes and presidential popularity stress the importance of disaggregating the data to discover the full political effects of unemployment. Stigler argued that there was no overall political response to unemployment because the unemployed were too few in number to make a substantial impact at the national level. He suggested that researchers focus on the political responses of groups affected differently by unemployment to determine if this disaggregated analysis could ascertain whether groups with higher levels of unemployment would show lower levels of support for the president than groups with average levels of unemployment.

When Schneider performed such an analysis, he found that for lower-income and lower-occupation groups unemployment did have a stronger effect. Similar findings were reported by Hibbs. Unfortunately, neither analysis controls for the political party of the incumbent as adequately as now appears necessary, so their findings cannot be considered definitive.[19] I did control for the president's political affiliation, adopted a more appropriate occupation category than the one described by Schneider, and examined not just the political response of upper-income/occupation and lower-income/occupation groups but also the actual unemployment rates among these different classes.

These changes provide a comparison of class popularity with class unemployment, rather than class popularity with aggregate unemployment. The results suggest that while unemployment has a strong political importance for presidents, its importance works through party affiliation rather than socioeconomic class. Appendix D demonstrates this in more detail. It shows, for example, that although political responses to Republican presidents among the young are affected by youthful unemployment, they are even more strongly affected by unemployment among married men. More surprising still is the non-existent political impact from unemployment among blacks, the group whose unemployment rates are the highest in the country and the group whose political reactions should be most responsive to fluctuations in unemployment if a socioeconomic class theory is accurate. Yet unemployment among this group is one of the very few for whom unemployment is not a significant predictor of presidential popularity for Republican presidents. (Because black support for presidents was not collected as a separate category until Nixon's tenure, figures for support for Democratic presidents are unreliable.)

All of this suggests that the class effects are not as strong as had been believed. The analysis of different group unemployment rates also suggests the politically relevant factor may not be unemployment of the group, but may instead be an estimate of the government's ability to manage the national economy. This finding corresponds with the Kinder and Kiewiet argument that collective rather than individual economic well-being has greater political relevance. Finding that different kinds of unemployment have divergent political significance—that it is not just the unemployment of the respondent's primary group that matters politically—is of great importance. It concerns policy makers and it concerns those who care about the public interest. Not least is its significance for the scholarly debate about the sociotropic versus the pocketbook voter. (More on this later.)

Still to be explained is the strange direction of unemployment's political impact on the popularity of Democratic presidents. No single explanation fully accounts for the irony of rising unemployment boosting a president's popularity except for partisan groups. The following attempt to explain this phenomenon should be viewed as only a preliminary analysis, to be expanded in later work.

The most logical place to begin is with that part of the political psychology of the American voter that deals with expectations and perceptions of the two parties on unemployment policy; that is, as unemployment increases, people may turn to the Democrats because they believe the Democrats will grapple with the problem more successfully. This reasoning seems sensible. Work on public perceptions of macroeconomic priorities suggests that the public sees clear party differences in economic priorities, with the Democrats emphasizing full employment and the Republicans emphasizing lower prices.[20] This difference in perception partly accounts for the group support base traditionally associated with the two parties. The young, nonwhite, lower-income and less-skilled occupation groups—whose concern with unemployment comes from their own potential joblessness—support the Democrats. Older, white, and upper-income and professional workers support the Republicans. Putting this together with recent work on expectations helps explain the seemingly anomalous finding on unemployment.

This piece in the puzzle comes from De Tocqueville's (1840) ingenious theory that the gap between the public's economic expectations and actual economic conditions will result in frustration and political unrest, even though actual conditions might be better than in the past.

Contemporary work by Alt (1979), Kuklinski and West (1981), and Monroe and Levi (1983) applies this general theory of expectations and modifies it to explain milder fluctuations in political support. Alt looks at contemporary Britain. Kuklinski and West explain U.S. congressional support, and Monroe and Levi explain American presidential popularity.

If we take these works as a whole—Hibbs, Weatherford, Tocqueville, Alt, Monroe and Levi, Kuklinski and West—we discover the beginnings of an explanation for the strange findings on unemployment, an explanation that again demonstrates the importance of partisan ties. If Democrats are expected to do more to control unemployment, then as unemployment becomes an increasingly serious problem, the general public might turn more toward a Democratic president, not out of gratitude for increasing unemployment, but out of fear that only a Democratic president will take the policy measures necessary to lower unemployment. Only when party affiliation is reintroduced directly into the model does it override the importance of this expectations phenomenon. When this is done, unemployment has a negative influence on the political support of Democrats, Republicans, and Independents, each of whose general partisan filter has already allowed for the expectations phenomenon.

This theory would be more satisfactory if voting rather than presidential popularity were being analyzed. Despite the difficulties in explaining this finding, however, it remains striking. It is hoped that later work in this area will offer a better explanation. Interestingly, the same finding is beginning to surface in comparative work on both Denmark and Canada.[21]

This general association of unemployment with public support of Democratic presidents explains why the earliest analysts, who focused on the heavily Republican 1950s, found unemployment had a negative impact on popularity, while more recent analysts who concentrated on a later period that contained as many observations for Democratic as for Republican presidents, found little evidence of such an impact. The explanation offered here corresponds with Kernell's finding that the political importance of unemployment and inflation vary according to the particular president. And it underscores the tremendous importance of allowing for prior partisan ties, an oversight in much of the earlier work in this area.

Are Economic Factors More Important Than Political Events?

Now that we have seen the crucial role partisan ties play in the process by which the economy influences presidential popularity, the next question we must ask is: What kinds of predictors are the most important determinants of presidential popularity? In Tables 4–1 through 4–3, economic predictors are consistently the most important, with the varying but strong impact of unemployment being the most important predictor for both Democratic and Republican presidents. Among Republican voters and for Republican presidents, the economy is slightly more important than it is for Democratic voters or Democratic presidents. In Table 4–1, which shows the popularity among voters of all presidents from 1965 to 1980, the model explains 84 percent of the total variance in Republican support for presidents, as opposed to 70 percent of the total variance for Democrats. When it comes to support for Democratic presidents (Table 4–2), unemployment and the stock market are the most important variables (in fact, they are the only two economic variables that are consistently significant influences on presidential popularity), with unemployment being a significant influence on the political support of twenty-one out of twenty-four groups and the stock market for nineteen out of twenty-four. In contrast, the honeymoon and nostalgia phenomenon existed for only eight of the twenty-four groups. None of the other noneconomic factors had even this much political influence. For Republican presidents (Table 4–3), unemployment was consistently significant and inflation frequently so. Noneconomic factors were also important, particularly the corruption variable, which was a key factor for fifteen of the twenty-four groups duing the Nixon–Ford years. This is not surprising; indeed, were corruption not a significant political consideration in political support for Republican presidents during the Watergate period it would seem most peculiar. This result again underlines the importance of including both economic and noneconomic predictors in our models.

Taken as a whole, Tables 4–1 through 4–4 suggest that the single most important economic predictor of presidential popularity is unemployment. They further suggest that macroeconomic predictors are more important politically than are redistributive predictors. In this regard, note that neither the tax variable nor the government expenditures variable that measures changes in government spending for social welfare is ever politically significant. Although it was hypothesized that there would be important differences in public attitudes toward government spending for social welfare or public aid, this did not turn out to be the case. Perhaps these expenditures are too far removed from the public view to be noticed by many people. This finding suggests the comparative political importance of macroeconomic and redistributive economic predictors. General economic conditions are more important politically than the government's redistributive policies. This was not what had been expected. Logically, it seemed that the redistributive areas should be more politically sensitive because groups would be competing for a greater share of scarce goods and would reward or blame the government according to how well they came out in the final distribution. The fact that this conclusion comes from a time-series analysis, not subject to the qualifications of cross-sectional data leveled by Kramer and Sears, reinforces the Kinder and Kiewiet discovery that collective economic conditions can outweigh individual or group economic situations. This finding about the public's political concern for the government's ability to promote overall welfare is encouraging for those involved in promoting a common social good or a public interest. It is possible, of course, that these first attempts to measure political reactions to governmental redistributive policies are simply too crude and that further empirical refinement is needed to detect the political response to redistributive policies. At present, however, macroeconomic conditions and policies appear to affect presidential popularity more than redistributive policies do.

An even more important finding concerning the relative political significance of individual, group, and macroeconomic conditions comes from an analysis of the political response to different group unemployment rates. All models were tested separately, using each of the nine different group measures of unemployment. Both the assumption of the rational actor and earlier work on income classes and unemployment suggest that group support for a president should be more strongly affected by unemployment among members of that group than by the overall national unemployment rate or by the unemployment rates for other groups.[22] Groups with especially high unemployment, such as blacks and people under 30, were expected to have stronger negative responses to the president than groups with lower levels of unemployment. Yet this did not turn out to be true. For Republican presidents, white-collar unemployment was the most important. It was more important for blue-collar workers, those under 30, women, and whites than was unemployment in their respective groups.[23] For Democratic presidents, unemployment among married men was the most important rate politically. It was more important for both women and men, for those under 30, and for blue-collar and white-collar workers than the unemployment among these groups. These findings also support the sociotropic voter theory that collective economic conditions are more important politically than are individual economic well-being. The coefficients for presidential popularity among nonwhites are particularly interesting here (see Appendix D). Although all measures of unemployment were significant influences on nonwhite support for the president, the three lowest beta coefficients are for black, blue-collar and youth unemployment—all the unemployed groups that are more heavily black in composition and therefore would be presumed to be more highly correlated with support for the president among blacks.

Cyclical Fluctuations and Political Influences

What about cyclical fluctuations? Impressionistic evidence in Chapter 3 suggested cyclical fluctuations are less important than earlier researchers believed. More systematic analysis confirms this. Clearly, cyclical variables are not important determinants of popularity when other variables are included in the model. For only one group is the honeymoon-nostalgia variable a significant predictor of support for all presidents. Its importance, however, does seem to be affected by partisan ties; it becomes a significant predictor of Democratic response to presidents, regardless of the president's political party, when we control for the impact of party affiliation. It is also significant for Republicans, those under 30, white- and blue-collar workers, Western and Catholic support for Democratic presidents and for female and Catholic support for Republican presidents. More importantly from a practical political point of view, overall national support for both Democratic and Republican presidents is affected slightly by the honeymoon and nostalgia phenomenon. But this effect is evident only after we control for the president's party affiliation by examining Democratic and Republican presidential terms as separate units. Our conclusions on the honeymoon-nostalgia phenomenon are qualified: While its effect is more limited than some analysts had suggested, the successful prediction of overall popularity—the kind reported in the press and correlated with voting—does require inclusion of the presidential honeymoon and end-of-term nostalgia periods. Failure to do so will lead to distorted notions of political reality.

Which political predictors are the most important? Here party ties again come into play. Popularity seems surprisingly unrelated to political events for Democratic presidents, perhaps because of the remarkable proclivity of Democratic presidential popularity to respond to economic events, particularly unemployment. Leadership was never a significant predictor. The rally variable was significant for only one group and corruption for only two. For Republican presidents, however, the findings were strikingly different. Both the rally and the corruption variables were significant predictors of support: Rally events successfully predicted support for nine groups, and corruption was a significant factor for fifteen groups. That corruption is an important predictor of Republican presidential popularity is hardly surprising, since the period studied included the Watergate scandal. Corruption's lack of political significance for Democratic presidents suggests several interesting possible explanations. While cynics, especially those with Republican sympathies, might suggest corruption is simply expected of Democrats, a more plausible explanation suggests the public is willing to tolerate a certain amount of corruption among politicians but that this tolerance was exhausted by the excess of the Watergate period. (If this is so, inclusion of a corruption variable in future work should follow a step-level function.)

Little Impact of Social Class

Is the economy's political significance greater among different income and occupational classes, as earlier analysts have suggested?[24] I found virtually no evidence to support this theory. Unemployment is a significant influence for support for both Republican and Democratic presidents among all income and occupational groups, although it shifts directions along party lines, as described earlier. If a class theory were valid here, unemployment would be a more important predictor of support among the lower-income and the lower-status occupation groups, those more vulnerable to its vicissitudes.[25] Yet the opposite is largely true. For Democratic presidents, unemployment has a much stronger political importance among professionals and upper-income groups than it does among white- or blue-collar workers or lower-income earners. The same is true with slight exceptions for support for Republican presidents. Furthermore, close examination of those groups most directly affected by unemployment—the blacks, women and the young—found their political support remarkably unrelated to unemployment rates for these groups. Taken in conjunction with the earlier noted importance of expectations of party priorities on unemployment, these findings suggest not a class explanation but one which stresses the importance of party ties and economic expectations. While unemployment has great political significance, then, its importance must be understood within the context of prior partisan loyalties. Again, we find that a simple rational economic explanation is greatly enhanced by introducing other less economic considerations into the model.

GENERAL CONCLUSIONS

What general conclusions can we draw from a comparison of these findings with those in the literature? In particular, how do these findings correspond with the traditional wisdom that increases in inflation and unemployment hurt popularity and increases in income help popularity? The most important general conclusion is that the economy's impact on popularity is strongly affected by political ties and party affiliation. This underlying partisanship must be allowed for in order to detect the more complex economic influences that counteract each other at the aggregate level. Beyond this, economic predictors are more important than political or cyclical predictors of presidential popularity. Unemployment, particularly among white-collar workers and among married men, is the single most important economic predictor. Actual macroeconomic conditions appear to be more important politically than governmental redistributive policies, and the economy's political importance is equally strong for all economic classes in American society.

The centrality of party is particularly interesting given recent discussions of the weakening and decline of American political parties. The findings presented here suggest the importance of partisan ties remains strong but is subtle, working through public perceptions of differing party priorities.[26] This, in turn, establishes different public expectations about economic performance, expectations that are key in determining the public's political response to the economy. This response is not at all a class response, certainly not in the general Marxist sense, which would argue that the two major U.S. parties do not differ on their economic priorities; nor is it a class response in a more limited sense, which suggests lower- or working-class respondents should be more concerned with unemployment and upper-income or upper-occupation groups more concerned with inflation.[27] Neither of these occurred.

Instead, a more explicit attempt to separate and analyze the political reaction to unemployment among those groups most dramatically affected by it—the young, blacks, and women—suggested a rather remarkable public concern for the economic well-being of the polity as a whole. Analysis suggested that a surprising number of voters respond to the president not so much on the basis of their individual situation, or even that of their immediate referrent group, but rather on the basis of a judgment of the president's ability to alleviate unemployment for the nation as a whole. The importance of national well being is in harmony with the sociotropic voter theory advanced by Kinder and his colleagues. This confirmation of the sociotropic voter theory is particularly important, since it comes from a time-series analysis using robust aggregate indicators of economic conditions and therefore does not suffer from either of the methodological criticisms dealing with cross-sectional survey data leveled by Kramer or Sears and Lau.[28]

This debate over a rational pocketbook voter versus a sociotropic voter is also important in directing us to the debate between economists and sociologists discussed by Brian Barry (1970). The economists developed a political man whose altruistic behavior is a mere quirk, a character trait almost to be smirked at. The sociologists tend to view altruistic behavior as desirable, a characteristic that aids in the peaceful continuation of society. The fact that the nature of political altruism is being raised in work on the presidency as an empirical question may result in new insight on this important issue.

Finally, what do these findings suggest concerning the fundamental nature of political man's response to the economy? Essentially, the response is a rational one. Not rational in the narrow sense conceived by Downs (1957), or Riker and Ordeshook (1973), or even the more extended rational model developed in Fiorina's retrospective voting theory, whereby voters extrapolate and then rationally choose between the two parties' future behavior on the basis of their past behavior. Instead, the pattern appears to be a subtle one whereby the political reaction to the economy is rational but is strongly influenced by partisan ties inherited or originating in earlier experiences. This provides both a partisan filter and economic expectations traditionally ignored by rational choice theorists. To consider those theoretical questions, let me step back and put the findings described above into the broader context of other work in this field.

NOTES

1. A strong correspondence between group voting patterns and the public support given the president in the public opinion polls, noted in the Prologue, gives these findings an even greater substantive political importance.

2. Most of the economic data discussed below are found in *The Survey of Current Business,* published by the United States Department of Commerce. Monthly data were averaged to construct a bimonthly time series corresponding to the bimonthly Gallup series. Figures on January and February unemployment, for example, are averaged to give one figure for unemployment during January/February. All data are presented in Appendix A.

3. In a more extreme argument, Stigler insists there is as much reason to assume unemployment will have positive political consequences because a voter who sees someone else lose a job may respond not with fear that he is next but rather with gratitude toward the government that has preserved his job. This proposition is fascinatingly clever. Whether it is accurate is another question.

4. Bach and Stephenson, for example, describe the redistributive aspects of inflation, usually considered a macroeconomic phenomenon. Inflation benefits debtors at the expense of creditors, hurts those on fixed incomes while helping those with mortgages, and is a tremendous boon to the government itself, insofar as it acts as a hidden form of taxation. This single example, which does not even address the question of which groups benefit most from the taxation aspect of inflation, shows how complex the issues are here.

5. See David Easton (1965, 1973) for a discussion of diffuse versus specific support for the incumbent political authorities.

6. The construction of these variables owes much to Tufte's (1978) analysis of political business cycles, where he notes the political importance of announcements of new policies to benefit key electoral groups, such as the government mailings announcing increased Social Security benefits just before November elections.

7. See Kenski 1977; Kernell 1977; Monroe 1978; or Stimson 1976.

8. Mueller also includes the beginning of each presidential term as a rally event, although this duplicates the beginning of the coalition-of-minorities variable and would seem to entail certain statistical difficulties. See Hibbs (1979) for a thorough statistical discussion of Mueller's work.

9. For a review, see Mueller 1973.

10. See, for example, any classic text, such as Koenig 1968 or Neustadt 1960.

11. Secretary of State Muskie's farewell address to the Department of State poignantly underlined the importance of leadership in politics. "But for the hostages I might not have been Secretary of State. And but for the hostages I might continue to be Secretary of State." Edmund Muskie, CBS News, January 11, 1981.

12. A few events are listed simply to signal to the reader that they were noted, but were not considered important enough to be included in the analysis. These events are followed by an "O."

13. All of the data were grouped into a bimonthly series to correspond with the data on group popularity. Each series will have a score of +1, +2, or -1, -2, etc., as noted above, depending on how many events occurred. At all other times, the series is set equal to zero. In many cases, an event coded "O" is not considered sufficient by itself to be entered as a +1 or a -1, but taken in conjunction with other events, it may go into the overall coding of -1, -2, etc., for a bimonthly period. Many of these events are listed here for information purposes, to serve as a general history of the time. All codings were done by four separate coders and checked by another coder. Disagreements were discussed and resolved by the four coders as a group.

14. See Chapter 3 or Mueller 1973.

15. See Monroe 1979 and Monroe and Laughlin 1983.

16. While there are still some economists who analyze economic events exclusively in terms of economic rationality

and economic efficiency, most economists who analyze economic policy making now conclude that the government's
economic decisions are made ". . . not by wise persons
immune from constitutency pressures, but by ordinary
politicians who are responsive to the demands of the voting
public" (Buchanan and Wagner 1977, 155). The impact of
this political competition on economic welfare and economic
policymaking is neither clearly nor definitively understood.
A traditional view, going back to the Federalist period,
argues that political competition, like economic competition,
will maximize welfare. (For various sides of this argument,
see Schumpeter 1962; Lowi 1969; Becker 1976; or Keech
1980.) Recent work on political business cycles, however,
suggests this political competition may result in suboptimal
economic policies as incumbents adopt policies that are
politically popular and will ensure their reelection. The
tension becomes acute when the choice of an economic policy
necessary to maximize immediate political gain involves
sacrificing long-term economic welfare or results in the
permanent exclusion of politically weak groups from the
economic gains enjoyed by the country as a whole. (See
Nordhaus 1975; Tufte 1978; Frey and Schneider 1979.)

On the other side of this politicoeconomic equation lies the
question about how the economy affects and determines
political choices and options. Here, again, the relationship
between politics and governmental economic policy is the
key. It is not clear whether the politician's main goal is
simply reelection, as is argued in the most extreme form by
Frey (1978), the achievement of certain policy options, as
Wittman suggests (1973, 1977), or some mixture of the
desire for reelection and influence over policy and power,
as most political scientists maintain (e.g., Fenno 1973).
(See Keech [1980] for a fuller discussion of this.) From
whichever side of the interaction our concern emanates,
however, it is clear that a key factor—in either the making
of economic policies or the election of political leaders—is
the public's response to economic conditions.

17. Durbin-Watson statistics tell whether the standard
errors are biased toward or away from statistical significance. They range from 0 to 4, with 0 denoting bias
toward significance and 4 indicating bias away from statistical significance. A value of 2 indicates no bias. The
exact range of figures that represents no autocorrelation
varies according to the number of variables and observations. For precise figures, see Durbin and Watson (1951
Table A—6).

18. Separate figures for those earning more than $15,000
a year were not collected during Johnson's incumbency.

The number of observations for this group is thus restricted to the Carter presidency and is too few to make reliable statistical tests of significance. Separate figures on popularity among those earning $10,000–15,000 were not collected until late in Johnson's term, bringing to 31 the number of observations for this income category. This may explain the inordinately high beta statistics.

19. There may be an additional problem with Schneider's findings. His classifications do not correspond to the data obtained from the Gallup agency, and when I attempted to replicate his findings using the Gallup data, I was unable to do so. My best attempts to replicate his findings suggest Schneider may have grouped farmers with unemployed workers, and put professional and white-collar workers in the same category.

20. Hibbs 1977, 1979; Weatherford 1978.

21. See Paldam and Schneider 1980; Erickson and Monroe 1981.

22. See Schneider 1978; Paldam and Schneider 1980.

23. See Appendix D for complete presentations of these findings.

24. See Schneider or Hibbs.

25. See Weatherford's work on the importance of distinguishing between class and status in this kind of analysis.

26. This centrality of party confirms the findings outlined in *The American Voter* and confirmed by Fiorina (1978), Rivers (1981), and Bell (1963). See also works by Hibbs and Vasilatos (1981), Tufte (1973), and Pomper (1975).

27. This is what Schneider (1978) and Jonung and Wadensjo (1979) found.

28. See Kramer 1983; Sears and Lau 1983.

Epilogue:
Toward an
Integrated Rational Theory
of Incumbent Support

How does the preceding empirical analysis help refine politicoeconomic models and broaden our understanding of political behavior? This is the subject of the Epilogue.

While the findings presented here are consistent with the general orientation of the pocketbook voter, they suggest important modifications in that theory. In particular, the economy's political influence is filtered through public expectations of differing economic priorities of the main political parties, with party ties serving as the simplifying mechanism used to link evaluations of past economic performance with the forecasting implicit in all but the simplest politicoeconomic models. Throughout the analysis, I have tried to note how the findings offer indirect evidence relevant for several important disciplinary debates concerning political behavior. First, they are consistent with the belief that the public perception of differing party priorities is a crucial determinant of electoral behavior. Second, they suggest voting and political support are not simple referenda on individual economic conditions but, instead, reflect public concern for group and national economic welfare and assessments of the president's managerial ability. Third, the findings are at variance with a class interpretation of political behavior. Finally, they suggest political behavior has rational origins, with economic conditions and expectations being more important than cyclical fluctuations.

Some of the specific findings presented in the preceding analysis, particularly employment's unusual political influence, detected only in a group analysis and heavily dependent on public expectations of different party economic priorities, alert us to a provocative question of potential theoretical interest: Are there other surprises concerning the economy's political impact and is there a way to resolve these anomalies by refining our traditional politicoeconomic theories? In short, can my findings on the economy's influence on presidential popularity yield broader insights into political behavior? I believe so. If we step back and examine these findings in relation to others in the field, certain contradictions and anomalies appear, both in the form of specific empirical findings and in the models that reflect broader theoretical orientations to understanding politics. These contradictions and anomalies are important in pointing to the need for theoretical clarification within contemporary political economy. This clarification centers on distinguishing between an economic decision-making process and economic motivations or goals. It is the distinction between understanding political behavior as a result of an economic process of calculations, regardless of the goals motivating this behavior, and understanding political behavior as being caused by economic motivations. This distinction alerts us to a longstanding and hidden philosophical disagreement between the sociological and the economic approach to social science over the fundamental motivations of human behavior. This disagreement centers on the need to revise our definition of rationality in social science and to construct a model of political behavior that integrates the sociological and economic approaches.

In a first attempt to do this, let me concentrate on four areas of discussion. First let me advance a theoretical clarification between the economic explanation as a decision-making process and as a motivation for political behavior. Second, I shall relate this to what I see as an extended historical debate between economists and sociologists over the fundamental motivations underlying political behavior. Third, I will argue that this debate runs so deeply within social science that it affects much empirical work in hidden ways. To document this, I shall present two examples of how this hidden disagreement has led to empirical controversies that could be resolved by reference to a broader theoretical framework, a framework that is essentially an integrated rational framework. Finally, I argue that the heart of the difficulty centers on the narrow definition of rationality utilized in political economy and in much of political science. In my conclusion, I suggest that my empirical analysis shares with virtually all the other major politicoeconomic models the fundamental premises of economic rationality. These premises, developed by classical economists and widely applied to political behavior after Downs's important development of an economic theory of democracy, underlie virtually all of the empirical analyses of political support, be it voting or popularity. Regardless of whether these models assume a retrospective, class, expectations, or sociotropic voting framework, all essentially offer only minor refinements or modifications in this classical economic model.

This classical economic model is essentially correct in its assumptions; when applied to political behavior, however, its illumination is so powerful that it blinds us to those aspects of behavior that it does not adequately explain. Future theoretical advances in the work begun by Downs will come not from further empirical application and tests of his model, but only from modifying the fundamental model on which his original work was based. In this Epilogue, I present the bare outline of such a modification by way of a critique of the economic rationality model, a critique aimed at stimulating development of what I shall call an economic ratiocination model of political behavior.

This economic ratiocination model of political behavior assumes political behavior is rational. It finds the classical economic rationality model too limiting, however, because it restricts politicoeconomic behavior to the conscious calculation of costs and benefits that define rationality for economists. A full understanding of political behavior must also allow for behavior emanating from impulses and goals buried deep within the preconscious and subconscious. While these impulses give behavior a quixotic element that puts them at variance with the economist's definition of rationality, an economic ratiocination model explicitly allows for such long-term and hidden influences of reason and behavior. Eventually, I hope this economic ratiocination model can be expanded to integrate the economic emphasis on rationality as a conscious calculation of costs and benefits with the social psychological emphasis on behavior derived from preconscious and subconscious impulses.[1]

POLITICAL BEHAVIOR:
THE PRODUCT OF AN ECONOMIC CALCULUS?
THE RESULT OF ECONOMIC CAUSES?

Any theory concerned with the economic influences on political support must first distinguish between economics as a method for understanding the behavioral process and economics as an explanation of the origin of the goals toward which this behavior is directed.[2]

The distinction between an economic explanation as a method and as a motive can be addressed relatively straightforwardly: The economic methodology stresses a behavioral process that is essentially rational. Although the precise definition of rational political behavior varies, it is usually defined as behavior in which the individual consistently pursues certain goals in accordance with some well-defined priorities and preferences; specific decisions, political or otherwise, are made subject to information costs and after assessing the costs and benefits for the individual.[3] Now, even the most fanatical economists admit that human behavior is not always consistent in its pursuit of goals and in the priorities these goals are assigned. But there is sufficient consistency, both at the macrolevel and for the individual over an extended time period, to yield remarkable explanatory and predictive power in politics, economics, and other areas of social interaction. Because of this, the economic method has enjoyed much vogue in the last 30 years and provides one of the leading approaches used in contemporary political analysis.[4]

The economic explanation as a motive for political support has an even longer history. Simply put, an economic explanation of politics views political behavior as originating in man's material goals and impulses. The emphasis is on the goals toward which the behavior is directed. The process by which these materialistic goals are advanced is not relevant, nor is it necessarily the same process stressed by an economic methodology. The distinction between an economic methodology and an economic explanation of political behavior can be clearly seen in one of Downs's examples. Downs argues that it is perfectly rational for a man to vote for candidate X rather than candidate Y, whom he prefers on the basis of his own cost-benefit calculation, if the man's wife supports candidate X and assuming the man wishes to please his wife. This demonstrates an economic process but is certainly not an economic explanation of the motive for voting.

This distinction between economics as methodology and economics as a motive draws attention to the distinction between process and goals, a distinction that focuses attention on the need for a theoretical clarification that is useful for specific works discussing economic influences on political support. This clarification concerns the sociological and the economic approaches to understanding political behavior. Even though all of the works discussed in this book have asked whether the economy affected political support, a question that necessarily stresses the economic explanation, not all have assumed that the public responds politically to the economy on the basis of rational calculations of cost and benefit, subject to information costs. Those who have not made this assumption can be classified as following a sociological approach. Those who have made this assumption can be said to follow an economic approach. The economic approach stresses the process by which political behavior emerges. It assumes this process is rational. The sociological approach stresses the goals toward which behavior is aimed at obtaining. The process itself is seldom discussed and is often implied to be a nonrational one.

ECONOMISTS VERSUS SOCIOLOGISTS: DIFFERENT APPROACHES TO UNDERSTANDING BEHAVIOR

The debate between economists and sociologists is a fundamental one that occurs when discussing both the causes of human behavior and the nature of the behavioral process. The heart of the debate, however, concerns the behavioral process. Economists emphasize intentional behavior in which an individual consciously seeks to further his perceived self-interest. The development of the individual goals that constitute the individual's conception of his self-interest are rarely, if ever, considered. The key to understanding behavior—political and economic—for an economist is rationality, generally defined to refer to the individual's attempts to maximize his perceived self-interest, subject to constraints of information and conflicting needs.[5]

While this classical economic concept of rationality has been discussed and refined by many different theorists, the most important refinement comes from Herbert Simon (1957) and concerns information availability, costs, and processing. Simon's work moves from the traditional concept of rationality to one heavily dependent on man's access to information and his actual computational capabilities. Simon concludes that many people seek not to maximize welfare but rather to achieve a certain minimum level of well-being; once this level is obtained, the individual remains largely indifferent to the varying satisfaction among alternatives and remains satisfied with any option that meets his minimum requirements.

All of the definitions of rationality, however, stress behavior designed to achieve certain goals. The goals themselves are never considered. Whether they appear reasonable or desirable in some objective sense is not discussed; only the process by which unspecified goals are obtained is relevant. Subconscious or preconscious motivations and impulses moving behavior are not considered by economists.

Juxtaposed to this concept of rational human behavior is what is often referred to as dispositional behavior, stressing attitudes, opinions, and personality traits and emphasizing learning theory rather than cost-benefit analysis. Graham Wallas, for example, disputes the importance of rationalism and intellectualism in political analysis and stresses man's unconscious attitudes. Wallas's ideas have influenced analysts who stress psychological factors or characteristics that are unconsciously related to political phenomena and the personality traits that serve as subconscious links between a disposition and political behavior.

This sociological approach thus emphasizes individual values and their formation, precisely that part of the process assumed as given and never discussed by the rational political economists. These alternative methods of analysis often end with little in common in their empirical conclusions since, like the fabled blind men describing an elephant, each feels a different part and therefore gains wildly divergent pictures of a common reality.

These alternative approaches to understanding human behavior have caused many schisms within political economy as a field. The nineteenth century break between historicists and theoreticians and the later fragmentation into socialists, Marxists, Marginalists, and Austrian schools of political economy, all emanated from disagreements about the centrality of rationality in the method of analyzing human behavior. Disciplinary divergences over the concept of rationality, however, seemed to end in the twentieth century with the development of econometrics, a development that occurred in both socialist and capitalist systems. In fact, econometrics merely obscured the persistent epistemological differences about the fundamental origins of human behavior by providing economists a common statistical technique and a common language.[6]

REPERCUSSIONS OF THE DEBATE
WITHIN POLITICAL SCIENCE

A similar development occurred within political science. Just as in economics, the econometric method spread to political science and sociology. Important ideological differences between these disciplines and economics over rationality became blurred, however, appearing as mere differences in measurement. This process was particularly striking in American departments since, despite its European origin, the major econometric work was done in the United States after the influx of European scholars during World War II.

The divergent views concerning the rational components of political behavior are best typified by the different analytical approaches that developed at the University of Chicago and Columbia University between 1920 and 1950. Chicago theorists stressed rational economic explanations of political behavior, while those at Columbia stressed sociological and ideological explanations. This divergence produced a dichotomized discipline, with both parts the poorer. Within political science, those concerned with the rational underpinnings of political behavior had been buffeted by shattering political and methodological events after World War I. The collapse of democracy in Germany and Italy, the deterioration of the Russian Revolution into civil war, the Stalinist purges and totalitarianism, the horror of World War II and inhumane treatment of civilian populations, the failure of decolonization to lead to democracy in Africa and Asia, the rise of the Cold War, and McCarthyism within the United States, all reawoke fears that the political progress promised by the pursuit of reason would not come to pass. Brian Barry argues that these upheavals exacerbated disciplinary differences concerning rationality, scarring at a critically formative period emerging contemporary political sociologists and political economists, just as the French Revolution had scarred the original sociologists and economists. (See Barry 1970.) Barry argues that the early nineteenth-century theories of national character were to reappear as theories of political culture. What earlier analysts had noted as a tendency for mass political participation to end in chaos and absolutism, reappeared as the theory of mass society. The post-World War II field of survey research uncovered many apparent inconsistencies in political attitudes, giving further evidence of human irrationality. Barry argues that the work of Talcott Parsons, in particular, reflected a conservative bias in political sociology. This has influenced sociologically oriented political analysts to ask: How can social order and social systems be maintained? Their answer was a common value system, an emphasis that stresses precisely that part of the process omitted or assumed as given by the economists: values or goals. Thus, contemporary political sociologists concluded that culture, ideology, groups, religion, and inherited memberships provided the essential motivations for human action and were the central factors to explain political behavior.

In contrast to this approach, political economists retained the Benthamite tradition that argued that men act rationally in pursuit of their goals. In addition to their methodological differences with political sociologists, political economists also differed radically in their professional analysis of the twentieth-century political upheavals. In contrast to the sociologists, they continued to stress self-interest and material gain, and continued largely to ignore group ties, ideology, and culture. Nowhere can these contrasting approaches be seen more clearly than in the analysis of voting behavior, that most central field of contemporary political science and one which involves the researcher in questions ranging from specific policy choices to normative concerns of democratic theory. Let us consider the analysis of the economy's political impact on presidential popularity as one example. To demonstrate why we need theoretical clarification concerning the extent to which the political process is rational or nonrational, let me outline a specific empirical disagreement that could be resolved by the adoption of a model that integrates both the rational and nonrational aspects of political behavior.

POLITICOECONOMIC MODELS: THE NEED FOR AN INTEGRATED RATIONAL APPROACH

Research on voting and other forms of political support is presently dominated by two schools: the rational choice theorists and the Michigan survey researchers. The differences in approach pursued by these schools create something akin to an epistemological barrier, with the rational choice theorists emphasizing abstract mathematical models and the survey researchers concentrating on the detailed empirical charting of public attitudes. As analysts from these two schools have turned to the study of the presidents' political support, and in particular, to the intricate relationships among presidential policies, general macroeconomic conditions, and voters' political response to economic change, many significant empirical discoveries have been made. Theoretical advances in this area, however, have remained limited by the perpetuation of the sharp epistemological division I have characterized as being represented by sociologists and economists. The result has produced simplistic explanations of presidential voting and policy making, with explanations tending to emphasize one of two views: voting as the outcome of partisan political battles, or voting as the product of strict cost-benefit calculations by voters for whom any preconscious responses to economic conditions are reduced to the catch-all of party identification.

Works on the economic influences on presidential popularity reflect these sharply contrasting explanations of political behavior. Rational choice explanations, on the one hand, have viewed presidential popularity as the result of rational causes, such as the economy, wars, and international crises. On the other hand, while some survey researchers have occasionally accepted certain elements of the rational choice framework, the majority has viewed presidential popularity as originating in inherited attitudes that are the product of group memberships and ideological predispositions beyond the individual's ability to understand consciously, much less control or change.[7]

Two examples of these sharply contrasting explanations of public support for the president are offered by John Mueller (1970, 1973) and James Stimson (1975, 1976). Mueller stresses rational causes, such as the economy, wars, and international crises, while Stimson emphasizes the psychological disposition of an uninformed public first to embrace and then to reject presidents almost at whim, though with a consistency that produces a pattern.

Mueller assumes a rational choice framework in which the public responds to the president on the basis of the economy in an uneven way, blaming him for economic deterioration but not giving him credit for economic improvement. Stimson's model takes the opposite tack: It stresses nonrational cyclical movements in public opinion that have little to do with presidential actions or economic events. Although Stimson neither develops nor refers to a specific theoretical orientation, it seems clear that his model is founded on an essentially nonrational base, at least so far as his central argument is concerned. This argument maintains that presidential popularity is more the reflection of unrealistic public expectations early in the term, followed by eventual disillusionment among the less well-informed segments of the public, than it is a reflection of a rational response to particular presidential actions or policies. Stimson examines the pattern of popularity for each president and finds a regularity that he argues is inevitable: high initial popularity during so-called honeymoon periods, followed by a gradual decline for three years, then a slight upsurge near the end of the term.

Stimson does not attempt to explain this cycle through presidential actions, arguing instead that "presidential approval may be almost wholly independent of the president's behavior in office" and is "a function largely of inevitable forces associated with time" (1976, 1). Essentially, Stimson's argument is this: The public response to the president is unrelated to specific presidential actions but follows a certain general and inevitable pattern for all presidents. Mueller sees the same pattern, but he explains it in psychological terms within a rational choice framework. Over time, various presidential actions antagonize different groups, who eventually join together in a coalition of disaffected minorities. This results in the gradual erosion of presidential popularity, which is halted only as the next election nears and the president is compelled to woo these groups. That the general cycles in presidential popularity can be explained by an argument that appeals to rationality seems obvious when one considers Mueller's coalition-of-minorities theory or the psychological arguments concerning stimulus familiarity. Stimson's failure to develop these explanations, therefore, seems significant.

This basic disagreement over the causes of the fluctuations in presidential popularity has continued beyond the original debate, with Kenski (1977a, 1977b, 1977c, 1979), Stimson and Le Gette (1975), and Zeller and Carmines (1978) insisting that time is the only explanatory variable, while Kernell (1978), Monroe (1978), and Frey and Schneider (1978), inter alia argue for more tangible reasons. All of these authors have built sophisticated econometric models and have produced interesting and convincing empirical results to confirm their models. As the preceding analysis in this book has demonstrated, however, empirical analysis that gives sufficient attention to these differing approaches to integrate both economic and sociological factors (e.g., the role of groups and leadership ability) will do much to minimize needless and often trivial empirical debate.

POLITICOECONOMIC MODELS

A theoretical clarification stressing the distinction between the sociological and the economic approaches to the political behavior process would not only eliminate disagreement over specific empirical findings. It would also improve the politicoeconomic models employed in this area.

Over the last 50 years, many models have been developed to explain the economy's political influence. The original policy models grew from a view of political behavior as the result of an informed choice between policy alternatives. In its classic form, policy models find informed citizens choosing between honest candidates on the basis of what the candidates say they will do if elected. Analysts emphasize voter policy preferences, the average voter, media presentation of views, and the like.[8]

While policy models are useful, they overlook certain obvious aspects of political behavior; e.g., single-issue candidates, voter difficulties in obtaining information, or the desire of candidates for fame rather than reelection or money, to mention just a few. In response to these short-comings, a pocketbook-voter model developed. Based largely on Downs's technical modification of the classical economic model, this model has become the single most important politicoeconomic model. Because it is based on Downs's original work, the modifications made in this model by analysts concerned with the economy's political influence have come to be known as a Downsian model with satisficing assumptions (see Kramer 1971).[9] Offering the many ad-vantages of parsimony in the economic tradition from which it sprang, this model advances a simplified rational analysis of voting by the simple but brilliant theoretical assumption that political support is a conscious cost-benefit calculation in which the individual's own economic condition is his chief information source. This assumption alleviates all the difficulties traditionally involved in specifying how voters obtain information on candidate and party policy prefer-ences, how this information is processed, and so on. The voter simply asks how he is doing economically and then rewards or blames the incumbent accordingly. The strength of this model is the strength of rationality: It does explain a remarkable degree of political behavior and it yields a high predictive value.

While all of the important later politicoeconomic models offer certain refinements in this basic Downsian model, all essentially accept the fundamental tenets of classical eco-nomics on which this original model is based; i.e., they assume political behavior emanates from individual self-interest through a conscious calculation of costs and bene-fits. The retrospective voting models argue for a particu-lar way in which this basic rational economic calculation is made using past events.[10] Class models emphasize the unit whose welfare is maximized in the calculation.[11] Party priority models and prospective voting models emphasize the route by which this estimation of past behavior is projected onto future behavior.[12]

One model that claims to offer an alternate approach to the basic Downsian model is the sociotropic voting model.

This model moves away from the simple pocketbook voter, who responds politically only on the basis of his own economic situation; it substitutes a voter who responds politically primarily to national economic conditions. The relevant political consideration is not one's personal economic situation but rather a judgment about national economic conditions. While there is much empirical evidence suggesting this occurs, the key weakness in the theory itself centers on its ambiguity over whether the sociotropic voter uses economic conditions as a measure of the president's economic managerial ability or whether he actually disregards his own condition in favor of his evaluation of the economic well-being of the country as a whole. These two phenomena are quite distinct.

Let us consider the first possibility. Assume the voter no longer asks: How am I doing economically under the incumbent president? Rather, he asks about the nation's economic condition. If he disregards his own situation because it does not correspond with national economic conditions and if he assumes these national conditions better reflect the managerial ability that the president brings to economic matters, and therefore his own long-run economic prospects, then this model simply extends the logic of the original pocketbook-voter model. It proposes behavior in which concern for public economic conditions sensitizes voters to their individual situations.[13] But it does not propose a fundamentally different approach to political behavior.

If, on the other hand, the sociotropic voting model posits voters who disregard their own welfare (both immediate and long-term) in order to respond politically to advance the common good, then the sociotropic voting theory proposes a radically different politicoeconomic behavior process. If this is so, then the sociotropic voting model views political behavior as the result of a rational calculation of group rather than individual interest. (It could be the latter only in so far as it assumes individual voters have goals that are public rather than private.) The critical point is that an entirely new kind of political animal is being proposed: a selfless, public-spirited man who not merely puts public goals into his individual utility function but actually puts them ahead of his own individual welfare. Such behavior seems unlikely to be common and should, therefore, be of limited predictive value. The alternative sociotropic claim, then, of voting as a referendum on managerial ability, seems a much stronger assumption.[14]

EXPECTATIONS MODELS

A recent category of models may actually be moving political science toward a new model of politicoeconomic behavior. These models are the ones developed to explain the process by which economic conditions relate to expectations. They consider the political impact of expectations of what actual economic conditions would be under different parties or candidates. They also consider how the expectations of differing party priorities are formed originally. The empirical analysis in Chapter 4 suggested both of these are critical determinants of the economy's political influence. These models, I believe, offer a new approach. While they do not explicitly discuss their underlying premises, some of these models—or at least certain elements of several models—offer the possibility of a basic modification in the Downsian model. Let me offer a very tentative discussion of these aspects and of their theoretical implications.

Expectations Models—Relation to
the Classical Economic Model

Elements of these expectations models are found in the economic literature as early as Keynes, and can be found in several of the politicoeconomicive models discussed earlier. Retrospective voting models, for example, are ones in which voters' observations about past behavior inform their expectations of future behavior. While accepting the premises of economic rationality, retrospective voting models differ from the policy models by stressing not the candidates' stated issue positions but rather the candidates' or incumbents' past behavior or the behavior of their party. This theory holds that voters note the performance (economic or otherwise) during an incumbent's term and compare this with what they believe the other candidate or party might do, using some weighting factor to discount future and past performance. The link providing continuity comes from party ties.[15] This theory is an important advance over the policy model insofar as it rejects political promises as accurate indicators of future performance in favor of an evaluation of past performance as an indicator of future behavior. Its weakness comes from its failure to deal with extremist candidates, with left/right splits within the parties, and with its limitation to strong party systems, since in multiparty systems with shifting coalition governments, the party link between past behavior and future behavior breaks down.

An additional theoretical weakness comes from the theory's failure to specify how independent calculations about the future are constructed. These forecasts appear to be what economists would call static expectations, in which the past is assumed to be the best predictor of the future. Prospective voting models offer only a slight advance in their discussion of how forecasts are constructed from evaluations of past behavior. The empirical work by Kuklinski and West finds independent measures of economic expectations are better predictors of voting than are past observations. Prospective voting models thus seem to propose using direct survey evidence to measure these expectations; but they fail to ask where or how these expectations are formed. While one possible route is the evaluation of past behavior (i.e., the static expectation phenomenon discussed above), presumably this solution is what originally caused the prospective voting model theorists to reject the retrospective voting models as too simple.

One alternative explanation comes from emphasizing the degree of accuracy in predicting future behavior from past behavior. It seems self-evident that the accuracy of one's predictions will affect the political response to an occurrence. Realistic expectations can cushion the political shock of an event, such as a recession, while unrealistic expectations can worsen it. While there is little explicit politicoeconomic work on this, the accuracy in prediction is usually measured either simply as the deviations from the norm or through an adaptive expectations model developed by neoclassical economists.[16] This model assumes that individuals, ignorant of the environment they face, form current expectations by an adaptive or error-correcting mechanism to allow for their past mistakes. In formal terms, the expected value of each economic variable is assumed to be a weighted moving average of past values for the same variable.

An alternate measurement of expectations has developed from the economic theory of rational expectations.[17] The rational expectations model assumes individuals use whatever information they have optimally.[18] This model has been criticized, however, for its assumption that individuals know the expectations of other individuals.[19] Such knowledge of what others will do is necessary for the rational expectations theorists to successfully predict the outcome of the economic process. But how can these expectations be known since they, too, are dependent on the expectations of others? To assume away this problem by saying that all individuals hold the same expectations, as the rational theorists do, does not seem justified.[20]

An Economic Ratiocination Model

While political science can benefit from economists' models, we must also learn from their mistakes. The difficulty in the expectations models developed by economists centers on the question of information and uncertainty. This difficulty was noted by Keynes in his early work on the effects of public expectations on economic activity, as related to business cycles. Despite interesting initial theoretical discussions of the problems of information acquisition and the formation of individual expectations, the difficulties in modeling expectations formation, which arise due to the highly subjective nature of these expectations, remained intractable. For the most part, therefore, postwar Keynesian economics ignored the role of economic expectations in explaining macroeconomic phenomena and assumed individuals possessed complete information. This assumption clearly is not true in political life. An economic ratiocination model may be useful here.

This economic ratiocination model, which takes its name from the somewhat archaic verb "ratiocinate," meaning "to carry on a process of reasoning," assumes a behavioral process that is essentially rational. The nonrational process, noted by sociologists, however, is integrated into this model via social psychological theories that emphasize behavior patterns that are formed in response to early life experiences. These early behavior patterns form the individual's expectations about what the political process should do for him. They shape the cognitive framework into which he assembles and interprets events and in which he processes new information. Finally, they determine his predilection for taking risks.

This economic ratiocination model assumes the kind of adaptive expectations mechanism used both by economists and by historians and political scientists concerned with the political consequences of rising economic expectations.[21] Originally developed to explain violent political change, this theory can be applied to less drastic political shifts in order to explain an anomaly often ignored in American political history: the continuing popularity of Franklin Delano Roosevelt. Elected first on grounds that fit into the simple Downsian framework, Roosevelt's popularity continued even after economic conditions failed to improve in any substantial way for many people. If we push the Downsian framework into a long lagged form and stress the calamitous impact of the Depression's first shock waves, we can perhaps explain this phenomenon by making all four of FDR's elections (or at least the three nonwar elections) referenda on the Hoover administration's dismal record. This does strain credibility somewhat, however, and has resulted in the Roosevelt elections being used to give credence to nonrational explanations of political behavior, explanations that stress symbolic gestures or party ties developed in critical elections. A more satisfactory explanation can be provided, however, using expectations theory: After the Depression's first shock, people did not expect much from their government. Their expectations had been drastically lowered.

An economic ratiocination model further modifies this explanation, however, to allow for the politically unsettling aspects of uncertainty. This moves analysis beyond a simple consideration of the political impact of economic expectations to include also the political importance of uncertainty over future economic events. In explaining short-term fluctuations in presidential popularity, for example, an economic ratiocination model would allow for economic conditions but would also contain some measure of economic expectations and uncertainty about the future. This allows us to stress both expectations and the psychological dislocation from uncertainty about the economic future, an uncertainty that has negative political consequences that are independent of public reaction to the gap between actual and expected economic conditions. The key is the need for certainty and predictability, rather than public pleasure at doing better than had been anticipated or displeasure at doing worse than had been expected. The uncertainty factor explains situations in which support for a president decreases because of an uncertain economic climate, despite the fact that this uncertainty may actually have resulted in the occurrence of better-than-expected economic conditions. While both the traditional theories of economic expectations and the uncertainty factors stress expectations of future events, the two theories accentuate quite distinct political psychologies.[22] It will not be easy to allow adequately for the role uncertainty plays in politicoeconomic life. Even the limited empirical work done in this area, however, can raise important theoretical concerns for us.[23]

Here I have few answers, only useful questions. How are expectations formed in a rational fashion? At what age? How are they shifted? And when do the unsettling effects of uncertainty become troubling enough to offset any joy felt at doing better than had been expected? The limited empirical work discussing short-term expectation formation suggests these expectations are rational in their construction, based on an evaluation of the past performance of another party. But these past judgments are then forecast, using some kind of adaptive expectations mechanism, coupled with the individual's need for certainty, into what the two parties are expected to do in the future. The certainty factor, the continuity between one administration and another, is provided by the party label. But we need to know more about how the need for certainty varies from individual to individual and about how individual needs for certainty are affected by group responses.[24]

Again, however, these advances only raise new questions for us. What weights do the voters attach to the parties' policies? How do the forecasts allow for gradual shifts in party positions? How do they allow for liberal-conservative splits within parties, especially for the oscillations of control in the parties by the different wings? The central question seems to be how information is received, processed, and accorded importance and how individual expectations are derived from the schematic framework carried in the individual voter's head. But where does this framework originate? And when and how is it modified? These questions cannot be answered here. They involve the literature on decision making and risk aversion, on both adaptive and rational economic expectations, on the relation between individual microlevel motives and macrolevel behavior, and the social psychology literature on levels of aspiration and the frustrations of need achievement that lead to cognitive dissonance and its resolution.[25]

These different literatures all suggest a rational framework, as modified by an economic ratiocination model, in the sense that the individual's views and expectations are all derived originally as part of his response to further his own self-interest. But the narrower rational economic man, popular with economists and social choice theorists, must be expanded to allow for the subconscious and preconscious drives to which Freud alerted us. This will serve as a link between economic man and the sociologist's emphasis on political behavior as emanating in dark, primitive, mysterious forces. It will wed the economists' emphasis on rationality as a conscious calculation of costs and benefits with the social psychologists' emphasis on behavior derived from preconscious and subconscious impulses. My guess is that such work will yield an integrated rational model similar to the economic ratiocination model outlined above. My conviction is that it will be the next major theoretical break-through in political science.

NOTES

1. Weber's work on Zweckrationality is relevant here. See Parsons 1951.

2. It could be perhaps argued that this distinction corresponds roughly to the distinction between epistemology and ontology, insofar as epistemology refers to the process of knowing reality, and ontology to the reality itself.

3. The information costs refer to the costs, including opportunity costs, involved in obtaining all information relevant to the choice.

4. For a discussion of this, see Harsanyi, in Sen and Williams 1982, 39–62.

5. Rationality as an explanatory concept applied to human behavior has been defined by many different theorists. The clearest classical statement of politics as the conscious calculation of needs and wants is Bentham's. The most important contemporary definition of rationality comes from Anthony Downs, who argues that rationality entails "maximizing output for a given input, or minimizing input for a given output" (Downs 1957). Robert Dahl and Charles Lindblom designate an action rational when it is correctly designed to maximize goal achievement, given the goal under consideration and the world as it actually exists. Gibson defines rationality as any behavior that considers the evidence in pursuit of goals, thereby raising the question of how information about this evidence is obtained.

6. See Spiegel, *Econometrics: A Supposed Merger, An Actual Obfuscation of Continuing Ideological Differences* (1971, 572). The term econometrics was coined by Rauar Frisch, a Norwegian economist and statistician, in the 1920s to refer to a science of measurement. The word gained widespread usage when Frisch and Irving Fisher inter alia founded the Econometric Society in 1930. The Cowles Commission (later the Cowles Foundation) was founded in 1932 as an affiliated research organization to coordinate theoretical and empirical work. This goal was in contrast to the National Bureau of Economic Research's emphasis on fact finding.

7. This sharp split is less evident after Fiorina's important work. See Chapter 1 (above) for a review.

8. In a more technically developed form, policy models can be expressed as issue-space or spatial models, in which positions on particular issues are treated as locations in

cognitive issue-space. These spatial models differ from simpler policy models in assuming candidates are more interested in being elected than in implementing specific policies. The underlying tenets, however, are the same.

9. See Downs 1957. This original work is actually much richer and more all-encompassing than what is usually referred to as "the Downsian model."

10. The best known retrospective voting model is Fiorina's original model.

11. For examples of class models, see the recent works by Weatherford or Schneider.

12. Examples of party models are the ones developed by Hibbs, Hibbs and Madsen, Jonung and Wadensjo, or Rosa and Amson. The best example of prospective voting models is the Kuklinski and West model. For reviews of all these models, see Chapter 1.

13. Kuklinski and West (1981) present evidence that this, in fact, is what occurs.

14. The prior sociotropic voter claim puts us into a world where collective goods are highly integrated into individual utility functions. This may be in a world of symbolic politics in which personal predicaments do not matter politically and in which global concerns are key. These models move out of the category of politicoeconomic models, however, and into the area of noneconomic models of political behavior. While there is good recent evidence reconfirming the importance of symbolic politics, this topic lies outside the range of the present discussion. See works by Markus and Converse (1979) suggesting candidates are more important than policies or party identification, or by Kelley and Mirer (1974) suggesting that party identification has political impact when there is no clear personal favorite, or by Kinder and Abelson (1981) suggesting that candidate personality is more important than economic concerns at either the individual or national level.

15. This links the retrospective voting models with the party priority models. See Fair 1978; Hibbs and Vasilatos 1982a, 1982b.

16. See Phelps 1970 (edited volume).

17. See the work done by John Muth or by Robert Lucas during the 1970s.

18. As evidence that this occurs, the rational expectation theorists argue that wages and prices adjust instantaneously to clear markets at all times.

19. See Frydman (February 1983) *Journal of Money, Credit and Banking* and (September 1982) *The American Economic Review*.

20. This difficulty must make us question whether

206 / PRESIDENTIAL POPULARITY AND THE ECONOMY

voters who do not know the rational expectations of others can produce a macrolevel rational expectation equilibrium.

21. The central work on this topic, of course, is Alexis de Tocqueville's (1840) analysis of the French Revolution. De Tocqueville argued that public support for political incumbents is determined not so much by actual economic conditions as by the gap between actual and anticipated economic reality. This explained two puzzling aspects of the French Revolution: (1) why the revolution occurred in France, instead of another country, and (2) why it occurred at that particular time. After all, France was one of the most economically developed countries in Europe, with the French peasant and bourgeois infinitely better off than his German or Russian counterpart. And economic conditions under Louis XVI were much better than they had been under his predecessors. De Tocqueville argued that the revolution occurred when and where it did precisely because conditions had been improving; it was the rate at which they were improving that had slowed and was outpaced by people's expectations of how fast things had progressed and were, therefore, expected to progress in the future. This gap between economic reality and what people had come to expect caused frustrations to outpace economic reality and culminated in revolt.

Since de Tocqueville's first work, many analysts have discussed situations in which political support was withdrawn from both incumbents and entire regimes, not because economic conditions had deteriorated but rather because conditions had failed to improve as quickly as past growth led the populace to expect. (See, for example, Davies 1962, 1969; Gurr 1970.) Recent analysts have refined the measurement techniques and applied the psychological concept of a revolution of rising expectations to less violent regime changes or to microlevel survey data. The most significant analyses of public opinion responses indicating the importance of economic expectations for more routinized expressions of support for political incumbents in representative democracies are Alt's important work on England and the analysis of American public opinion by Hibbs and by Kuklinski and West (Alt 1979; Hibbs 1981; Kuklinski and West 1981).

22. They also suggest different choices for policy makers.

23. In an earlier joint work on American presidential popularity (Monroe and Levi 1983), I counterposed the traditional theory of a revolution of rising expectations with a theory stressing the political consequences of uncertainty concerning future economic conditions. This work con-

sidered the importance of economic expectations for mass public support for American presidents from 1950 to 1975.

In particular, short-term fluctuations in the Gallup Poll indicators of presidential popularity were explained through measurements of economic expectations and uncertainty about key economic events collected since 1946 by Joseph Livingston. These data were analyzed in a standard multivariate statistical analysis to determine the political importance of the gap between actual and expected inflation, the gap between actual and expected economic growth, uncertainty about inflation, and uncertainty about economic growth. Two additional variables were also included to avoid specification error; the first measured military involvement in Korea and Vietnam, and the second measured public shifts in attitudes toward the president resulting both from political activity around elections and from the honeymoon phenomenon following inaugurations.

By considering both the degree to which presidential popularity responds to the difference between actual and expected economic experience and the degree to which presidential popularity responds simply to uncertainty concerning economic conditions, we were able to test the two alternative theories of short-term political-economic interaction discussed above: the traditional theory of a revolution of rising expectations, and the theory stressing the political consequences of uncertainty concerning future economic conditions, a theory that argues that presidential popularity rises when there is certainty about the economic future and falls when there is uncertainty.

While this is not the place to reproduce the findings from an earlier analysis, the results were both remarkable and highly significant for public policy. The gap between expected and actual results of the empirical analysis suggested that both economic expectations and economic uncertainty have serious political consequences. Expectations of inflation were not significant, suggesting that the satisfaction of those who gain is offset by the dissatisfaction of those who lose from inflation. What does seem to disturb people is the tremendous uncertainty concerning future inflation. And this uncertainty carried great political costs for the incumbent president. (See Monroe and Levi 1983.)

24. See Schelling 1978.

25. This relates quite closely to the Brody and Sniderman work suggesting the middle class blames the government for individual economic distress; i.e., they focus on structural explanations rather than internalizing the blame, as working class respondents do. (See Brody and Sniderman 1977 or Chapter 1 for a review.)

Bibliography

Abramowitz, A. I. 1979. Electoral Accountability in 1978: Comparison of Voting for U.S. Senators and Representatives. Presented at the annual meeting of the American Political Science Association, Washington, D.C.

Abramson, P. R. 1975. *Generational Change in American Politics*. Lexington, Massachusetts: Lexington Books.

Akerman, J. 1947. Political Economic Cycles. *Kyklos* 1:107–17.

Almond, G. A., and G. B. Powell, Jr. 1966. *Comparative Politics: A Developmental Approach*. Boston: Little, Brown.

Almond, G. A., and S. Vera. 1963. *The Civic Culture: Political Attitudes and Democracy in Five Nations*. Princeton: Princeton University Press.

Alt, J. E. 1979. *The Politics of Economic Decline*. Cambridge: Cambridge University Press.

————. 1980. Democracy and Public Expenditure. *Political Science Paper* No. 44. Presented to the colloquium, "Les Consequences Économiques de la Démocratie," Université Rene Descartes, Paris, January 18–19, 1980.

Alt, J. E., and K. A. Chrystal. 1983. *Political Economics*. Berkeley: University of California Press.

Alt, J. E., and J. T. Woolley. 1982. Reaction, Functions, Optimization, and Politics: Modeling the Political Economy of Macroeconomic Policy. *American Journal of Political Science* 26(4):709–40.

Andersen, K. 1979. *The Creation of a Democratic Majority, 1928–1936*. Chicago: University of Chicago Press.

Arcelus, F. 1978. Effects of Aggregate Economic Variables on the Distribution of House Seats. Paper presented at the 1978 Annual Meeting of the Midwest Political Science Association, Chicago, Illinois, April 20–22, 1978.

Arcelus, F., and A. H. Meltzer. 1975a. The Effect of Aggregate Economic Conditions on Congressional Elections. *American Political Science Review* 69(4):1232–39.

————. 1975b. Aggregate Economic Variables and Votes for Congress: A Rejoinder. *American Political Science Review* 69(4):1266–69.

Arendt, H. 1958. *The Human Condition.* Chicago: University of Chicago Press.

Atesoglu, H. T., and R. Congleton. 1982. Economic Conditions and National Elections, Post-sample Forecasts of the Kramer Equations. *The American Political Science Review* 76(4):873–75.

Bach, G. L., and J. B. Stephenson. 1974. Inflation and the Redistribution of Wealth. *The Review of Economics and Statistics* 61(1):1–13.

Bachrach, P. 1967. *The Theory of Democratic Elitism.* Boston: Little, Brown.

Barnhart, J. D. 1925. Rainfall and the Populist Party in Nebraska. *American Political Science Review* 19(3):527–40.

Barry, B. 1970. *Sociologists, Economists and Democracy.* London: Collier-Macmillan.

Bean, L. 1940. *Ballot Behavior.* Washington, D.C.: American Council on Public Affairs.

————. 1948. *How to Predict Elections.* New York: Knopf.

Beck, N. 1981. Linkages Between Political Pressures and Economic Policy-Making: Monetary and Fiscal Policy in the Post-War United States. Prepared for delivery at the 1981 Annual Meeting of the American Political Science Association, New York, September 3–6, 1981.

Becker, G. 1976. *Economic Approach to Human Behavior.* Chicago: University of Chicago Press.

Bell, D., ed. 1963. *The Radical Right: The New American Right.* New York: Doubleday.

Benedict, R. 1946. *The Chrysanthemum and the Sword.* Boston: Houghton Mifflin.

Bloom, H. S., and H. D. Price. 1975. Comment. *American Political Science Review.* 69(4):1240–54.

Boddy, R., and J. Crotty. 1975. Class Conflict and Macropolicy: The Political Business Cycle. *Review of Radical Political Economics,* 1:1–19.

Britannia Yearbooks. 1965–78. Chicago: Encyclopedia Britannia.

Brittan, S. 1962. *Observer* (December 2).

Broder, I., and A. Lichtman. 1980. Modeling the Past: A Note on the Search for Proper Form. *Social Science Working Paper* 358. Pasadena: California Institute of Technology.

Brody, R. A. 1978. The Puzzle of Political Participation in America. In *The New American Political System,* ed. Anthony King. Washington, D.C.: American Enterprise Institute for Public Policy Research. 287–324.

————. 1980. Public Evaluations and Expectations and

the Future of the Presidency. Delivered at the Conference on the Future of the Presidency, University of Virginia, November 29–30, 1979.

Brody, R. A., and B. Grofman. 1982. Choice vs. Involvement in Electoral Participation. *Political Behavior* 4(1):83–92.

Brody, R. A., and B. I. Page. 1973. Indifference, Alienation and Rational Decisions. *Public Choice* 15: 1–17.

————. 1975. The Impacts of Events on Presidential Popularity: The Johnson and Nixon Administrations. In *Perspectives on the Presidency,* ed. Aaron Wildavsky, 136–48. Boston: Little, Brown.

Brody, R. A., and P. M. Sniderman. 1977. From Life Space to Polling Place: The Relevance of Personal Concerns for Voting Behavior. *British Journal of Political Science* 7 (July):337–60.

Buchanan, J., and R. E. Wagner. 1977. *Democracy in Deficit: The Political Legacy of Lord Keynes.* New York: Academic Press.

Burnham, W. D. 1970. *Critical Elections and the Mainsprings of American Politics.* New York: Norton.

Butler, D., and D. Stokes. 1969. *Political Change in Britain: Forces Changing Electoral Choice.* 2nd ed. New York: St. Martin's Press.

Cameron, D. 1976. Inequality and the state: A political-economic comparison. Paper for the annual meeting of the American Political Science Association, Chicago, September 1976.

————. 1978. The Expansion of Public Economy: A Comparative Analysis. *American Political Science Review* 72:1243–61.

Campbell, A., P. S. Converse, and D. E. Stokes. 1960. *Elections and the Political Order.* New York: John Wiley.

Campbell, A., P. S. Converse, W. S. Miller, and D. E. Stokes. 1960. *The American Voter.* New York: Wiley.

Carmines, E. D., and J. A. Stimson. 1980. The Two Faces of Issue Voting. *American Political Science Review* 74:7891.

Chappell, H. W., Jr., and W. R. Keech. 1981. Welfare Consequences of the Six-Year Presidential Term Evaluated in the Context of a Model of the U.S. Economy. Paper presented at the Annual Meeting of Public Choice Society, New Orleans, Louisiana, March 13–15, 1981.

Chilcote, Ronald H. 1981. *Theories of Comparative Politics.* Boulder, Colorado: Westview Press.

Chrystal, K. A., and J. E. Alt. 1979a. Some Problems in

Formulating and Testing a Politico-Economic Model of the U.K. University of Essex Discussion Paper.
──────. 1979b. Public Sector Behavior: The Status of the Political Business Cycle. Discussion Paper, No. 128, presented at the University of Essex. Mimeo.

Clark, W. 1943. *Economic Aspects of a President's Popularity*. Philadelphia: University of Pennsylvania Press.

Conforto, B. M., and R. Y. Shapiro. 1980. Presidential Performance, the Economy and the Public's Evaluation of Economic Conditions. *Journal of Politics* 42:49–67.

Converse, P. 1957. The Shifting Role of Class in American Politics. In *Readings in Social Psychology,* ed. E. Maccoby et al. New York: Holt.
──────. 1975. Public Opinion and Voting Behavior. In F. I. Greenstein and N. W. Polsby, eds. *Handbook of Political Science* 4:75–156.

Cowart, A. T. 1978. The Economic Policies of European Governments, Parts I and II: Monetary Policy and Fiscal Policy. *British Journal of Political Science* 8:285–311, 425–39.

Crewe, I., B. Sarlvik, and J. Alt. 1977. Partisan Dealignment in Britain, 1964-1974. *British Journal of Political Science* 7:129–90.

Crick, B. 1959. *The American Science of Politics*. London: Routledge and Kegan Paul.
──────. 1962. *In Defense of Politics*. London: Weidenfeld and Nicolson.

Dahl, R. A. 1961. *Who Governs?* New Haven: Yale University Press.

Davies, J. 1969. The J curve of Rising and Declining Satisfactions as a Cause of Some Great Revolutions and a Continued Rebellion. In *Violence in America: Historical and Comparative Perspectives,* ed. H. D. Graham and T. R. Gurr. Washington, D.C.: National Commission on the Causes and Prevention of Violence.

Davis, O., M. Hinich, and P. Ordeshook. 1970. An Expository Development of a Mathematical Model of the Electoral Process. *American Political Science Review* 64:426–48.

Dennis, J. 1981a. Public Support for Congress. *Political Behavior* 4(3):319–50.
──────. 1981b. On Being an Independent Partisan Supporter. Paper prepared for delivery at the 1981 Annual Meeting of the Midwest Political Science Association, Cincinnati, Ohio, April 15–18, 1981.
──────. 1981c. Some Properties of Measures of Partisanship. Paper prepared for delivery at the 1981 Annual Meeting of the American Political Science Association,

New York, September 3–6, 1981.

Doe, P. 1982. Issue Preferences and Candidate Choice in Presidential Primaries. *American Journal of Political Science* 26:n.p.

Downs, A. 1957. *An Economic Theory of Democracy.* New York: Harper and Row.

Durant, H. 1965. Indirect Influences on Voting Behavior. *Polls* 1:3–10.

Durbin, J., and G. S. Watson. 1951. Testing for Serial Correlation in Least Squares Regression. II *Biometrika* 38:159–78.

Easton, D. 1953. *The Political System: An Inquiry into the State of Political Science.* New York: Alfred A. Knopf.

————. 1965. *A Systems Analysis of Political Life.* New York: Wiley.

————. 1973. Theoretical Approaches to Political Support. Paper presented at the National Science Foundation Conference on Political Support and Alienation, Madison, Wisconsin.

Easton, D., and J. Dennis. 1969. *Children in the Political System: Origins of Political Legitimacy.* New York: McGraw-Hill.

Erickson, L., and K. R. Monroe. 1981. The Economic, Political and Cyclical Components. Paper presented at the 1981 meetings of the Canadian Political Science Association.

Erikson, Robert S. 1971. The Advantage of Incumbency in Congressional Elections. *Polity* 3:395–405.

Facts on File Yearbook. New York: Facts on File, xxix, xxxx.

Fair, R. C. 1978. The Effect of Economic Events on Votes for the President. *Review of Economics and Statistics* 60:159–75.

Feldman, S. 1981. Economic Individualism and Mass Belief Systems. Paper prepared for delivery at the annual meeting of the Midwest Political Science Association, Cincinnati, Ohio, April 15–18, 1981.

————. 1982. Economic Self-Interest and Political Behavior. *American Journal of Political Science* 26: 446–66.

Fenno, R. F. 1973. *Congressmen in Committees.* Boston: Little, Brown.

————. 1975. If, As Ralph Nader Says, Congress Is "The Broken Branch," How Come We Love Our Congressmen So Much? In N. J. Ornstein, ed. *Congress in Change.* New York: Praeger.

Ferejohn, J. A., and M. P. Fiorina. 1979. The Decline in Turnout in Presidential Elections. Paper presented at the Conference on Voter Turnout, San Diego, California, May 16–19, 1979.

Festinger, L. 1957. *A Theory of Cognitive Dissonance.* Evanston: Row, Peterson.

Finkelstein, M. O., and H. E. Robbins. 1973. Mathematical Probability in Election Challenges. *Columbia Law Review* 73(241):242–48.

Fiorina, M. P. 1974. *Representatives, Roll Calls and Constituencies.* Lexington, Massachusetts: Lexington Books.

—————. 1978. Economic Retrospective Voting in American Elections: A Microanalysis. *American Journal of Political Science* 22(2):426–43.

—————. 1981a. *Retrospective Voting in American National Elections.* New Haven: Yale University Press.

—————. 1981b. Short and Long-Term Effects of Economic Conditions on Individual Voting Decisions. In *Contemporary Political Economy,* ed. D. A. Hibbs, Jr., and H. Fassbender. Amsterdam: North Holland, 73–100.

Flanigan, W. 1973. *Political Behavior of the American Electorate.* Boston: Allyn and Bacon.

Flanigan, W., and N. Zingale. 1975. *Political Behavior of the American Electorate.* Boston: Allyn and Bacon.

Frey, B. S. 1974. The Politico-Economic System: A Simulation Model. *Kyklos* 27(2):227–54.

—————. 1978a. Economic and Personality Determinants of Presidential Popularity. *Empirical Economics* 3(2): 79–89.

—————. 1978b. *Modern Political Economy.* New York: John Wiley.

—————. 1978c. Politico-economic Models and Cycles. *Journal of Public Economics* (9):203–20.

—————. 1979. Politometrics of Government Behavior in a Democracy. *Scandinavian Journal of Economics* 81:308–22.

Frey, B. S., and F. Schneider. 1975. On the Modeling of Politico-Economic Interdependence. *European Journal of Political Science* 3:339–60.

—————. 1978a. Economic and Personality Determinants of Presidential Popularity. *Empirical Economics* 3:79–89.

—————. 1978b. An Empirical Study of Politico-Economic Interaction in the United States. *Review of Economics and Statistics* 60(2):174–83.

—————. 1978c. A Politico-Economic Model of the United Kingdom. *Economic Journal* 88:243–53.

—————. 1978d. An Empirical Study of Politico-Economic

Interaction in the U.S. *Review of Economics and Statistics* 45:174–83.

———. 1979. An Econometric Model with an Endogenous Government Sector. *Public Choice* 34(1):29–43.

———. 1980. Popularity Functions: The Case of the U.S. and West Germany. In *Model of Political Economy,* ed. Paul Whiteley. London: Sage.

———. 1981. Central Bank Behavior: A Positive Empirical Analysis. *Journal of Monetary Economics* 7:291–315.

———. 1982. Politico-Economic Models in Competition with Alternative Models: Who Predicts Better? Delivered at the International Political Science Association Round Table Conference, Nijmegen, Netherlands, February 23–25, 1982.

Frey, B. S. and H. Garbers. 1971. "Politico-Econometrics"—On Estimation in Political Economy. *Political Studies* 19:316–20.

Frey, B. S., and H. Weck. 1981. Estimating the Shadow Economy: A "Naive" approach. Paper presented at the European Public Choice Society Conference, University College, Oxford, April 9–10, 1981.

Friedman, M. 1953. *Essays in Positive Economics.* Chicago: University of Chicago Press.

Gallup Opinion Index 1965–80. Princeton, New Jersey.

Ginsburgh, V., and P. Michel. 1980. Random Timing of Elections and the Political Business Cycle. Discussion Paper no. 8043: Center for Operations Research and Econometrics, Université Catholique de Louvain.

Ginzberg, E., and G. J. Vojta. 1981. Service Sector of the Economy. *Scientific American* 244:14, 48–55.

Glazer, N., and D. P. Moynihan. 1969. Beyond the Melting Pot. In *Ethnic Group Politics,* ed. H. A. Bailey and E. Katz. Columbus: Charles E. Merrill.

Golden, D., and J. Poterba. 1980. The Price of Popularity: The Political Business Cycle Reexamined. *American Journal of Political Science* 24:696–714.

Goodhart, C. A. E., and R. J. Bhansali. 1970. Political Economy. *Political Studies* 18:43–106.

Goodman, S., and G. H. Kramer. 1975. Comment on Arcelus and Meltzer, The Effect of Aggregate Economic Conditions on Congressional Elections. *American Political Science Review* 69(4):1255–65.

Gordon, R. J. 1975. The Demand for and Supply of Inflation. *Journal of Law and Economics* 18:807–36.

Gosnell, H., and W. Coleman. 1940. Political Trends in Industrial America: Pennsylvania an Example. *Public Opinion Quarterly* 473–86.

Greenstein, F. I. 1965. *Children and Politics.* New Haven: Yale University Press.

Gurr, T. R. 1970. *Why Men Rebel.* Princeton, N.J.: Princeton University Press.

Heider, F. 1958. *Psychology of Interpersonal Relations.* New York: John Wiley.

Hibbing, J. R., and J. R. Alford. 1981. The Electoral Impact of Economic Conditions: Who is Held Responsible? *American Journal of Political Science* 24:423–40.

Hibbs, D. A., Jr. 1974. Problems of Statistical Estimation and Causal Inferences in Time-series and Regression Models. In *Sociological Methodology 1973–1974,* ed. H. L. Costner, 473–86. San Francisco: Jossey-Bass.

——————. 1976. Industrial Conflict in Advanced Societies. *American Political Science Review* 70(4):1033–58.

——————. 1977. Political Parties and Macroeconomic Policy. *American Political Science Review* 71(4):1467–87.

——————. 1978. On the Political Economy of Long-run Trends in Strike Activity. *British Journal of Political Science* 8:153–75.

——————. 1979a. Letter. *American Political Science Review* 73:185–90.

——————. 1979b. The Mass Public and Macroeconomic Policy: The Dynamic of Public Opinion Toward Unemployment and Inflation. *American Journal of Political Science* 23(4):705–31.

——————. 1981. Public Concern about Inflation and Unemployment in the United States: Trends, Correlates and Political Implications. Paper written for the National Bureau of Economic Research, Massachusetts.

——————. 1982b. More on Economic Performance in Britain: A Reply to William R. Keech. *American Political Science Review* 76:282–84.

——————. 1982c. Economic Outcomes and Political Support for British Governments among Occupational Classes: A Dynamic Analysis. *American Political Science Review* 76(2):259–79.

——————. 1982d. On the Demand for Economic Outcomes: Macroeconomic Performance and Mass Political Support in The United States, Great Britain and Germany. *Journal of Politics* 44(2):426–62.

Hibbs, D. A., Jr., and H. Fassbender, eds. 1981. *Contemporary Political Economy.* Amsterdam: North Holland.

Hibbs, D. A., Jr., and H. J. Madsen. 1981a. The Impact of Economic Performance on Electoral Support in Sweden, 1967–1978. *Scandinavian Political Studies* 4:33–56.

——————. 1981b. Public Reactions to the Growth of

Taxation and Government Expenditure. *World Politics* 23(3):413–35.

Hibbs, D. A., Jr., and N. Vasilatos. 1981. Economics and Politics in France: Economic Performance and Mass Political Support for Presidents Pompidou and Giscard d'Estaing. *European Journal of Political Research* 9(2): 133–45.

————. 1982a. The Dynamics of Political Support for American Presidents Among Occupational and Partisan Groups. *American Journal of Political Science* 26829: 312–332.

Hinckley, B. Forthcoming. House Reelections and Senate Defeats: The Role of the Challenger. *British Journal of Political Science.* 1979 paper.

Hinich, M. J. 1979. Voting as an Act of Contribution. Paper presented at the Conference on Voter Turnout, San Diego, California, May 16–19, 1979.

Hirsch, R., and J. H. Goldthorpe, eds. 1978. *The Political Economy of Inflation.* Cambridge, Mass.: Harvard University Press.

Hollis, M., and E. J. Nell. 1975. *Rational Economic Man.* Cambridge: Cambridge University Press.

Hollister, R., and J. Palmer. 1972. The Impact of Inflation on the Poor. In *Redistribution to the Rich and Poor,* ed. K. Boulding and M. Pfaff. Belmont, Calif.: Wadsworth.

Holm, J. D., and J. P. Robinson. 1980. Ideological and Issue Voting in The American Electorate: Measurement, Trends and an Alternative Model. Paper presented at the Annual Meetings of the American Political Science Association, Washington, D.C., August 28–31, 1980.

Hotelling, H. 1929. Stability in Competition. *Economic Journal* (39):41–57.

Inoguchi, T. 1980. Economic Conditions and Mass Support in Japan, 1960–1976. In *Models of Political Economy,* ed. P. Whiteley, 121–51. London: Sage.

Isaak, A. 1969. *Scope and Methods of Political Science.* Homewood, Ill.: Dorsey Press.

Jackson, J. E. 1975. Issues, Party Choices, and Presidential Votes. *American Journal of Political Science.* 19:161–86.

Jacobson, G. C., and S. Kernell. 1981. *Strategy and Choice in Congressional Elections.* New Haven: Yale University Press.

Jonung, L. 1981. Perceived and Expected Rates of Inflation in Sweden. *American Economic Review* 71(5):961–68.

Jonung, L., and E. Wadensjo. 1979. The Effects of Unemployment, Inflation and Real Income Growth on

Government Popularity in Sweden. *Scandinavian Journal of Economics* 81:343–53.

—————. 1981. Popularity Functions for Sweden—A Disaggregated Approach. Some Preliminary Results. Paper presented at the Meetings of the Public Choice Society, European Section, Oxford, March 1981.

Kagan, M. R., and G. A. Caldeira. 1975. I Like the Looks of his Face: Elements of Electoral Choice, 1952–1972. Paper delivered at the annual meeting of the American Political Science Association, San Francisco, California, September 2–5, 1975.

Kahneman, D., and Tversky, A. 1973. On the Psychology of Prediction. *Psychological Review* 80:237–51.

Kaplan, N. 1955. Reference Group Theory and Voting Behavior. Unpublished doctoral dissertation, Columbia University.

Katona, G. 1963. *Psychological Analysis of Economic Behavior.* New York: McGraw-Hill.

—————. 1975. *Psychological Economics.* New York: Elsevier.

—————. 1976. Persistence on Belief in Personal Financial Progress. In *Economic Means for Human Needs, ed. B. Strumpel, 83–106.* Ann Arbor, Mich.: Institute for Social Research.

Katona, G., B. Strumpel, and E. Zahn. 1971. *Aspirations and Affluence.* New York: McGraw Hill.

Keech, W. R. 1980. Elections and Macroeconomic Policy Optimization. *American Journal of Political Science* 24(2):345–67.

—————. 1982. Of Honeymoons and Economic Performance: Comment on Hibbs. *American Political Science Review* 76(2):280–81.

Keech, W. R., and C. P. Simon. 1983. Inflation, Unemployment and Electoral Terms: When Can Reform of Political Institutions Improve Macroeconomic Policy. In *The Political Process and Economic Change,* ed. K. R. Monroe. New York: Agathon.

Keesings' Contemporary Archives. 1979. London: Keesings' Publications, 25.

Kelley, H. H. 1967. Attribution Theory in Social Psychology. In *Nebraska Symposium on Motivation,* ed. D. Levine. Lincoln: University of Nebraska Press.

Kelley, S., Jr., and T. Mirer. 1974. The Simple Act of Voting. *American Political Science Review* 68:572–91.

Kenski, H. 1977a. Inflation and Presidential Popularity. *Public Opinion Quarterly* 41:86–90.

—————. 1977b. The Impact of Economic Conditions on Presidential Popularity. *Journal of Politics* 39:764–73.

—————. 1977c. The Impact of Economic Conditions on Presidential Popularity from Eisenhower to Nixon. *Presidential Studies Quarterly* 7:114–26.

—————. 1979. The Impact of Unemployment on Congressional Elections, 1958–1974: A Cross Sectional Analysis. *American Politics Quarterly* 7(April):147–57.

Keohane, R. 1978. Economics, Inflation and the Role of the State. *World Politics* 31:108–28.

Kernell, S. 1977. Explaining Presidential Popularity. *American Political Science Review* 72(2):506–22.

—————. 1978. Presidential Popularity and Negative Voting: An Alternative Explanation of the Midterm Congressional Decline of the President's Party. *American Political Science Review* 71(1):44–65.

—————. 1980. Strategy and Ideology: The Politics of Unemployment and Inflation in Modern Capitalist Democracies. Revision of a paper delivered at the Annual Meeting of the American Political Science Association, Washington, D.C., August 1980.

Kerr, W. A. 1944. A Quantitative Study of Political Behavior, 1840–1950. *Journal of Social Psychology* 60(1):273–81.

Key, V. O., Jr. 1949. *Southern Politics in State and Nation*. New York: Knopf.

—————. 1955. A Theory of Critical Elections. *Journal of Politics* 60(1):273–81.

—————. 1961. *Public Opinion and American Democracy*. New York: Knopf.

—————. 1966. (With the assistance of Milton Cummings, Jr.) *The Responsible Electorate: Rationality in Presidential Voting, 1936–1960*. Cambridge, Mass.: Belknap Press.

Keynes, J. M. 1936. *A General Theory of Employment, Interest and Money*. London: Macmillan.

Kiewiet, D. R. 1980a. The Effects of Personal Economic Problems Upon Voting in American National Elections. Paper presented at the Annual Meeting of the Conference Group on the Political Economy of Advanced Industrial Societies, Washington, D.C., August 28–30, 1980.

—————. 1980b. *The Electoral Effects of Economic Issues*. Ph.D. dissertation, Yale University.

—————. 1981a. Policy-Oriented Voting in Response to Economic Issues. *American Political Science Review* 75(June):448–59.

—————. 1983. *Micromotives and Macropolitics*. Chicago: University of Chicago Press.

Kiewiet, D. R., and D. R. Kinder. 1978. Political Consequences of Economic Concerns—Personal and Collective.

Paper presented at the Annual Meeting of American Political Science Association, New York, August 31– September 3, 1978.

—————. 1979. Economic Discontent and Political Behavior: The Role of Personal Grievances and Collective Economic Judgments in Congressional Voting. *American Journal of Political Science* 23(3):495–527.

Kinder, D. R. 1981. Presidents, Prosperity and Public Opinion. *Public Opinion Quarterly* 45(1):1–21.

Kinder, D. R., and R. P. Abelson. 1981. Appraising Presidential Candidates: Personality and Affect in the 1980 Campaign. Paper prepared for the 1981 annual meeting of the American Political Science Association, New York, September 3–6, 1981.

Kinder, D. R., and D. R. Kiewiet. 1981. Sociotropic Politics: the American Case. *British Journal of Political Science* 11(April):129–61.

Kinder, D. R., and W. Mebane. 1983. Politics and Economics in Everyday Life. In *The Political Process and Economic Change,* ed. K. R. Monroe. New York: Agathon Press.

Kinder, D. R., M. D. Peters, R. P. Abelson, and S. T. Fiske. 1980. Presidential Prototypes. *Political Behavior* 2:315–38.

King, M. R., and R. E. O'Connor. 1981. The Contribution of the ISR Voting Studies: Review and Critique. Paper prepared for delivery at the 1981 Annual Meeting of the American Political Science Association, New York, September 3–6, 1981.

Kirchgassner, G. 1981. *On the Theory of Optimal Government Behavior.* Zurich: Center for Economic Research, Swiss Federal Institute of Technology.

—————. 1979. Popularity of the Government and Opposition in a 2-Party and a 3-Party System. Zurich: Eidgenossische Technische Hochschule. Mimeo.

Klorman, R. 1978. Trend in Personal Finances and the Vote. *Public Opinion Quarterly* 42(1):31–48.

Koenig, L. W. 1975. *The Chief Executive.* New York: Harcourt, Brace, Jovanovich.

Koestler, A., and J. R. Smythies, eds. 1969. *Beyond Reductionism.* New York: Macmillan Company.

Kramer, G. H. 1971. Short-term Fluctuations in U.S. Voting Behavior, 1896–1964. *American Political Science Review* 65(1):131–43.

—————. 1983. The Ecological Fallacy Revisited: Aggregate Versus Individual-Level Findings on Economics and Elections and Sociotropic Voting. *American Political Science Review* 77(1):92–111.

Kramer, G. H., and S. Lepper. 1972. Congressional Elections. In *Dimensions of Quantitative Research in History,* ed. W. O. Aydelotte. Princeton: Princeton University Press.

Kramer, W. 1977. A Dynamical Model of Political Equilibrium. *Journal of Economic Theory* 16:310–34.

Kuckerman, A. S., and M. I. Lichbach. 1977. Stability and Change in European Electoriates. *World Politics.* 29:269–319.

Kuklinski, J. H., and D. M. West. 1981. Economic Expectations and Voting Behavior in United States House and Senate Elections. *American Political Science Review* 75(June):436–47.

Ladd, E. C., and C. D. Hadley. 1978. *Transformations of the American Party System.* New York: Norton.

Lafay, J. D. 1977. Les Consequences Électorales de la Conjoncture Économique: Essais de Previsism chiffree pour Mars 1978. *Vie et sciences economique* 75(October):1–7.

————. 1980. Demande de politiques économiques et mouvement de popularite. Poitiers: Faculte des Science Economiques. Mimeo.

————. 1981. The Impact of Economic Variables on Political Behavior in France. In *Contemporary Political Economy,* ed. D. A. Hibbs, Jr., and H. Fassbender, 137–49. Amsterdam: North Holland.

Lane, R. E. 1959. *Political Life: Why People Get Involved in Politics.* New York: The Free Press.

Langer, W. L., ed. N.d. *An Encyclopedia of World History.* Boston: Houghton Mifflin.

Lasswell, H. D. 1930. *Psychopathology and Politics.* New York: The Viking Press.

Lau, R. R., and D. O. Sears. 1981. Cognitive Links between Economic Grievances and Political Responses. *Political Behavior* 3(4):279–302.

Lazarsfeld, P. F., B. Berelson, and H. Gaudet. 1944. *The People's Choice.* New York: Duell.

Lee, F. P. 1979. Presidential Elite Images of the American Presidency. Paper presented at the Annual Meeting of the American Political Science Association, Washington, D.C., August 31–September 3, 1979.

Lee, J. R. 1975. Presidential Choice: Limits of Leadership in Foreign Policy. Unpublished Ph.D. dissertation, Yale University.

Lee, J. R., and J. S. Milstein. 1973. A Political Economy of the Vietnam War, 1965–1972. *Peace Science Society International* 21:41–63.

Lekachman, R. 1966. *The Age of Keynes.* New York:

Random House.

Lepper, S. J. 1974. Voting Behavior and Aggregate Policy Targets. *Public Choice* 18:67–82.

Lewis, A. The King Must Die. *St. Louis Post Dispatch.* January 13, 1981.

Lewis-Beck, M. S. 1980. Economic Conditions and Executive Popularity: The French Experience. *American Journal of Political Science* 24:306–23.

Lewis-Beck, M. S., and P. Bellucci. 1982. Economic Influences on Legislative Elections in Multiparty Systems: France and Italy. *Political Behavior* 4(1):93–107.

Lewis-Beck, M., and I. W. Rice. 1982. Presidential Popularity and Presidential Vote. *Public Opinion Quarterly* 46:534–37.

Li, R. P. Y. 1976. Public Policy and Short-term Fluctuations in U.S. Voting Behavior: A Reformulation and Expansion. *Political Methodology* 3:49–70.

Lieberson, J. 1981. The Silent Majority. *The New York Review of Books.* 28(16):34–36.

Lindberg, L., and C. Maier, eds. 1983. *The Political Economy of Global Inflation and Recession.* Washington, D.C.: The Brookings Institution.

Lindberg, L. N. 1980. Inflation and Perspectives on the Political-Economic Transformations of the 1970's. Paper prepared for delivery at the 1980 Annual Meeting of the American Political Science Association, New York, September 3–6, 1981.

Lindblom, C. E. 1977. *Politics and Markets: The World's Political-Economic Systems.* New York: Basic Books.

Linehan, W. J., and P. A. Schrodt. 1979. Size, Competitiveness, and the Probability of Influencing an Election. Paper presented at the Conference on Voter Turnout, San Diego, May 16–19, 1979.

Lowi, T. J. 1969. *The End of Liberalism: Ideology, Policy and the Crisis of Public Authority.* New York: Norton.

Luce, R. D. 1959. Analyzing the Social Process Underlying Group Voting Patterns. In *American Voting Behavior,* ed. E. Burdick and A. J. Brodbeck, 330–51. New York: Free Press.

Luke, T. 1978. The Limits of Rational Choice Theory: A Critique. Paper prepared for delivery at the 1978 Annual Meeting of the American Political Science Association, New York, August 31–September 3, 1978.

Mackuen, M. 1980. Social Communication and the Mass Policy Agenda. In *More Than News,* ed. M. Mackuen and S. Coombs. Beverly Hills: Sage.

—————. 1980. Individual Motives, Social Networks, and the Media's Shaping of Policy Orientations. Paper presented at the American Political Science Association, Washington, D.C., August 28–31, 1980.

──────. 1983. Political Drama, Economic Conditions, and the Dynamics of Presidential Popularity. *American Journal of Political Science* 27.

MacRae, C. D. 1977. A Political Model of the Business Cycle. *Journal of Political Economy* 85(2):239–63.

Madsen, H. J. 1980. Electoral Outcomes and Macroeconomic Policies: The Scandinavian Cases. In *Models of Political Economy,* ed. Paul Whiteley, 15–46. London: Sage.

Maier, C. S. 1978. The Politics of Inflation in the Twentieth Century. In *The Political Economy of Inflation,* ed. F. Hirsh and J. Goldthorpe. Cambridge: Harvard University Press.

Markus, G. B. 1981. Political Attitudes During an Election Year: A Report on the 1980 NES Panel Study. Paper prepared for the 1981 Annual Meeting of the American Political Science Association, New York, September 3–6, 1981.

Markus, G. B., and P. E. Converse. 1979. A Dynamic Simultaneous Equation Model of Electoral Choice. *American Political Science Review* 73:1055–70.

McCombs, M., and D. Shaw. 1972. The Agenda-Setting Function of the Mass Media. *Public Opinion Quarterly* 36:176–87.

McLeod, J. and J. Byrnes. 1974. Another Look at the Agenda-Setting Function of the Press. *Communication Research* 1:131–66.

Meier, K. J. 1975. Party Identification and Vote Choice: The Causal Relationship. *Western Political Quarterly* 28:496–505.

Meltzer, A. H., and M. Vellrath. 1975. The Effects of Economic Policies on Votes for the Presidency: Some Evidence from Recent Elections. *Journal of Law and Economics* 18:781–98.

Miller, A., P. Gurin, and G. Gurin. 1979. Group Consciousness and Political Participation. Paper presented at conference on Voter Turnout, San Diego, May 16–19, 1979.

Miller, A. H., and W. E. Miller. 1977. Partisanship and Performance: "Rational" Choice in the 1976 Presidential Election. Paper presented to the American Political Science Association.

Miller, W. L., and M. Mackie. 1973. The Electoral Cycle and the Asymmetry of Conditions and Political Popularity. *Political Studies* 21(3):263–79.

Monroe, K. R. 1978. Economic Influences on Presidential

Popularity. *Public Opinion Quarterly* 42(3):360–69.
————. 1979. Econometric Analyses of Electoral Behavior: A Critical Review. *Political Behavior* 9(2): 137–73.
————. 1981. Presidential Popularity: An Almon Distributed Lag Model. *Political Methodology* 6(4):43–69.
Monroe, K. R., and M. D. Levi. 1983. Economic Expectations, Economic Uncertainty and Presidential Popularity. In *The Political Process and Economic Change,* ed. K. R. Monroe. New York: Agathon Press.
Monroe, K. R., and D. M. Laughlin. 1983. Economic Influences on Presidential Popularity Among Political and Socioeconomic Groups. *Political Behavior.* 5(3):309–45.
Morris, R. B., and J. B. Morris. 1976. *Encyclopedia of American History: Bicentennial Edition.* New York: Harper and Row.
Mueller, J. E. 1970. Presidential Popularity from Truman to Johnson. *American Political Science Review* 64(1): 18–34.
————. 1971. Trends in Popular Support for the Wars in Korea and Vietnam. *American Political Science Review* 65(3):358–75.
————. 1973. *War, Presidents and Public Opinion.* New York: John Wiley.
Neprash, J. 1932. *The Brookhart Campaign in Iowa, 1920–1926.* New York: Columbia University Press.
Neustadt, R. 1960. *Presidential Power: The Politics of Leadership.* New York: Knopf.
New York Times Index. New York: The New York Times Company.
Nie, N. (with S. Verba, and J. Petrock). 1976. *The Changing American Voter.* Cambridge, Mass.: Harvard University Press.
Nisbett, R., and L. Ross. 1980. *Human Inference: Strategies and Shortcomings of Social Judgment.* Englewood Cliffs: Prentice-Hall, Inc.
Nordhaus, W. D. 1975. The Political Business Cycle. *Review of Economic Studies* 42(2):169–90.
Norpoth, H., and T. Yantek. 1981. Deflating a Popular Myth: or, Can Political Economy Survive Box-Jenkins and Live to Find True Significance? Paper prepared for delivery at the 1981 Annual Meeting of the American Political Science Association, New York, September 3–6, 1981.
Ogburn, W. F., and L. Coombs. 1940. The Economic Factor in the Roosevelt Elections. *American Political Science Review* 34(4):719–27.
Okun, A. M. 1981. *Prices and Quantities.* Washington,

D.C.: The Brookings Institute.

Owens, J. R., and E. C. Olson. 1980. Economic Fluctuations and Congressional Elections. *American Journal of Political Science* 24:469–93.

Page, B. I. 1977. Elections and Social Choice: The State of the Evidence. *American Journal of Political Science* 21(3):639–68.

Paldam, M. 1980. Economic Conditions and 145 National Elections. Institute of Economics, University of Aarhus. Mimeo.

—————. 1981a. An Essay on the Rationality of Economic Policy—the Test Case of the Electional Cycle. *Public Choice* 36.

—————. 1981b. A Preliminary Survey of the Theories and Findings on Vote and Popularity Functions. *European Journal of Political Research* 9:181–99.

Paldam, M., and P. J. Pedersen. 1982. The Macroeconomic Strike Model: A Study of 17 Countries, 1948–75. *Industrial and Labor Relations Review* 35:504–21.

Paldam, M., and F. Schneider. 1980. The Macro- Economic Aspects of Government and Opposition Popularity in Denmark 1957–1978. *Nationalokonomisk Tidskrift* 118(2).

Palmer, J. L., and M. C. Barth. 1978. Distributional Effects of Inflation and Higher Unemployment. In *Improving Measures of Economic Well-being* ed. M. Moon and E. Smolensky, 201–39. New York: Academic Press.

Parenti, M. 1967. Ethnic Politics and the Persistence of Ethnic Identification. *American Political Science Review* 61(September):717–26.

Parker, G. R. 1979. Trends in Party Preferences, 1949–1976. *American Politics Quarterly* 7(2):132–46.

Parsons, T. 1937. *The Structure of Social Action.* Glencoe, Ill.: The Free Press.

—————. 1951. *The Social System.* New York: The Free Press.

Payne, J. L. 1979. Inflation, Unemployment, and Left-wing Political Parties: A Reanalysis. *American Political Science Review* 73:181–85.

Pearson, F. A., and W. I. Myers. 1948. Prices and Presidents. *Farm Economics* 163(September):4210–18.

Peretz, P. 1978. Who Gets What, How and Why: The Economic Effects of Party Change. Paper prepared for delivery at the annual meeting of the American Political Science Association.

Petrocik, J. R. 1980. Conceptual Sources of Voting Behavior. In *The Electorate Reconsidered,* ed. J. C. Pierce and J. L. Sullivan, 257–78. Beverly Hills: Sage.

Petrocik, J. R. 1981a. Voter Turnout and Electoral Oscil-
lation. *American Politics Quarterly* 9(2):161–80.
————. 1981b. *Party Coalitions: Realignment and the
Decline of the New Deal System.* Chicago: University of
Chicago Press.
Pierson, J. E. 1975. Presidential Popularity and Midterm
Voting at Different Electoral Levels. *American Journal
of Political Science* 19(4):683–94.
Pissarides, C. A. 1980. British Government Popularity
and Economic Performance. *Economic Journal* 90:569–81.
Plamenatz, J. 1958. *The English Utilitarians.* 2d rev. ed.
Reprint with minor corrections in 1966. Oxford: Basil
Blackwell.
Pollard, W. 1978. Effects of Economic Conditions on
Elections—A Study Controlling for Political Variables.
Paper presented at the Meetings of the Public Choice
Society, New Orleans, March 1978.
Pomper, G. M. 1975. *Voter's Choice: Varieties of Ameri-
can Behavior.* New York: Dodd Mead.
Popkin, S., J. W. Gorman, C. Phillips, and J. A. Smith.
1976. Comment: What Have You Done For Me Lately?
Toward an Investment Theory of Voting. *American
Political Science Review* 70:779–805.
Presser, S., and J. Converse. 1976–77. On Stimson's
Interpretation of Declines in Presidential Popularity.
Public Opinion Quarterly 40(Winter):538–41.
Prysby, C. L. 1979. Mass Policy Orientations on Economic
Issues in Post Industrial America. *Journal of Politics*
41(2):543–65.
Przeworski, A. 1974. Contextual Models of Political Be-
havior. *Political Methodology* 1:27–61.
Public Opinion. 1981. Early Expectations: Comparing Chief
Executives. (February/March):538–41.
Rees, A., et al. 1962. The Effect of Economic Conditions
on Congressional Elections, 1946–1958. *Review of Eco-
nomics and Statistics* 44:458–65.
Rice, S. A. 1928. *Quantitative Aspects of Politics.* New
York: Knopf.
Riker, W. H. 1973. Discussion (of Stigler's paper).
American Economic Review 63(2):178–79.
Riker, W. H., and P. C. Ordeshook. 1968. A Theory of
the Calculus of Voting. *American Political Science
Review* 62(1):25–42.
————. 1973. *An Introduction to Positive Political
Theory.* Englewood Cliffs: Prentice-Hall.
Roelofs, H. M. 1976. *Ideology and Myth in American
Politics.* Boston: Little, Brown.
Rosa, J. J., and D. Amson. 1976. Conditions Economiques

et Elections: Une Analyse Politico-Econometrique (1920–1973). *Revue francaise de science politique* 26:1101–24. English version in Whitely 1980, 101–20.

Rosenberg, M. J. 1960. An Analysis of Affective-Cognitive Consistency. In *Attitude Organization and Change,* ed. C. I. Hovland and M. J. Rosenberg. New Haven: Yale University Press.

Rosenberg, S. 1977. New Approaches to the Analysis of Personal Constructs in Person Perception. In *Nebraska Symposium on Motivation,* vol. 24, ed. D. Levine. Lincoln: Nebraska University Press.

Rosenstone, S. J. 1982. Economic Adversity and Voter Turnout. *American Journal of Political Science* 26(1): 25–46.

Rosenstone, S. J., and E. H. Lazarus. 1981. Third Party Voting in America. Paper prepared for delivery at the 1981 Annual Meeting of the American Political Science Association, New York, September 3–6, 1981.

Rudebusch, T. 1979. Mathematics and Politics: A Critique of Rational Choice Theory. Paper prepared for delivery at the 1979 Annual Meeting of the Southwestern Political Science Association.

Rusk, J. G. 1981. The Michigan Evaluation Studies: A Critical Evaluation. Paper prepared for delivery at the 1981 Annual Meeting of the American Political Science Association, New York, September 3–6, 1981.

Russell, R. R. 1983. Can Income Policies Work? In *The Political Process and Economic Change,* ed. K. R. Monroe. New York: Agathon Press.

Sabine, G. 1939. Logic and Social Studies. *Philosophical Review* 48(March):155–76.

Scalia, L. J. 1981. The Voting Act as a Function of Exogenous Factors: A Group Approach. Undergraduate honors thesis, New York University.

Schelling, T. C. 1978. *Micromotives and Macrobehavior.* New York: W. W. Norton and Co.

Schlenker, B. R., D. R. Forsyth, M. R. Leary, and R. S. Miller. 1980. Self-presentational Analysis of the Effects of Incentive on Attitude Change Following Counterattitudinal Behavior. *Journal of Personality and Social Psychology* 39:553–77.

Schlozman, K. L., and S. Verba. 1979. *Injury to Insult: Unemployment, Class, and Political Response.* Cambridge, Mass.: Harvard University Press.

Schneider, F. 1978. Different (income) Classes and Presidential Popularity: An Empirical Analysis. *Munich Social Science Review* 2:53–69.

Schneider, F., and W. W. Pommerehne. 1980. Politico-

Economic Interactions in Australia: Some Empirical Evidence. *Economic Record* 56:113–31.

Schneider, F., W. W. Pommerehne, and B. S. Frey. 1981. Politico-economic interdependence in a direct democracy: The case of Switzerland. In *Contemporary Political Economy,* ed. D. A. Hibbs, Jr. and H. Fassbender, 231–48. Amsterdam: North Holland.

Schumpeter, J. A. 1962. *Capitalism, Socialism and Democracy.* New York: Harper and Row.

Sears, D. O., and J. Citrin. 1982. *Tax Revolt: Something for Nothing in California.* Cambridge, Mass.: Harvard University Press.

Sears, D. O., and R. R. Lau. 1983. Inducing Apparently Self-Interested Political Preferences. *American Journal of Political Science* (in press).

Sears, D. O., R. R. Lau, T. R. Tyler, and H. M. Allen, Jr. 1980. Self-interest vs. Symbolic Politics in Policy Attitudes and 1976 Presidential Voting. *American Political Science Review* 74:670–84.

Sen, A., and B. Williams, eds. *Utilitarianism and Beyond.* Cambridge: Cambridge University Press.

Shabad, G., and K. Andersen. 1979. Candidate Evaluation by Men and Women. *Public Opinion Quarterly* 43:18–35.

Shinn, D. C. N.d. Towards a Model for Presidential Influence in Congress. Paper prepared for the Institute of Social and Policy Studies, Yale University.

Sigelman, L. 1979. Presidential Popularity and Presidential Elections. *Public Opinion Quarterly* 43:532–34.

Sigelman, L., and P. J. Conover. 1981. The Dynamics of Presidential Support During International Conflict Situations: The Iranian Hostage Crisis. *Political Behavior* 3(4):303–18.

Simon, H. A. 1957. *Models of Man.* New York: John Wiley.

Sniderman, P. M., and R. A. Brody. 1977. Coping: The Ethic of Self-reliance. *American Journal of Political Science* 27:501–21.

Stigler, G. 1973. General Economic Conditions and National Elections. *American Economic Review* 63(2):160–67.

Stimson, J. A. 1976. Public Support for American Presidents: A Cycle Model. *Public Opinion Quarterly* 40(1):1–21.

————. 1976–77. On Disillusion with the Expectation/Disillusion Theory: A Rejoinder. *Public Opinion Quarterly* 40(Winter):541–43.

Stimson, J. A., and C. LeGette. 1975. Public Support for American Presidents: Does Anything but Time Matter?

Paper presented at the Annual Meeting of the American Political Science Association. San Francisco, September 2–5, 1975.

Stokes, D. E. 1966. Some Dynamic Elements of Contests for the Presidency. *American Political Science Review* 60:19–28.

Stone, P. J. 1970. Expectations of a Better Personal Future: A Two-component Model. *Public Opinion Quarterly* 34(Fall):346–59.

Tan, A. 1980. Mass Media Use, Issue Knowledge and Political Involvement. *Public Opinion Quarterly* 44: 241–48.

Tibbitts, C. 1931. Majority Votes and the Business Cycle. *American Journal of Sociology* 36(4):596–606.

Tipton, L., R. Haney, and J. Basehart. 1975. Media Agenda Setting in City and State Election Campaigns. *Journalism Quarterly* 52:15–22.

Thurow, L. C. 1980. *The Zero Sum Society: Distributions and the Possibility of Income Change.* New York: Basic Books.

Tocqueville, A. de. 1840. *The Old Regime and the French Revolution.* New York: Harper.

Truman, D. B. 1951. *The Governmental Process.* New York: Knopf.

Tufte, E. R. 1973. The Relationship Between Seats and Votes in Two-party Systems. *American Political Science Review* 67(2):540–54.

—————. 1975. Determinants of the Outcomes of Midterm Congressional Elections. *American Political Science Review* 69(3):812–26.

—————. 1978. *Political Control of the Economy.* Princeton: Princeton University Press.

Tulis, J. 1981. Public Policy and the Rhetorical Presidency. Paper prepared for delivery at the 1981 Annual Meeting of the American Political Science Association, New York, September 3–6, 1981.

Wagner, R. E. 1980. Boom and Bust: The Political Economy of Economic Disorder. *Journal of Libertarian Studies* (Winter):1–37.

Wallas, G. 1981. *Human Nature in Politics.* New York: Transaction Books.

Weatherford, M. S. 1978. Economic Conditions and Electoral Outcomes: Class Differences in the Political Response to Recession. *American Journal of Political Science* 22(4):917–38.

—————. 1981. How Economic Events Affect Electoral Outcomes: A Model of Political Translation. *Micropolitics* 1(3):269–93.

——————. 1982. Recessions and Social Classes: Economic Impacts and Political Opinions. *Political Behavior* 4(1): 7–32.

——————. 1983. Parties and Classes in the Political Response to Economic Conditions. *The Political Process and Economic Change,* ed. K. R. Monroe. New York: Agathon Press.

Weisberg, H. F., and B. Grofman. 1979. Candidate Evaluations and Turnout. Paper presented at the Conference on Voter Turnout, San Diego, May 16–19, 1979.

Whiteley, Paul, ed. 1980. *Models of Political Economy.* London: Sage Publications.

Wides, J. W. 1976. Self-perceived Economic Change and Political Orientations: A Preliminary Exploration. *American Politics Quarterly* 4(October):395–411.

Wilkinson, T., and H. Hart. 1950. Prosperity and Political Victory. *Public Opinion Quarterly,* 331–35.

Winters, R., et al. 1981. Political Behavior and American Public Policy: The Case of the Political Business Cycle. In *The Handbook of Political Science,* ed. S. Long. New York: Plenum.

Wittman, D. 1973. Parties as Utility Maximizers. *American Political Science Review.* 67(June):490–99.

——————. 1977. Candidates with Policy Preferences: A Dynamic Model. *Journal of Economic Theory* 14:180–89.

Wolfinger, R. E. 1965. The Development and Persistence of Ethnic Voting. *American Political Science Review* 59(December):896–908.

The World Almanac and Book of Facts. 1980. New York: Newspaper Enterprise Association.

Wright, G. 1974. The Political Economy of New Deal Spending: An Econometric Analysis. *Review of Economics and Statistics* 41(1):30–38.

Zeller, R. A., and E. G. Carmines. 1978. *Statistical Analysis of Social Data.* Chicago: Rand McNally.

Zinser, J. E., K. R. Hausafus, and P. A. Dawson. 1979. The Rational Allocation of Time and Electoral Participation. Paper presented at the Conference on Voter Turnout, San Diego, May 16–19, 1979.

Zukin, C. 1977. A Reconsideration of the Effects of Information on Partisan Stability. *Public Opinion Quarterly* 41:244–54.

Appendixes

APPENDIX A

Appendix A contains the bimonthly data series on group support for the president, group unemployment figures, personal income, a price index, and the Standard and Poor stock market index. All series begin in April 1965 and end in February 1980, unless otherwise noted. It is hoped that the inclusion of these data series will facilitate the work of future scholars who will build on the work begun here.

APPENDIX A-1. Presidential Popularity: Percent Approval by National Total

Date	National	Date	National	Date	National
6504	67.0	7004	54.7	7504	39.0
6506	67.0	7006	58.0	7506	47.7
6508	67.0	7008	58.0	7508	45.5
6510	64.0	7010	57.0	7510	47.0
6512	64.0	7012	54.5	7512	42.5
6602	61.0	7102	53.0	7602	45.5
6604	57.0	7104	51.7	7604	48.7
6606	50.0	7106	48.7	7606	46.0
6608	53.5	7108	50.0	7608	48.5
6610	47.0	7110	54.0	7610	51.0
6612	46.0	7112	49.0	7612	53.0
6702	46.3	7202	50.5	7702	68.5
6704	45.3	7204	54.5	7704	69.4
6706	47.3	7206	61.0	7706	63.8
6708	43.0	7208	56.0	7708	54.6
6710	38.5	7210	62.0	7710	54.6
6712	43.5	7212	59.0	7712	56.0
6802	43.5	7302	66.0	7802	51.0
6804	42.0	7304	54.0	7804	46.8
6806	41.5	7306	45.0	7806	42.2
6808	37.5	7308	35.7	7808	40.2
6810	42.0	7310	30.5	7810	49.0

APPENDIX A-1. Continued

Date	National	Date	National	Date	National
6812	45.3	7312	30.0	7812	51.3
6902	60.0	7402	26.7	7902	43.0
6904	63.0	7404	25.0	7904	40.5
6906	64.0	7406	27.0	7906	31.8
6908	61.7	7408	71.0	7908	29.7
6910	58.0	7410	58.9	7910	29.0
6912	63.5	7412	45.7	7912	47.2
7002	62.7	7502	38.0	8002	56.3

APPENDIX A-2. Presidential Popularity: Percent Approval by Political Affiliation

Date	Republican	Democrat	Independent
6504	51.0	77.0	62.0
6506	49.5	80.5	60.0
6508	50.0	77.0	57.0
6510	45.0	79.0	55.0
6512	46.8	75.3	60.3
6602	43.0	75.0	46.0
6604	36.5	72.5	48.5
6606	32.5	61.0	40.5
6608	30.0	65.0	47.0
6610	27.5	62.0	46.0
6612	28.0	66.0	40.0
6702	25.0	62.5	39.5
6704	26.5	60.5	40.5
6706	30.0	61.0	42.0
6708	26.5	58.0	37.0
6710	22.0	53.0	33.0
6712	24.5	62.0	37.5
6802	26.0	61.0	36.5
6804	32.0	58.5	30.0
6806	24.0	56.0	38.0
6808	23.5	51.0	31.0
6810	28.0	58.0	35.0

APPENDIX A-2. Continued

Date	Republican	Democrat	Independent
6902	66.0	53.0	53.3
6904	84.0	49.0	63.0
6906	83.0	52.0	61.0
6908	83.0	51.5	64.0
6910	80.0	44.0	58.0
6912	87.0	54.0	65.0
7002	85.0	46.0	65.5
7004	81.0	40.0	56.0
7006	81.5	42.5	60.0
7008	82.0	40.0	56.0
7010	82.0	44.0	57.0
7012	82.0	37.0	54.5
7102	76.0	36.0	50.0
7104	82.0	36.0	53.5
7106	78.5	33.5	47.0
7108	73.0	34.0	46.0
7110	81.0	38.0	49.0
7112	80.0	34.5	46.5
7202	80.0	32.0	51.0
7204	84.5	39.0	57.0
7206	89.0	46.0	63.0
7208	86.0	39.0	61.0
7210	89.0	46.0	60.0
7212	87.0	42.0	60.0
7302	89.0	51.0	71.0
7304	91.0	47.0	69.0
7306	74.0	24.0	48.0
7308	63.8	21.8	37.3
7310	58.5	16.0	30.5
7312	54.0	17.0	27.5
7402	53.8	12.3	27.0
7404	54.0	12.5	24.0
7406	52.0	16.0	27.0
7408	77.0	68.0	70.0
7410	73.0	44.0	56.0
7412	60.0	32.0	43.0
7502	63.0	28.0	38.0
7504	60.5	29.0	39.5
7506	69.0	40.5	55.5
7508	65.0	37.0	46.0
7510	71.0	34.0	50.0
7512	59.5	30.0	40.0

APPENDIX A-2. Continued

Date	Republican	Democrat	Independent
7602	66.0	35.0	50.0
7604	72.0	35.0	49.0
7606	68.0	35.0	46.0
7608	71.0	38.0	49.0
7610	74.0	41.0	52.0
7610	80.0	40.0	54.0
7702	49.0	77.0	60.0
7704	56.0	81.0	70.0
7706	52.0	73.0	59.0
7708	46.2	71.6	57.6
7710	40.6	70.3	56.3
7712	35.0	69.0	55.0
7802	34.0	60.0	53.0
7804	25.0	51.0	36.0
7806	26.5	51.5	38.5
7808	28.0	52.0	41.0
7810	29.5	57.5	46.5
7812	31.0	63.0	52.0
7902	24.0	55.0	43.0
7904	22.0	52.0	38.0
7906	19.0	34.0	28.0
7908	18.0	41.0	29.0
7910	17.0	64.0	44.0
7912	39.0	62.0	48.0
8002	43.0	65.0	48.0

APPENDIX A-3. Presidential Popularity: Percent Approval by Income Level

Date	A	B	C	D	E	F	G
6504				64.0	72.0	64.0	69.0
6506				66.0	70.0	68.0	63.5
6508				64.0	68.0	65.0	68.0
6510				64.0	66.0	65.0	59.0
6512				62.3	70.5	61.0	61.8
6602				60.0	60.0	63.0	53.0

APPENDIX A-3. Continued

Date	A	B	C	D	E	F	G
6604				54.3	60.8	56.8	55.8
6606				46.0	52.5	50.5	48.5
6608				51.0	52.0	55.0	49.0
6610				46.5	48.5	49.0	47.5
6612				47.0	53.0	42.0	53.0
6702			43.3	44.3	47.8	49.3	48.0
6704			41.5	43.5	45.0	45.5	49.0
6706			47.5	47.5	48.0	43.5	45.5
6708			42.5	43.5	44.5	43.0	41.5
6710			36.0	37.5	37.5	36.5	41.5
6712			41.5	44.0	44.5	45.0	40.0
6802			40.0	42.5	45.0	44.5	51.0
6804			40.0	41.5	44.0	45.0	44.0
6806			40.0	41.0	40.0	51.0	41.0
6808			33.0	34.5	36.5	39.0	45.0
6810			42.0	41.0	41.0	48.0	38.0
6812			38.0	41.0	47.0	43.0	45.0
6902			58.3	58.5	57.5	53.5	53.5
6904			67.0	65.0	63.5	63.5	56.0
6906			67.0	66.0	62.0	62.0	55.0
6908			67.0	67.5	61.5	57.5	57.0
6910		62.0	59.5	61.0	54.0	58.0	50.5
6912		70.0	69.0	69.0	64.0	63.0	65.0
7002		72.5	67.5	63.5	60.0	61.0	53.0
7004		62.0	58.0	58.0	51.0	52.5	50.0
7006		66.0	62.0	60.0	52.5	58.0	50.0
7008		56.0	60.0	57.0	49.0	50.0	54.0
7010		71.0	60.0	57.0	54.0	49.0	52.0
7012		54.5	60.5	57.0	51.5	46.0	51.5
7102		54.0	55.0	50.0	48.0	45.0	38.0
7104		58.0	60.0	50.5	51.5	45.5	42.0
7106		48.0	53.0	50.5	51.5	47.0	40.0
7108		49.0	45.0	48.0	47.0	48.0	50.0
7110		58.0	57.0	57.0	48.0	49.0	44.0
7112		58.5	48.0	50.0	49.0	46.5	41.0
7202		54.0	55.0	42.0	55.0	49.0	40.0
7204		60.0	57.5	51.0	56.0	52.5	44.5
7206		66.0	60.0	60.5	57.0	56.0	49.0
7208		65.5	63.0	62.5	56.5	56.0	54.0
7210		65.0	66.0	65.0	56.0	56.0	61.0
7212		64.0	67.0	55.0	55.0	58.0	48.0
7302		68.0	71.0	67.0	72.0	57.0	56.0

APPENDIX A-3. Continued

Date	A	B	C	D	E	F	G
7304		73.0	70.0	62.0	62.0	60.0	57.0
7306		53.0	50.0	39.0	44.0	31.0	47.0
7308		43.8	38.0	36.8	33.5	29.3	32.3
7310		32.0	33.0	29.0	33.0	26.5	21.5
7312	34.5	27.5	29.5	31.5	26.0	29.5	28.0
7402	30.5	26.0	25.8	28.0	23.3	26.5	23.0
7404	27.5	27.0	26.0	20.0	24.0	26.5	22.0
7406	26.0	27.0	33.0	20.0	26.0	30.0	29.0
7408	75.9	74.9	76.7	65.0	65.0	64.0	64.0
7410	63.0	58.0	55.0	50.0	49.0	43.0	52.0
7412	45.0	45.0	47.0	46.0	33.0	38.0	34.0
7502	45.0	41.0	37.0	41.0	39.0	32.0	31.0
7504	45.5	40.5	45.5	36.0	31.0	33.5	28.5
7506	58.5	58.5	54.5	53.0	47.0	40.0	32.5
7508	59.0	49.0	44.0	41.0	42.0	38.0	41.0
7510	57.0	53.0	54.0	42.0	41.0	29.0	27.0
7512	43.5	40.0	44.0	36.5	35.5	35.0	41.5
7602	50.0	52.0	46.0	49.0	37.0	40.0	36.0
7604	54.0	55.0	45.0	43.0	38.0	50.0	40.0
7606	55.0	45.0	44.0	43.0	41.0	38.0	40.0
7608	57.0	47.0	46.0	45.0	43.0	40.0	42.0
7610	59.0	49.0	48.0	47.0	45.0	42.0	44.0
7612	61.0	57.0	53.0	49.0	43.0	49.0	44.0
7702	64.0	67.0	66.7	65.9	65.9	64.0	64.0
7704	74.0	72.0	73.0	74.0	69.0	68.0	64.0
7706	63.0	66.0	66.0	64.0	56.0	59.0	64.0
7708	59.0	62.7	62.2	63.7	57.3	59.3	61.2
7710	55.0	59.3	58.6	63.0	58.0	59.6	58.6
7712	51.2	56.0	55.0	63.0	60.0	60.0	56.0
7802	48.0	57.0	50.0	47.0	60.0	52.0	50.0
7804	33.0	40.0	44.0	45.0	47.0	41.0	45.0
7806	37.0	39.0	44.5	46.0	43.0	45.0	51.5
7808	41.0	38.0	45.0	47.0	39.0	49.0	58.0
7810	41.3	45.3	48.3	49.0	50.5	47.8	52.0
7812	51.0	52.0	50.0	52.0	49.0	61.0	58.0
7902	44.0	46.0	47.0	35.0	42.0	43.0	39.0
7904	39.0	41.0	44.0	36.0	38.0	41.0	46.0
7906	21.0	31.0	31.0	33.0	30.0	26.0	40.0
7908	31.0	30.0	34.0	31.0	34.0	34.0	38.0
7910	45.0	48.0	48.0	45.0	48.0	53.0	51.0

APPENDIX A-3. Continued

7912	27.5	33.0	30.0	37.5	37.5	34.0	34.0
8002	55.0	57.0	53.0	57.0	57.0	56.0	56.0

```
A = $20,000 and over
B = $15,000 - $19,999 (or $15,000 and over)
C = $10,000 - $14,999 (or $10,000 and over)
D = $ 7,000 - $ 9,999 (or $ 7,000 and over)
E = $ 5,000 - $ 6,999
F = $ 3,000 - $ 4,999
G = Under $ 3,000
```

APPENDIX A-4. Presidential Popularity: Percent Approval by Occupation

Date	Prof & Bus	White Collar	Manual	Farmers	Nonlabor Force	Clerical
6504	67.0	64.0	69.0	63.0		
6506	65.5	61.5	72.5	58.5		
6508	65.0	56.0	69.0	69.0		
6510	62.0	63.0	70.0	48.0		
6512	62.3	66.3	67.0	54.5		
6602	55.0	60.0	64.0	53.0		
6604	53.3	57.3	61.0	44.8		
6606	47.0	52.0	51.5	40.0		
6808	47.0	50.0	59.0	28.0		
6610	46.0	50.5	49.5	35.0		
6612	44.0	46.0	53.0	42.0		
6702	41.5	44.3	50.3	36.3		
6704	42.5	50.0	45.5	31.5		
6706	49.0	48.5	46.0	32.0		
6708	42.0	47.0	46.0	34.0		
6710	34.5	39.5	41.0	29.5		
6712	44.0	43.5	45.5	27.5		
6802	40.5	43.0	47.0	26.5		
6804	39.0	41.0	45.0	33.0		
6806	43.0	37.0	45.0	29.0		
6808	36.0	36.0	37.5	26.0		
6810	38.0	39.0	46.0	35.0		
6812	38.0	45.0	45.0	37.0		
6902	59.5	56.3	55.3	58.0		

APPENDIX A-4. Continued

Date	Prof & Bus	White Collar	Manual	Farmers	Nonlabor Force	Clerical
6904	69.5	64.0	60.5	65.5		
6906	69.0	69.0	61.0	52.0		
6908	68.5	68.0	62.5	63.5		
6910	60.5	65.0	55.0	59.5		
6912	67.0	73.0	65.0	68.0		
7002	69.5	66.0	59.0	59.5		
7004	61.5	59.5	49.5	67.0		
7006	64.0	55.5	55.5	68.0		
7008	60.0	60.0	49.0	63.0		
7010	64.0	64.0	53.0	64.0		
7012	56.5	61.5	51.5	58.5		
7102	56.0	41.0	50.0	53.0		
7104	59.0	59.5	47.5	56.5		
7106	52.5	53.5	45.0	58.0		
7108	51.0	45.0	44.0	47.0		
7110	63.0	57.0	45.0	65.0		
7112	59.0	50.0	42.5	50.0		
7202	54.0	55.0	42.0	55.0		
7204	69.0	64.0	57.0	77.0		
7206	63.0	56.0	52.0	59.0		
7208	63.5	59.0	55.0	60.0		
7210	66.0	62.0	58.0	67.0		70.0
7212	63.0	66.0	55.0	56.0		70.5
7302	68.0	58.0	66.0	67.0		71.0
7304	67.0	54.0	63.0	74.0	76.0	
7306	54.0	50.0	41.0	46.0		53.0
7308	41.0	34.3	33.5	38.0		
7310	29.5	30.5	29.0	39.5		
7312	32.0	31.0	25.0	32.5		
7402	27.0	33.8	23.5	39.0	28.3	
7404	29.5	26.0	20.5		28.5	
7406	26.0	24.0	26.0		32.0	
7408	78.0	72.0	65.0		73.0	
7410	60.0	52.0	52.0		52.0	
7412	49.0	44.0	38.0		43.0	
7502	43.0	43.0	36.0		37.0	
7504	47.0	48.0	37.5		34.0	
7506	61.5	58.5	50.0		43.5	
7508	57.0	45.0	42.0		42.0	
7510	61.0	61.0	42.0		39.0	
7512	45.5	46.0	36.5		37.5	

APPENDIX A-4. Continued

Date	Prof & Bus	White Collar	Manual	Farmers	Nonlabor Force	Clerical
7602	53.0	47.0	44.0		40.0	
7604	56.0	47.0	47.0		44.0	
7606	54.0	41.0	41.0		47.0	
7608	56.0	44.0	44.0		50.0	
7610	58.0	47.0	47.0		53.0	
7612	60.0	49.0	49.0		56.0	
7702	64.0	70.0	67.0		62.0	
7704	76.0	78.0	73.0		65.0	
7706	67.0	59.0	66.0		57.0	
7708	62.6	60.0	63.0		56.0	
7710	58.3	61.0	60.0		55.6	
7712	54.0	62.0	57.0		55.0	
7802	52.0	48.0	55.0		50.0	
7804	34.0	46.0	44.0		43.0	
7806	40.0	35.0	44.0		45.0	35.0
7808	35.0	38.0	47.0	53.0	45.0	38.0
7810	45.0	40.3	47.0		46.8	40.3
7812	51.0	49.0	54.0		55.0	
7902	41.0	36.0	48.0		41.0	
7904	42.0	47.0	38.0		42.0	
7906	24.0	31.0	30.0		28.0	
7908	29.0	28.0	34.0		33.0	
7910	49.0	48.0	47.0		44.0	
7912	47.0	54.0	51.0		58.0	
8002	53.0	53.0	53.0		58.0	

APPENDIX A-5. Presidential Popularity: Percent Approval by Race

Date	White	Nonwhite	Date	White	Nonwhite
6504	64		7210	68	26
6506	64		7212	62	27
6508	64		7302	69.5	43

APPENDIX A-5.   Continued

Date	White	Nonwhite	Date	White	Nonwhite
6510	60		7304	50	13
6512	62		7306	43	19
6602	58		7308	36	13
6604	54		7310	33	11.5
6606	46		7312	32.5	13.5
6608	48		7402	29	09.6
6610	44		7404	27.5	09.5
6612	46		7406	30	15
6702	44		7408	74	51
6704	42.5		7410	56	38
6706	45		7412	45	21
6708	41		7502	41	24
6710	36.5		7504	42	23
6712	42		7506	55	26
6802	42.5		7508	47	35
6804	41		7510	50	23
6806	41		7512	42	26
6808	35		7602	47	33
6810	39		7604	50	36
6812	42		7606	48	27
6902	56		7608	52	27
6904	64.5		7610	55	27
6906	66		7612	58	27
6908	66		7702	66	62
6910	59.2	38.5	7704	71	78
6912	68	44	7706	63	64
7002	66	35	7708	60	66
7004	59	20.5	7710	57	68
7006	61.5	30	7712	54	70
7008	58	21	7802	51	54
7010	61	25	7804	39	59
7012	56.5	31.5	7806	46.5	56.5
7102	52	33	7808	42	54
7104	56	24	7810	46.5	57.5
7106	52	26	7812	51	61
7108	50	25	7902	43	48
7110	57	21	7904	39	53
7112	51.5	24	7906	26	43
7202	25	23	7908	30	43
7204	57	24	7910	44	67
7206	65	37	7912	31	36
7208	60	28	8002	55	60

APPENDIX A-6. Presidential Popularity: Percent Approval by Region

Date	East	Midwest	South	West
6504	79	70	52	63
6506	78	67.5	52.5	71
6508	71	67	60	66
6510	77	65	47	63
6512	74.3	65.3	52.6	56.3
6602	72	59	42	66
6604	65	57	46.3	57
6606	55	50	41.5	45
6608	60	52	40	52
6610	56.6	44.6	40	45.5
6612	62	46	40	43
6702	55.3	46.6	39.6	43
6704	52	43.5	40	42.5
6706	53	46	38.5	50
6708	48.5	45	35	44.5
6710	45	35.5	33	39
6712	52	40.5	36	47
6802	49	43.5	40.5	46
6804	50	39.5	37.5	46.5
6806	50	45	38	33
6808	42.5	36.5	32	36
6810	49	41	32	44
6812	51	44	34	42
6902	53	60	54	55.6
6904	61.5	63	65	64
6906	66	60	62	67
6908	62	63	66.5	64
6910	55.5	58	59.5	59
6912	63	71	71	60
7002	60	62.5	65.5	61
7004	51.5	55	60	56.5
7006	55.5	54	65.5	58.5
7008	53	55	55	58
7010	59	53	64	54
7012	53	51.5	59	55
7102	50	48	52	47
7104	53	54	54	48
7106	48	47.5	52	48
7108	46	47	51	45
7110	54	52	56	52
7112	51	47.5	52	44
7202	47	48	57	44

APPENDIX A-6. Continued

Date	East	Midwest	South	West
7204	58.5	52.5	62.5	51.5
7206	62	57	68	59
7208	55	55	67	43
7210	57	57	66	55
7212	57	60	65	50
7302	64	65	71.5	61.5
7304	41	45	51	42
7306	36	40	44	35
7308	32.5	32.5	36.5	33
7310	27	31	35.5	27
7312	22.5	29.5	38	30
7402	21.3	28.6	32.6	22.6
7404	21	25.5	30	23
7406	24	28	33	25
7408	67.0	76.0	68.0	72.0
7410	52	55	53	54
7412	43	45	37	43
7502	36	43	36	39
7504	37.5	40.5	38.5	37
7506	51	50	52.5	52.5
7508	44	46	47	45
7510	45	51	45	48
7512	36.5	45	41	37
7602	40	47	47	51
7604	44	48	51	51
7606	38	49	49	46
7608	28	34	30	40
7610	36	36	31	41
7612	63.2	65.6	73.7	57.1
7702	63.2	65.6	73.7	57.1
7704	72	74	70	71
7706	63	60	62	70
7708	61	51.6	61	63.2
7710	59	55.3	60	58.6
7712	57	53	59	53
7802	50	53	54	49
7804	41	39	40	41
7806	40.0	42.0	42.5	41.5
7808	39.0	45.0	45.0	42.0
7810	45.0	49.0	49.5	46.0
7812	52	53	54	50
7902	47	38	46	42

APPENDIX A-6.   Continued

Date	East	Midwest	South	West
7904	41	41	43	35
7906	25	25	32	33
7908	29	30	37	31
7910	50	40	50	49
7912	48	55	58	43
8002	54	55	64	44

APPENDIX A-7.   Presidential Popularity: Percent Approval by Sex

Date	Male	Female	Date	Male	Female
6504	67.0	66.0	7210	64.0	58.0
6506	69.5	65.0	7212	63.5	58.5
6508	65.0	65.5	7302	66.5	65.0
6510	64.0	63.0	7304	44.0	46.0
6512	63.5	64.0	7306	42.0	37.0
6602	62.0	57.0	7308	33.0	34.0
6604	58.0	55.3	7310	32.5	29.0
6606	51.0	46.5	7312	30.5	29.0
6608	54.0	49.0	7402	27.0	26.0
6610	50.5	44.0	7404	26.5	24.0
6612	52.0	45.0	7406	29.0	27.0
6702	49.0	44.3	7408	70.0	71.0
6704	46.0	43.5	7410	52.0	54.0
6706	47.5	45.5	7412	37.0	47.0
6708	42.5	43.5	7502	37.0	39.0
6710	40.5	36.5	7504	37.0	40.5
6712	45.0	42.5	7506	53.0	50.0
6802	43.5	45.5	7508	43.0	47.0
6804	44.0	42.0	7510	47.0	47.0
6806	45.0	40.0	7512	40.0	40.0
6808	38.0	36.0	7602	47.0	44.0
6810	40.0	43.0	7604	48.0	48.0
6812	45.0	41.0	7606	46.0	45.0
6902	56.3	57.0	7608	48.0	48.0

APPENDIX A-7. Continued

Date	Male	Female		Date	Male	Female
6904	65.5	61.5		7610	50.0	51.0
6906	66.0	60.0		7612	53.0	54.0
6908	64.5	63.0		7702	67.0	64.3
6910	61.0	55.5		7704	71.0	72.0
6912	71.0	63.0		7706	63.0	63.0
7002	66.5	58.5		7708	60.2	61.0
7004	57.0	53.5		7710	57.6	59.0
7006	59.5	55.5		7712	55.0	57.0
7008	60.0	51.0		7802	53.0	51.0
7010	61.0	55.0		7804	41.0	40.0
7012	58.5	50.5		7806	44.0	42.0
7102	53.0	47.0		7808	42.0	41.3
7104	55.0	51.0		7810	46.0	45.8
7106	49.3	47.8		7812	55.0	49.0
7108	51.5	50.0		7902	43.0	44.0
7110	55.0	52.0		7904	39.0	42.0
7112	51.5	48.0		7906	28.0	28.0
7202	52.0	47.0		7908	32.0	32.0
7204	57.5	54.0		7910	48.0	46.0
7206	62.0	57.0		7912	29.7	34.0
7208	62.5	55.5		8002	53.0	57.0

APPENDIX A-8. Presidential Popularity: Percent Approval by Age

Date	18-20	21-29	30-49	50
6504		75	68	63
6506		69	67.5	66
6508		67	68	63
6510		70	64	60
6512		69	67	60
6602		66	62	54
6604		60	58	54
6606		53	50.5	44
6608		57	54	46

APPENDIX A-8.   Continued

Date	18-20	21-29	30-49	50
6610		49	49.5	44
6612		51	50	46
6702		44.3	44.3	48.5
6704		47.5	46	43
6706		47.5	46	47
6708		44.5	42.5	42.5
6710		39.5	39.5	36
6712		43	46	41
6802		40.5	44.5	46.5
6804		40	41	46
6806		35	43	45
6808		33	37	39
6810		41	41	42
6812		41	41	46
6902		56	54.6	57
6904		66.5	64	60.5
6906		66	63	62
6908		65.5	64.5	62
6910		61.5	57	57
6912		66	67	67
7002		61.5	62.5	63
7004		59	53.5	55.5
7006		56	60	57
7008		49	56	58
7010		52	60	59
7012		54	54	55.5
7102		49	50	48
7104	45	52.5	55.5	52.5
7106	37	44.5	52	49.5
7108	46	45	45	52
7110	42	48	55	58
7112	45.5	46	50.5	49.5
7202	43	45	53	50
7204	49	47	55	55
7206	56	54	54.5	61.5
7208	55.5	54.5	56.0	62.8
7210	55	55	57	63
7212	53	59.5	61	63.5
7302	62.0	60.0	67.0	87.1
7304	57.0	68.0	65.0	68.0
7306	40	47	47	47
7308	28.5	29.5	35.3	39

APPENDIX A-8. Continued

Date	18-20	21-29	30-49	50
7310	28.5	32	30	31.5
7312	26.5	22.5	29.5	33.5
7402	24	24	26	30
7404	18.5	19.5	25.5	29.5
7406	22	21	27	32
7408	64	74	69	74
7410	52	58	54	53
7412	42	48	41	42
7502	38	41	40	37
7504	42.5	40.5	38	37
7506	52	52	54	48.5
7508	44	52	47	42
7510	49	53	48	44
7512	43.5	47.5	40.5	36
7602	56	50	44	41
7604	55	53	50	44
7606	48	41	47	45
7608	50	47	47	48.5
7610	52	53	47	52
7612	55	58	47	56
7702	70	72	65	63
7704	76	78	71	68
7706	65	67	65	59
7708	63.0	65.6	62.2	56.3
7710	61.0	64.8	59.6	54.3
7712	59	63	57	52
7802	55	59	50	51
7804	47	39	39	39
7806	49	40	40	40
7808	51	41	41	41
7810	51.5	47.5	46.5	46.5
7812	52	54	52	52
7902	46	55	44	38
7904	46	43	41	37
7906	31	38	24	28
7908	35	32	30	33
7910	51	61	48	42
7912	32	39	27	35
8002	56	51	56	56

APPENDIX A-9. Presidential Popularity: Percent Approval by Religion

Date	Protestant	Catholic	Date	Protestant	Catholic
6504	60.0	81.0	7210	65.5	57.0
6506	61.5	81.5	7212	65.5	57.5
6508	63.0	73.0	7302	68.5	68.0
6510	59.0	76.0	7304	60.5	53.5
6512	58.8	74.3	7306	51.0	39.0
6602	53.0	65.0	7308	41.3	32.3
6604	52.0	72.0	7310	35.0	24.5
6606	43.5	61.5	7312	35.0	22.0
6608	45.0	70.0	7402	31.0	20.5
6610	41.5	60.0	7404	30.0	19.5
6612	43.0	60.0	7406	34.0	21.0
6702	42.0	58.8	7408	71.0	73.0
6704	40.0	54.0	7410	58.0	52.0
6706	41.5	57.5	7412	45.0	43.0
6708	39.5	52.5	7502	41.0	38.0
6710	33.5	49.5	7504	41.5	36.5
6712	38.5	58.0	7506	52.5	50.5
6802	41.5	53.5	7508	48.0	45.0
6804	40.5	51.5	7510	50.0	49.0
6806	39.0	53.0	7512	43.0	37.0
6808	34.0	44.0	7602	48.0	44.0
6810	38.0	50.0	7604	52.0	46.0
6812	37.0	60.0	7606	48.0	46.0
6902	59.0	56.5	7608	50.0	48.5
6904	66.5	61.0	7610	52.0	53.0
6906	65.0	65.0	7612	54.0	56.0
6908	66.0	63.0	7702	67.0	63.0
6910	61.0	55.0	7704	71.0	74.0
6912	71.0	66.0	7706	63.0	63.0
7002	65.0	62.0	7708	60.2	62.0
7004	59.0	53.5	7710	57.6	61.0
7006	63.5	52.0	7712	55.0	60.0
7008	57.0	54.0	7802	50.0	57.0
7010	59.0	59.0	7804	41.0	39.0
7012	58.5	51.0	7806	42.0	42.0
7102	54.0	46.0	7808	43.0	45.0
7104	57.0	50.5	7810	48.5	50.0
7106	53.0	46.0	7812	54.0	55.0
7108	51.0	45.0	7902	41.0	45.0
7110	56.0	51.0	7904	41.0	40.0
7112	52.5	47.5	7906	29.0	28.0

APPENDIX A-9. Continued

Date	Protestant	Catholic		Date	Protestant	Catholic
7202	54.0	48.0		7908	31.0	31.0
7204	61.0	55.5		7910	47.0	42.0
7206	66.0	61.0		7912	52.0	53.0
7208	60.0	57.0		8002	56.0	55.0

APPENDIX A-10. Unemployment Group Data (bimonthly)

Date	unp	male	fmle	yuth	mmen	blk	wht	whcl	blcl
6504	4.90	3.60	4.80	16.70	2.65	9.10	4.40	2.50	5.80
6506	4.75	3.45	4.65	15.95	2.50	8.45	4.35	2.50	5.65
6508	4.60	3.25	4.60	15.05	2.40	7.85	4.20	2.35	5.40
6510	4.40	3.10	4.35	14.20	2.35	8.05	3.95	2.20	5.15
6512	4.30	2.95	4.15	14.60	2.15	7.75	3.80	2.05	4.95
6602	4.05	2.70	4.15	13.20	1.95	7.35	3.65	2.25	4.50
6604	3.80	2.65	3.75	12.65	1.90	6.95	3.40	2.05	4.20
6606	3.80	2.55	3.70	12.95	1.85	7.25	3.35	2.00	4.20
6608	3.85	2.45	3.90	13.30	1.85	7.40	3.45	2.00	4.25
6610	3.80	2.50	3.80	12.70	1.95	7.75	3.30	2.00	4.45
6612	3.70	2.35	3.85	12.70	1.80	7.20	3.25	2.15	4.00
6702	3.70	2.40	3.70	12.00	1.80	7.30	3.25	1.90	4.25
6704	3.70	2.25	4.15	12.05	1.75	7.00	3.30	2.05	4.20
6706	3.75	2.35	4.10	12.10	1.85	7.30	3.35	2.00	4.40
6708	3.90	2.50	4.15	12.65	1.90	7.70	3.45	2.05	4.60
6710	3.85	2.35	4.05	13.10	1.85	7.00	3.45	2.20	4.45
6712	4.10	2.35	4.85	13.90	1.80	8.30	3.55	2.40	4.70
6802	3.75	2.25	4.00	13.40	1.75	7.10	3.35	2.15	4.35
6804	3.65	2.30	3.95	12.15	1.70	6.85	3.25	2.05	4.35
6806	3.60	2.15	3.75	12.70	1.65	6.85	3.15	1.95	4.20
6808	3.65	2.20	3.70	12.95	1.65	6.80	3.25	1.95	3.95
6810	3.60	2.15	3.75	12.80	1.60	6.60	3.25	2.05	4.25
6812	3.60	2.20	3.80	12.40	1.60	6.95	3.15	2.00	4.05
6902	3.35	1.90	3.50	12.45	1.50	6.25	3.00	1.95	3.75
6904	3.35	1.95	3.60	12.00	1.40	6.05	3.00	1.90	3.70
6906	3.45	1.95	3.70	12.65	1.45	6.55	3.10	1.90	3.85
6908	3.45	2.00	3.70	12.05	1.50	6.60	3.05	2.05	3.75
6910	3.50	2.15	3.75	12.25	1.55	6.45	3.20	2.20	3.80

APPENDIX A-10. Continued

Date	unp	male	fmle	yuth	mmen	blk	wht	whcl	blcl
6912	3.80	2.35	3.85	12.90	1.65	6.65	3.50	2.30	4.30
7002	3.50	2.15	3.55	11.80	1.60	5.95	3.20	2.10	4.25
7004	4.05	2.65	3.90	13.55	1.95	6.80	3.70	2.30	4.80
7006	4.55	3.05	4.45	14.55	2.25	7.75	4.10	2.70	5.40
7008	4.85	3.40	4.70	14.55	2.50	8.15	4.40	2.70	6.15
7010	5.05	3.70	4.85	15.00	2.75	8.35	4.70	2.90	6.70
7012	5.45	4.00	5.00	16.75	2.95	9.05	5.10	2.95	7.30
7102	6.05	4.40	5.70	17.70	3.30	9.25	5.55	3.70	7.60
7104	5.95	4.30	5.65	17.20	3.25	9.55	5.45	3.50	7.50
7106	6.00	4.35	5.85	17.25	3.20	9.65	5.55	3.70	7.45
7108	5.95	4.40	5.75	16.80	3.15	9.95	5.45	3.40	7.30
7110	6.00	4.40	5.75	16.80	3.15	9.95	5.50	3.50	7.35
7112	5.90	4.40	5.60	16.80	3.15	10.40	5.35	3.40	7.40
7202	6.00	4.35	5.80	17.00	3.25	9.90	5.50	3.50	7.50
7204	5.85	4.15	5.35	18.00	2.95	10.75	5.25	3.50	7.05
7206	5.85	4.20	5.45	17.05	2.85	9.85	5.30	3.35	6.85
7208	5.65	4.05	5.65	15.30	2.85	9.75	5.15	3.35	6.60
7210	5.60	3.90	5.60	16.10	2.65	9.85	5.05	3.45	6.45
7212	5.50	3.85	5.45	15.80	2.80	10.00	5.00	3.45	6.00
7302	5.15	3.45	5.05	15.65	2.45	9.85	4.60	3.20	5.70
7304	5.05	3.40	5.10	15.00	2.40	8.95	4.60	3.05	5.65
7306	5.00	3.40	4.85	14.70	2.45	9.10	4.45	3.00	5.45
7308	4.85	3.30	4.75	14.55	2.30	9.00	4.35	2.90	5.30
7310	4.70	3.10	4.80	14.35	2.10	9.00	4.15	2.90	5.20
7312	4.65	3.00	4.60	14.15	2.10	8.80	4.15	2.75	5.10
7402	4.75	3.00	4.85	14.45	2.15	8.75	4.30	2.95	5.30
7404	5.20	3.45	5.10	15.25	2.35	9.20	4.65	3.15	5.95
7406	5.05	3.45	5.00	14.50	2.35	9.00	4.55	2.90	6.15
7408	5.20	3.45	5.10	15.70	2.40	9.15	4.75	3.20	6.00
7410	5.35	3.70	5.25	15.75	2.70	9.40	4.85	3.25	6.40
7412	5.90	4.10	5.65	16.90	2.90	10.40	5.40	3.40	7.20
7502	6.90	4.95	6.90	17.75	3.55	12.05	6.15	3.95	8.80
7504	8.20	6.10	8.10	20.35	4.60	13.45	7.45	4.55	10.95
7506	8.80	6.90	8.55	20.50	5.40	14.40	8.05	4.65	12.75
7508	8.90	7.15	8.35	20.50	5.75	14.20	8.20	5.10	12.80
7510	8.40	6.80	7.80	20.10	5.20	13.50	7.75	4.70	11.80
7512	8.45	7.05	7.65	19.60	5.25	14.25	7.75	4.75	11.35
7602	8.30	6.70	7.90	19.25	4.80	13.75	7.55	4.75	10.65
7604	7.70	5.85	7.45	19.25	4.15	13.40	6.95	4.60	9.35
7606	7.50	5.55	7.25	19.15	4.05	12.80	6.80	4.65	9.00
7608	7.45	5.75	7.00	18.45	4.20	12.85	6.75	4.50	9.15
7610	7.85	6.00	7.70	18.90	4.35	13.25	7.10	4.80	9.75

APPENDIX A-10. Continued

Date	unp	male	fmle	yuth	mmen	blk	wht	whcl	blcl
7612	7.85	6.15	7.60	18.90	4.45	13.10	7.20	4.60	9.80
7702	7.90	6.25	7.50	19.10	4.40	13.45	7.20	4.60	9.65
7704	7.50	5.70	7.05	18.60	3.95	12.85	6.75	4.55	8.65
7706	7.25	5.20	7.10	18.30	3.75	12.60	6.50	4.55	8.20
7708	7.10	5.15	6.90	18.25	3.50	13.05	6.30	4.25	7.90
7710	6.95	5.15	7.00	17.45	3.45	13.80	6.10	4.15	8.20
7712	6.80	5.10	6.90	17.70	3.45	13.40	6.00	4.15	7.90
7802	6.55	4.75	6.85	16.35	3.25	13.20	5.70	4.10	7.40
7804	6.20	4.60	5.90	16.70	2.90	12.25	5.40	3.55	7.10
7806	6.10	4.35	5.75	17.10	2.90	12.10	5.25	3.45	6.80
7808	5.90	4.05	6.20	15.35	2.80	12.10	5.05	3.55	6.55
7810	6.05	4.10	6.30	15.95	2.75	12.10	5.25	3.65	6.95
7812	5.90	4.00	5.80	16.45	2.70	11.30	5.20	3.40	6.95
7902	5.85	4.05	5.80	16.35	2.50	11.65	5.10	3.40	6.70
7904	5.75	4.00	5.70	15.90	2.60	11.55	5.00	3.35	6.40
7906	5.75	4.00	5.70	16.00	2.65	11.50	4.95	3.35	6.75
7908	5.70	3.90	5.80	16.05	2.55	11.45	4.95	3.30	6.60
7910	5.85	4.15	5.70	15.90	2.95	10.90	5.10	3.40	7.20
7912	5.85	4.20	5.60	16.30	2.90	11.15	5.10	3.35	7.15
8002	5.85	4.25	5.65	15.95	2.85	11.10	5.10	3.25	7.35
8004	6.10	4.65	5.75	16.40	3.25	11.65	5.35	3.40	7.85

unp = aggregate unemployment
male = male unemployment
fmle = female unemployment
yuth = youth (16 to 19 years) unemployment
mmen = married men unemployment
blk = black unemployment
wht = white unemployment
whcl = white collar unemployment
blcl = blue collar unemployment

APPENDIX A-11. Standard and Poor Stock Market Index, Consumer Price Index, and Personal Income (bimonthly)

Date	Standard and Poor Stock Market Index	Consumer Price Index	Personal Income
6504	87.40	93.85	524.40
6506	87.16	94.45	533.30

APPENDIX A-11. Continued

Date	Standard and Poor Stock Market Index	Consumer Price Index	Personal Income
6508	85.70	94.70	540.45
6510	90.38	94.85	555.35
6512	91.94	95.10	560.80
6602	93.00	95.70	568.05
6604	90.24	96.50	576.35
6606	86.42	96.95	582.15
6608	83.24	97.65	590.75
6610	77.47	98.30	599.30
6612	81.16	98.55	606.70
6702	85.90	98.65	612.95
6704	90.19	99.00	617.75
6706	92.01	99.55	623.85
6708	93.79	100.35	633.10
6710	95.73	100.85	638.90
6712	93.98	101.45	649.40
6802	92.89	102.15	659.95
6804	92.38	102.95	673.55
6806	99.18	103.70	684.35
6808	99.20	104.65	695.20
6810	102.55	105.40	705.55
6812	105.95	106.25	714.95
6902	101.75	106.90	723.45
6904	100.30	108.35	735.75
6906	101.87	109.35	745.50
6908	94.44	110.45	756.80
6910	95.01	111.40	766.15
6912	93.66	112.55	774.30
7002	88.73	113.60	781.80
7004	87.30	115.35	798.70
7006	75.82	116.00	801.70
7008	76.82	116.80	807.15
7010	83.47	117.80	814.25
7012	87.16	118.80	818.30
7102	95.30	119.30	831.15
7104	101.30	120.00	840.65
7106	100.66	121.15	858.60
7108	98.12	121.95	865.75
7110	98.34	122.30	873.50
7112	95.97	122.85	884.90
7202	104.25	123.50	903.70
7204	108.25	124.15	916.50
7206	107.85	124.85	923.45

APPENDIX A-11. Continued

Date	Standard and Poor Stock Market Index	Consumer Price Index	Personal Income
7208	109.10	125.60	936.45
7210	109.50	126.40	955.30
7212	116.30	127.05	978.05
7302	116.30	127.90	993.25
7304	111.35	129.60	1007.45
7306	106.00	131.50	1022.65
7308	104.80	132.85	1041.45
7310	107.70	136.05	1085.60
7312	98.39	137.55	1103.55
7402	94.78	139.50	1110.20
7404	94.95	142.60	1121.15
7406	89.73	144.80	1139.35
7408	79.42	148.10	1163.35
7410	68.78	151.10	1181.50
7412	69.40	153.60	1187.75
7502	76.33	154.30	1202.90
7504	84.25	155.20	1207.00
7506	91.25	156.90	1231.20
7508	89.10	160.00	1253.20
7510	86.62	161.00	1283.05
7512	89.38	162.50	1298.50
7602	98.75	162.80	1326.10
7604	101.50	162.90	1347.20
7606	101.46	164.20	1366.65
7608	103.74	165.80	1383.15
7610	103.67	166.80	1397.95
7612	102.92	167.70	1430.45
7702	102.38	170.40	1465.65
7704	99.81	172.90	1504.60
7706	99.02	174.90	1520.80
7708	98.96	175.70	1544.10
7710	94.98	176.50	1572.55
7712	94.05	177.90	1612.20
7802	89.61	180.30	1620.25
7804	90.76	183.10	1657.85
7806	97.53	186.40	1688.90
7808	100.55	188.30	1725.15
7810	102.22	190.90	1756.55
7812	95.41	193.90	1796.70
7902	98.97	197.90	1827.85
7904	101.09	202.50	1876.40
7906	100.73	206.20	1898.35

APPENDIX A-11.   Continued

Date	Standard and Poor Stock Market Index	Consumer Price Index	Personal Income
7908	105.04	209.50	1939.86
7910	106.54	224.60	1970.68
7912	105.72	244.80	2016.90
8002	113.10	250.30	2048.45

SP = Standard and Poor Index
CPI = Consumer Price Index
PI = Personal Income

APPENDIX A-12.   Tax Rating (bimonthly)

Date	Rating	Date	Rating	Date	Rating
6502	0	7002	0	7502	0
6504	2	7004	0	7504	1
6506	1	7006	1	7506	0
6508	2	7008	0	7508	0
6510	0	7010	0	7510	0
6512	0	7012	3	7512	4
6602	0	7102	0	7602	0
6604	0	7104	1	7604	1
6606	1	7106	3	7606	1
6608	0	7108	1	7608	1
6610	2	7110	0	7610	2
6612	0	7112	3	7612	0
6702	0	7202	0	7702	0
6704	0	7204	0	7704	1
6706	1	7206	3	7706	0
6708	0	7208	2	7708	1
6710	1	7210	1	7710	1
6712	0	7212	0	7712	-1
6802	0	7302	0	7802	0
6804	0	7304	0	7804	0
6806	0	7306	1	7806	0
6808	0	7308	-1	7808	0
6810	1	7310	1	7810	2
6812	0	7312	1	7812	1

APPENDIX A-12. Continued

Date	Rating	Date	Rating	Date	Rating
6902	0	7402	0	7902	1
6904	0	7404	0	7904	0
6906	0	7406	0	7906	1
6908	-1	7408	0	7908	2
6910	0	7410	2	7910	1
6912	2	7412	0	7912	4

APPENDIX B

The 1960 to 1965 period was one of economic growth and expansion in the United States. 1960 to 1965 saw declining unemployment, as the U.S. economy moved close to fulfilling its full productive potential. After a period of relatively low inflation, but with unemployment averaging greater than 5 percent from 1958 on, a shift began in 1960. Thereafter, the gap between unemployment and inflation closed, with the average annual change in the consumer price index approaching or outpacing unemployment until mid-1970. 1965 was a good year for both inflation and unemployment. Unemployment stood at 4.1 percent at the end of 1965, close to the interim goal set by Kennedy's *1962 Economic Report of the President,* and less than any other unemployment rate achieved since the mid-1950s. Inflation continued at the relatively low level it had followed since 1952, remaining well below 5 percent from 1952 on, with prices actually declining during 1954–55. 1965 continued this general low price level but, in retrospect, can be seen to be the last of the good years. To a great extent, government policies were responsible for this. The increasing expenditures for the Vietnam War plus the Great Society programs led directly to the inflation that has plagued policy makers and the public since 1965. Thus, the contraction of the 1980s can be said to be the payment for the boom of the late 1960s that resulted from stimulative fiscal policies.

1965 was a boom year. Unemployment reached 3.9 percent, a 13-year low and the level considered "full employment" by many economists. Most major groups in American society made income gains in 1966, as real income continued to increase for the sixth successive year. Overall economic growth was slightly greater than 5 percent for the third straight year as gross national product expanded by a record $58 billion (in 1966 dollars) to reach $740 billion. The key to this boom was, in part, the $10 billion addition to defense expenditures as a result of the Vietnam War, the increased state and local spending coupled with heavy federal expenditures for social welfare programs, and the business investments that resulted in large part from the first two phenomena.

By the end of 1966, certain problems in the economic expansion were becoming evident. There were strains in some financial markets. Demand outpaced supply in several sectors and prices were beginning to increase, although they were still within the 1952 to 1965 range. As a result of the increased demand, imports increased, thereby reducing the foreign trade surplus and slowing the desired progress toward equilibrium in balance of payments. As a result of all of this, government policy during and after 1966 shifted toward a more restrictive monetary policy to restrain the economy. The expansionary tax policy of 1964 to 1965 was abandoned. As of March 1966, restrictive tax policies were adopted, with excise tax cuts being postponed and income tax payments accelerated. Although fiscal policy also was used to slow the expansion—for example, the January 1966 budget held down defense spending—the principal government mechanism was tight monetary policy.

1967 began a period of readjustment at home and uncertainty abroad about the U.S. position in the international economy. While it was not as good a year as 1966, it was, in retrospect, the last of seven years of a strong economic expansion. Domestic economic growth was slow in the first half of the year at approximately a 1 percent annual rate; it increased vigorously the last half of the year, however, at an annual rate of 4.5 percent. Unemployment was 3.8 percent, comparable to the 1966 rate and lower than any previous year since 1953. Income rose, with real disposable income per capita up 3.2 percent, less than the annual 3.9 percent annual rate from 1961 to 1966 but well above the 2.3 percent annual average from 1945 to 1966. The main economic problem centered on the international situation, with uncertainty over the November devaluation of the British pound leading to a speculation against gold that was stopped only by concerted cooperative action on the part of several major powers. A constant problem since 1957, the balance of payments deficit worsened in 1967, thereby adding to the fears and uncertainty at the international level. The year ended with fear of an international financial crisis as a result of the deteriorating U.S. balance of payments, and the speculation against gold and currencies.

1968 was a year of growth soured by inflation. The real gross national product increased by 5 percent but average real money after-tax income increased by roughly 3 percent. The balance of payments problem decreased in magnitude, with the best ratio in 11 years occurring in 1968. Confidence in the dollar abroad, however, remained shaky. And inflation grew, with consumer prices up 4 percent and wholesale prices up 2.5 percent. This was largely the result of government policies, particularly the excessive and inappropriate stimulus by the government late in 1967 and early in 1968. A tax increase, designed to slow this, was not passed in time to have the desired effect; growth early in 1968 was at a 6.5 percent annual rate described by the President's Council of Economic Advisers as "hectic" (1969 Report), slowing to a 4 percent annual rate at the end of 1968 primarily because of tighter monetary policy by the Federal Reserve Board.

1969 was a shift year. It marks the point at which it became clear that the economic pattern predominant in the 1950s and 1960s was no longer existent. Stagflation became more evident and America's international economic preeminence became less so. As traditional government fiscal and monetary policies seemed less able to moderate, much less direct, the country's economic cycles, key presidential advisors on economic affairs began to disagree more openly on the kind of policy to follow. The problem was the entrenched inflation generated from the mounting budget deficits and rapid monetary expansion for the Vietnam War, plus the domestic welfare programs.

By the beginning of 1969, production, incomes, and prices were all increasing rapidly from the momentum of earlier fiscal and monetary policies. By midyear, however, there was some slowing due to the constraint of the anti-inflationary policies in 1968. Particularly effective were the mid-1968 tax increase, the tighter fiscal policy decreasing projected federal outlays, and the more restrictive monetary policy followed by the Federal Reserve Board. The economic improvement was less than it might have been, however, because of the uncertainty among professional economic policy makers concerning the relative importance of the rising budget deficit versus rapid monetary expansion in causing the inflation of 1965 to 1968. According to one view, the government needed to stabilize the budget in its current (1969) position of moderate surpluses. An opposing view held that the key was reduced rate of monetary growth. This professional confusion led to the government opting for some of both, a policy that had little impact on inflation.

The economic movement in 1970 was somewhat clearer, reflecting in part the new Republican administration's different economic priorities, stressing a steadier expansion with less concern for unemployment and more for inflation. This difference was noted by Nixon in his *1971 Economic Report of the President*. His speech highlights the political attractions of a political business cycle: "1970 was the year in which we paid for the excesses of 1966, 1967, and 1968, when federal spending went $40 billion beyond full employment revenues. But we are now nearing the end of these payments, and 1971 will be a better year, leading to a good year in 1972 and to a new steadiness of expansion in the years beyond." In other words, we have now paid for the Democrats' excesses and, thanks to Republican policies, 1971 will be better, but 1972, an election year, will be downright good.

In 1970, inflation and unemployment were higher than the key economic analysts had expected and aggregate demand (in money terms) and real output were lower than expected. The rate of inflation slowed somewhat, from an annual increase in the consumer price index of 6 percent (from June 1969 to June 1970) to a 4.6 percent increase in the last half of 1970. Unemployment increased as a result of the shift from a wartime to a peacetime economy, with lower defense spending and a 1.1 million worker reduction in defense employment in 1970. The cutback in social welfare policies and the ten-week General Motors auto strike also kept unemployment high. The stock market had one of its worst declines in 40 years.

1971 was a big year for economic headlines and great bursts of government activity to ensure economic well being; it was less successful in terms of its actual results. The year began with the now perennial problems of high inflation and high unemployment plus an uncertain international situation. The economy was continuing its shift from a military to civilian output. Defense spending decreased again and despite the stimulus/contraction of 1970, unemployment remained at 6.1 percent in May, after only a slight decrease earlier in the year. Inflation did not slow appreciably and the balance of payments continued to deteriorate.

Because of this, Nixon announced a major economic policy shift on 15 August 1971, a policy that baffled many of his loyal political followers. He froze prices, wages, and rents for 90 days and moved into a modified extension of this policy in Phase II, which established a more flexible system of mandatory controls. A temporary surcharge (usually 10 percent) was placed on dutiable imports. And Nixon suspended the convertibility of dollars into gold or other reserve assets for the first time since 1934. The last move was followed by a December meeting of major industrial powers to establish a new set of international currency relationships. Tax revisions also were enacted in December 1971.

Nixon's policies had the obvious outcome: Inflation slowed, to 3 percent by 1972. Unemployment decreased roughly 1 percent between December 1971 and December 1972. Real wages and corporate profits increased and the rate of growth of real output accelerated, with the 6.5 percent rise in real gross national product being better than had been expected. 1972 strike activity was the lowest in almost ten years. On the international scene, however, the uncertainty remained. And for the first time, there seemed to be an increased public awareness of the role foreign energy played in the domestic economy.

Inflation remained the major economic problem in 1973, with the President's Council of Economic Advisers referring to it as a "Hydra-headed monster" (*1974 Economic Report of the President,* 21). Fueled at various times by wages, by prices, by food, or by energy, it was caused by both international problems and by domestic policies.

Although many government programs were developed to combat inflation, none seemed to work. Restrictive fiscal and monetary policies did little to help.[2] Because the high price of oil decreased the demand for large cars, auto production was cut back sharply. General productivity slowed, with real output rising at only 4 percent in 1973 versus 6 percent in 1972. Along with this came decreased foreign demand for U.S. goods.

However bad 1973 looked at year's end, however, its appeal grew greatly as 1974 unfolded. For 1974 was a year politely characterized as "very difficult for the American economy" (*1975 Economic Report of the President,* 35). It was, in fact, the worst recession of the post-World War II period. It began with the Arab oil embargo, which led to spiraling oil prices, long gas lines, and short tempers. As if that were not enough, the decline in real output and the rise of prices were the greatest of any peacetime year since World War II. Living standards fell and unemployment increased to 6.6 percent from 4.7 percent in 1973. As a result, consumers cut back on real expenditures, especially for energy and automobiles. A partial midyear recovery was not enough to pull up the yearly average; and 1974 ended with demand and output falling rapidly, with the worst decline in home building in 30 years, and with unemployment and inflation still high.

The picture in 1975 failed to improve much. Inflation did drop appreciably in 1975, from a 12.1 percent annual rate in 1974 to a 7.3 percent rate in 1976, demonstrating that tight monetary policy worked. But unemployment also increased. And productivity fell, beginning with an annual drop of 9.2 percent in the first quarter; thereafter, it grew, but slowly. By the end of the year, the government had shifted to a policy of slow expansion and the beginnings of a slow three-year recovery occurred at the end of 1975.

1976 was a year of erratic growth, with a slow first quarter but an overall increase of 6.2 percent for the entire year. The inflation rate moderated and unemployment decreased 1 percent from the 1975 rate. 1977 picked up on the slow real growth in the last part of 1976, with growth early in 1977 being especially strong and an overall increase in real gross national product of 4.9 percent. Unemployment hovered around 8 percent early in the spring and then fell to 7 percent in the summer and fall, reaching 6.4 percent at year's end. Living standards increased, with real per capita disposable income up 4.9 percent for 1977. The government responded to a midyear slump in the economic recovery with quick fiscal stimulation that kept the slowdown from worsening late in the year. The major economic problem continued to be inflation, however, with the consumer price index holding at an annual 6 to 6.5 percent increase since 1975, due partly to the inflation deeply imbedded in the wage-cost-price structure. Increases for food and energy added to this increase.

1978 was a year in which inflation and the international value of the dollar were the main economic problems, with unemployment falling and output rising. The year's economic growth was uneven, however, with a severe winter and a coal strike hurting first quarter growth. And although all major demographic groups experienced economic gains, the growth in real income was less than in the previous three years. The importance of inflation for income can be quickly seen in comparative figures. For example, real disposable personal income per capita rose 2.5 percent in 1978 versus 4.6 percent in 1977 and an annual average of 3.2 percent from 1975 to 1978. Inflation continued to accelerate in 1978 with the consumer price index rising to around 9.2 percent from November 1977 to November 1978. (This compares with 6.8 percent for the prior

November 1976 to November 1977 year.) And as a precursor of what was yet to come, nominal interest rates approached an historic high.

Government policy did not help curb inflation in 1978, which was probably worse than overall economic conditions otherwise justified. 1979 saw increased fiscal and monetary restraint to slow inflation. Rising OPEC oil prices, however, made this difficult and the consumer price index increased to 13 percent in 1979. The lower price of the dollar during 1978 helped exports. Unemployment held between 5.7 percent and 5.9 percent throughout the year. The year ended with a certain amount of economic uncertainty—not lessened by the political events in Iran and Afghanistan—as experts were surprised that the economy held firm enough not to dip into recession again, given the tight money policies plus the OPEC increases. In part this was because consumer's expectations had shifted on inflation. Once inflation was not seen as a temporary phenomenon, it no longer deterred anyone from making purchases. In addition to this, the monetary restraint no longer produced the abrupt changes of credit that once used to bring an end to economic expansion, raising for some economists the question of the usefulness of monetary policy and suggesting the importance of the public's inflationary expectations.

1980 ended the five-year recovery and expansion following the 1964–75 recession, with an extremely brief 1980 recession and much uncertainty about future economic developments after the newly elected Reagan administration's proposed shift in economic policies. The economic performance was erratic, if not volatile. Real gross national product decreased at a record rate in the second quarter and thereafter advanced, making the 1980 recession one of the briefest on record. Interest rates soared to a record high, then dropped, went on to new peaks and then dropped again—all within a period of nine months. Unemployment was also erratic, at 6 percent in December 1979, 6.3 percent in March 1980, 7.6 percent in May 1980, and holding between 7.4 percent and 7.6 percent the rest of the year. The consumer price index rose to 9.9 percent and the overall gross national product grew 3.1 percent the first quarter, declined by 9.9 percent the second quarter, and held steady at roughly 3.1 percent for the last of the year. Clearly, the 1980 economic performance was inconsistent and as baffling to professional economists as it was to the voters.

NOTES

1.   The importance of the General Motors strike can be
seen by looking at the unemployment (in annual terms): 5.9
percent from July to December 1969; 6 percent from January to June 1970; 4.6 percent from June to November 1970;
but back up to nearly 6 percent in December due largely to
the strike.   The President's Council of Economic Advisers
estimate that General Motors productivity approximates 1.5
percent of the total U.S. national output, providing new
understanding to the old chestnut about what is good for
General Motors being good for the country.
2.   The money supply grew at 6.1 percent in 1973
versus 7.7 percent in 1972.   This assumes a narrow definition is adopted.   The rate is 8.8 percent in 1973 versus
10.9 percent in 1972 if a broader definition is accepted.

APPENDIX C

The following events were judged the most important ones
by four coders working independently, based on a pre-
selection by seven source books that listed the major
political events during the 1965 to 1980 period.   Differing
weights or even different selections might be made by other
readers.   The list of events and the codings used to create
the systematic measurements of political factors that influenced presidential popularity are listed in full here.   It
is hoped that later scholars can expand and refine this
instrument.

APPENDIX C-1.   Key Political Events Affecting Presidential Popularity,
1965-1980

Year	Date	Event	Rating
1965	January 4	State of Union address	0
	April 27	Dominican Republic intervention	R
	August 6	Voting Rights Act	L
	August 10	Housing Act	L
	August 11	Los Angeles race riots	L
	September	Department of Housing and Urban Development established	L

APPENDIX C-1. Continued

Year	Date	Event	Rating
1966	January	Price and wage controls	L
	June 29	Bombing raids extended to oil dumps in North Vietnam	L
	July 12	Chicago race riots	L
	October 15	Department of Transportation established	L
	November 3	Model Cities program instituted	L
	November 8	Congressional elections	L
1967	March 16	US-Soviet Consular Treaty	L
	April 25	Outer Space Treaty	L
	June 23	Glassboro Summit	L
	July 12	Newark race riots	L
	July 23	Detroit race riots	L
	July	Middle East crisis	O
1968	January 25	Pueblo seizure	R
	February	Viet Cong Tet offensive and Korean crisis continues	R
	February 29	Kerner Commission report	O
	March 12	McCarthy victory in New Hampshire primary	L
	March 16	Robert Kennedy announces presidential candidacy	L
	March 31	Johnson announces he will not seek reelection; announces partial bombing halt	L
	April	Open Housing laws, North Vietnam agrees to preliminary peace talks	L
	April 23-30	Columbia University demonstrations	L
	April 27	Hubert Humphrey announces presidential candidacy	L
	June 6	Robert Kennedy assassinated	R
	June 19	Omnibus Crime Control and Safe Streets Act	L
	August 29	Democratic Convention nominates Humphrey; street riots outside convention hall	L
	November 5	Nixon elected	O
	December	Pueblo crew released	O

APPENDIX C-1. Continued

Year	Date	Event	Rating
1969	January	Nixon takes office	O
	April	Paris Peace Talks	L
	July	Income tax surcharge	O
	July 20	Moon landing	R
	August	Nixon antiballistic missile program	L
	September	Nixon welfare program	L
	November 3	Withdrawal of troops from Vietnam	L
	November 16	My Lai massacre reported	L
	November 21	Haynsworth nomination to Supreme Court blocked	L
1970	April 8	Carswell nomination to Supreme Court blocked	L
	April 30	Nixon order Cambodian invasion	L
	May 4	Kent State protest later sparks further protests	L
	June	Cambodian fighting	O
	July 29	Criminal legislation introduced (no-knock, preventive detention)	L
	November 3	White House attacks press; Agnew's Iowa speech	L
	November	Republican losses in congressional elections	L
	November 25	Interior Department Secretary Hickel fired	L
1971	February 8	Laos invaded	L
	March 24	Supersonic Transport Program defeated	L
	June 15	Injunction against printing Pentagon Papers	O
	June 28	Ellsberg indicted on theft of government property and violation of espionage act	C
	June 30	Supreme Court denies injunction	L
	July 1	Pentagon Papers published	L
	September 3	Berlin Accord	O
	September 21	Selective Service extends draft	L
	September	Nixon economic program; Wage-	

APPENDIX C-1. Continued

Year	Date	Event	Rating
		price freeze	0
	December	Announce Phase II of economic program	0
1972	February 21-28	Nixon's China trip	R
	February 15	Seabed Arms Treaty	L
	April 7	Federal Elections Campaign Act	C
	April 16	Bombing of Haiphong	L
	May 15	Wallace shot	0
	May 22-30	Nixon visits Moscow	L
	June 17	Watergate breakin	C
	June 19	White House denies knowledge of Watergate breakin	0
	July 10-13	Democratic convention nominates McGovern	0
	July 31	Eagleton discloses earlier mental health problems and withdraws as vice-presidential nominee	0
	August 8	Shriver selected by Democrats	0
	August 21-23	Republican Convention nominates Nixon and Agnew	0
	September 2	Washington Post disclosures on Watergate	C
	November 7	Presidential election; Nixon wins	L
1973	January	Peace settlement announced	0
	January 3-8	Trials of Watergate burglars open	C
	February 12	Devaluation of dollar; Nixon impoundments	0
	February 28	Grey confirmation hearings	L
	April 5	Grey asks Nixon to withdraw his nomination	C
	April 27	Grey resigns from F.B.I.	C
	April 30	Halderman, Ehrlichman resign; Dean fired; Kleindeinst resigns; Richardson appointed; Nixon's speech on Watergate	C
	May 11	Ellsberg charges dismissed	L
	May 17-		

APPENDIX C-1.   Continued

Year	Date	Event	Rating
	August 7	Ervin committee hearings	C
	May 18	Cox appointed special prosecutor	C
	May 22	Nixon concedes coverup, but professes own innocence	C
	June 14	Magruder admits to perjury; implicates Dean	C
	June 17-25	Nixon-Brezhnev summit	L
	June 25-29	Dean implicates president in coverup; enemies list and plumbers unit disclosed	C
	June 29	Nixon says will cease bombing of Cambodia by August 15	L
	July 10-12	Mitchell testimony at Watergate hearings	C
	July 16	Butterfield reveals existence of White House tapes	C
	July 16	Katzenbach admits to having raised money for Watergate defendants	O
	July 17-23	Nixon refuses to release tapes to Ervin committee (July 17) or to Cox (July 23)	C
	August 29	Sirica orders Nixon to release tapes, Watergate Tapes released; Nixon's speech on Watergate to explain tapes	C
	October 6	Yom Kippur War	O
	October 12	US Court of Appeals upholds Sirica; Nixon proposes Stennis compromise; rejected by Cox	C
	October 20	Saturday Night Massacre	C
	October 28	Nixon releases tapes under public pressure; 16 impeachment resolutions related to Watergate scandals, ITT, milk fund, Hughes gifts, and San Clemente-Key Biscayne estates are introduced to the House	C
	October 30	Impeachment proceedings; preliminary resolutions introduced	C
	November 1	Saxbe, Jaworski appointed	C
	November 26	18-minute tape gap discovered	C

APPENDIX C-1.   Continued

Year	Date	Event	Rating
1974	January	Middle East crisis	O
	January 4	Nixon refuses to comply with tape subpoena	C
	January 18	Suez disengagement agreement signed between Israel and Egypt	L
	February	Energy crisis worsens	O
	February 6	House ratifies impeachment investigation resolution	C
	February 13	Washington Energy Conference with 13 major oil-consuming countries	O
	February 28	United States and Egypt resume diplomatic relations	L
	March 1	Seven White House and Nixon-campaign officials indicted for involvement in Watergate breakin or coverup	C
	March 18	Oil embargo on US lifted by 7 OPEC members	O
	March 28	Kissinger returns from Moscow; no substantive progress in SALT II talks	O
	March	Issue of impeachment and/or resignation of Nixon becomes more acute	O
	April 3	Presidential tax fraud surfaces	C
	April 11	House subpoenas Nixon's tapes	C
	April 28	Vexco, Stans, and Mitchell found innocent	C
	April 29	Nixon releases transcripts of tapes	C
	May	Transcript controversy worsens	O
	May 1	Watergate transcripts published	C
	May 9	Impeachment hearings resume	C
	May 22	Nixon refuses to release additional tapes	C
	May 31	Supreme Court to consider Nixon's refusal to release additional tapes	C
	June 3	Colson pleads guilty to obstructing justice in Ellsberg trial; charges dropped	C

APPENDIX C-1. Continued

Year	Date	Event	Rating
	June 11	Kissinger threatens to resign over accusation that he participated in illegal wiretapping at White House	C
	June 12-18	Nixon goes to Middle East	L
	June 15	Supreme Court considers whether grand jury had right to name Nixon as "unindicted co-conspirator"	C
	June 20	House Committee reveals transcript discrepancies	C
	June 26	NATO countries sign declaration of principles	O
	June 27-July 3	Nixon to Moscow for summit with Brezhnev	L
	July 24	Supreme Court rules against Nixon's executive privilege	C
	July 27	Committee votes to impeach Nixon	C
	August 5	Nixon releases ["smoking gun"] tapes revealing his awareness of coverup	C
	August 6	Kissinger cleared in wiretap controversy	C
	August 8-9	Nixon yields to pressure and resigns	C
	August 9	Ford becomes president	R
	August 19	US Ambassador to Cyprus killed	O
	August 20	Rockefeller nominated for Vice Presidency	O
	September 2	Ford signs law to ensure pension benefits are saved	O
	September 8	Ford pardons Nixon	L
	September 12	Court-ordered busing leads to widespread school boycotting in Boston	O
	September 19	Nixon subpoenaed as witness in Watergate coverup trial	C
	October 1	Watergate coverup trial opens	C
	October 15	National Guard mobilized in busing violence in Boson	O
	October 17	Ford defends the Nixon pardon	L

APPENDIX C-1. Continued

Year	Date	Event	Rating
	October 18	Ford and Congress agree on trade benefits to USSR	L
	November 18	Ford begins East Asia tour	O
	November 20	Antitrust suit against ATT brought by Department of Justice	O
	November 24	Ford and Brezhnev reach tentative agreement on nuclear weapons limits	L
	November 27	Republican losses in congressional elections	L
	November 29	Nixon too ill to testify at Watergate trial	O
	December 5	Sirica rules Nixon does not have to testify	O
	December 10	Rep. Wilbur Mills resigns position as Chairman of Ways and Means because of scandal with Fannie Fox	C
	December 19	Rockefeller becomes Vice President	L
	December 31	CIA domestic spying reported	L
1975	January 1	Watergate verdicts announced; convictions of principals	C
	January 14	Kissinger announces USSR will not accept Ford's agreement on trade and emigration	O
	February 5	US ends military aid to Turkey	O
	February 26	US Honorary Consul slain in Argentina	O
	March 18	100,000 South Vietnamese refugees flee Vietnam	O
	March 23	Kissinger fails at peacemaking in Middle East	O
	March 29	Ford signs tax cut bill	O
	April 10	Ford requests $972 million for South Vietnam aid	O
	April 11-12	Ford closes Embassy in Phnom Penh; evacuates Americans	L
	April 17	Khmer Rouge leftists have victory in Cambodia	O

APPENDIX C-1. Continued

Year	Date	Event	Rating
	April 29	US military involvement in Vietnam ends	L
	April 30	Saigon liberated by communists	O
	May 12-13	Mayaguez captured	R
	July 24-25	House rejects Ford's lifting of ban on military aid to Turkey	L
	July 26	Ford begins European tour	O
	August 21	US lifts export ban on Cuba	L
	September 5, 22	Attempts to assassinate Ford	R
	September 27	OPEC raises oil prices by 10 percent	O
	October 20	US-Soviet grain agreement	O
	November 26	Ford approves aid to New York City	O
	December 1-5	Ford visits China; meets with Mao	L
	December 19	US Senate votes to end military end to Angola	O
1976	January 25	House committee reports on US intelligence agencies	C
	January 30	Supreme Court rules Federal Election Campaign Act is unconstitutional according to First Amendment	C
	February 3	Lockheed scandal breaks	C
	February 17	Ford announces reorganization of intelligence agencies	C
	February 24	Ford wins New Hampshire primary	L
	February 28	Ford denounces Castro for aid to Angola	L
	May 8	Kelley, FBI apologize for some Hoover FBI activities	O
	May 19	Senate establishes committee on intelligence	O
	June 3	Congressional sex scandal involving Congressman Hays	O
	June 16	US Ambassador to Lebanon killed	O
	July 2	Vietnam unified	O
	July 4	Bicentennial celebration	R
	July 15	Carter nominated by Democrats	O
	August 11	Restructuring of FBI	O
	August 19	Ford nominated by Republicans	O

APPENDIX C-1. Continued

Year	Date	Event	Rating
	September 20	Carter's _Playboy_ interview released	O
	September 23	Ford/Carter debates begin	L
	October 4	Earl Butz resigns as Secretary of Agriculture	O
	November 2	Carter wins presidential election	L
	November 24	Human rights abuses brought to attention of United Nations by US ambassador	O
1977	January	Wage-price controls discussed	O
	January 9	Ford pardons "Tokyo Rose"	L
	January 21	Ford pardons Vietnam draft evaders;	L
		Carter inaugurated	O
	January 26	US rebukes Czechoslovakia on human rights	O
	March 5	Carter's phone calls from citizens	L
	March 30	USSR rejects US plan for limitation of arms	L
	April 20	Carter unveils energy plan	O
	May 2	Carter's arms limitation plans criticized in US	L
	May 5	Congress votes against aid to Vietnam	O
	May 30	US and Cuba exchange diplomats	O
	June	Public reaction to Carter's energy plan	O
	June 30	B-1 bomber plans shelved	L
	July 15	Carter approves admission of Indo-Chinese refugees to US	L
	July 20	CIA experiments in behavior control revealed	C
	August 4	Energy Department created	L
	September 21	Burt Lance resigns	C
	November 20	Korean influence investigation opens	C
	December	Panama Canal accords signed	O
	December 6	US coal miners strike	O

APPENDIX C-1. Continued

Year	Date	Event	Rating
1978	January 6	Carter overseas tour ends	0
	January 10	Nicaraguan violence reaches new level	0
	January 10	US-Japan trade accord signed	0
	January 31	Nicaraguan national strike	0
	February 2-8	Sadat visits US	0
	February 10	Vietnamese ambassador to UN accused of spying	L
	March 9	Park Tong Sun testifies before House Ethics Committee	C
	March 13	Taft-Hartley Act invoked in US coal miners strike	0
	April 6	Carter signs legislation raising mandatory retirement age	0
	April 7	Neutron bomb deferred	L
	April 10	Attorney General Bell announces indictments of three former FBI officials	C
	April 17	NY Stock Exchange sets record	0
	April 18	Panama Canal Treaty signed	L
	April 21	Troop withdrawal from Korea	L
	May 11	Rioting in Teheran	0
	May 15	US Senate approves jet sales to Saudi Arabia and Egypt in Middle East package	L
	May 31	Congress votes to request South Korea to make former Ambassador Kim testify before committee on standards of official conduct	C
	June 6	California mandates tax cuts by passing Proposition #13	L
	June 26	Carter Campaign Committee fined for illegal use of airplane during campaign	C
	June 28	Supreme Court rules on affirmative action in Bakke Case	0
	July 12	Andrew Young declares US also holds political prisoners; public calls for his resignation or impeachment	L
	September 5-17	Middle East peace talks at	

APPENDIX C-1.   Continued

Year	Date	Event	Rating
		Camp David	L
	September 8	Iran imposes martial law	O
	October 6	ERA deadline extended by Senate	L
	October 15	Energy package passed	L
	October 21	Cuban prisoners admitted to US	L
	October 31	Iranian oil workers strike	O
	November 1	Carter's new monetary policy helps to bolster US dollars abroad	O
	November	Republican gains in Congress	L
	November	Representative Diggs relected to Congress despite November conviction in payroll kickback scheme; expulsion later considered but rejected by House, pending appeal	C
	November 18	Murder of US congressman in Guyana triggers mass suicide among cult group	R
	November 30–December 2	US embassy in Tripoli attacked by mob; no injuries; other anti-US demonstrations in Indian, Bangkok, and Kuwait	R
	December 15	US-China establish full diplomatic relations; president criticized over severing of ties with Taiwan	L
	December 17	OPEC raises oil prices	O
	Decmeber 27	Senator Talmadge charged with violating Senate rules	C
	December 27	Iran crisis; Bakhtiar asked to establish civilian government	O
1979	January 31	New China policy instituted; Taiwan status shifts	L
	February 1-11	Khomeini returns to Iran; Bakhtiar resigns; Bazargan appointed head of government	O
	February	Farmers demonstrate in Washington	O
	February 14	US embassy in Iran attacked by	

APPENDIX C-1. Continued

Year	Date	Event	Rating
		leftist guerrillas; 100 employees including Ambassador Sullivan held hostage 2 hours before being freed by Khomeini supporters	R
	February 14	US ambassador to Afghanistan abducted then killed in raid; US protests the role of Soviet advisors in raid	R
	March 26	Egypt-Israel sign formal peace treaty in Washington, based on Camp David agreements	L
	March 28	Accident on Three Mile Island; US nuclear policies criticized	L
	March 29	Carter given 18 percent approval of handling of economy in Gallup Poll	O
	April 6	US aid to Pakistan cut due to Bhutto execution and Pakistan nuclear policies	O
	May 9	Salt II	L
	May 23	Lance indicted	C
	June 8	Carter approves MX missile	L
	June 12	Carter proposed national health insurance plan	L
	July 15	Carter's domestic energy speech	L
	July 16	Disclosures of CIA spying on anti-war students	O
	July 17	Shifts in Carter cabinet	L
	July 31	House censures Diggs	C
	August 15	Andrew Young resigns over questions of his dealings with the PLO	L
	September 5	Vance warns USSR about combat brigade in Cuba	O
	September 14	FBI slander of Jean Seberg disclosed	O
	October 6	Federal Reserve tightens money; market reacts	O
	October 11	Senate denounces Talmadge	C
	October 15-16	Military coup to overthrow President Amin crushed by	

APPENDIX C-1. Continued

Year	Date	Event	Rating
		local Afghan troops	O
	October 22	Shah to New York for medical	
		treatment	L
	October 25	South Korean President Park	
		assassinated	O
	November 1	Chrysler loan proposed by	
		Carter administration	O
	November 4	500 Iranian students seize US	
		embassy; take hostages; demand	
		return of Shah; US refuses;	
		Iran rebuffs mediation;	
		Bazargan resigns	R
	November 7	Ted Kennedy announces his	
		presidential candidacy	O
	November 9	US Senate Foreign Relations	
		Committee recommends SALT;	
		close vote, 9 to 6	L
	November 11	US embassy in Beirut seized,	
		dispersed by Syrian troops	R
	November 13	Reagan announces his	
		presidential candidacy	O
	November 14	US freezes Iranian assets	
		by executive order	L
	November 14	Diggs conviction upheld	C
	November 21	US embassy in Islamabad	
		attacked; anti-US attacks in	
		other Moslem countries after	
		Grand Mosque in Mecca taken	
		over	R
	November 29	US Special Prosecutor named	
		in Jordan cocaine charges	C
	December 4	US Security Council calls for	
		release of US hostages;	
		Waldheim contacts Iranians	O
	December 4	Carter presidential candidacy	
		announced	O
	December 10	Reports of increasing Soviet	
		supports and advisors to	
		Afghanistan	O
	December 10	NBC interview with Marine	
		hostage in Iran	O
	December 11	Gallup Poll (first time in	

APPENDIX C-1. Continued

Year	Date	Event	Rating
		nearly two years) shows Carter (49%) ahead of Kennedy (40%) in national opinion poll; jump largest in four decades of Gallup organization polling	O
	December 12	Most Iranian diplomats ordered out of the country	L
	December 15	Shah leaves for Panama	O
	December 20	Senate committee backs away from SALT	O
	December 21	Congress okays $3.5 billion loan to Chrysler	O
	December 27	Amin ousted in Afghanistan in Soviet backed coup	R
	December 28	Carter warns Brezhnev on Afghanistan	R
1980	January 1-3	Waldheim trip to Iran regarding US hostages	O
	January 2	Carter vetoes Agent Orange Study Bill	O
	January 4	Carter curtails grain sale to USSR because of Afghanistan	L
	January 5	GOP debate in Iowa: Baker, Crane, Anderson, Connally, Dole, Bush; attack Carter foreign policy	O
	January 7	US to buy grain earmarked USSR	O
	January 7	Carter signs Chrysler aid bill	O
	January 8	Carter announces more retaliation measures against Iran	L
	January 12	Brezhnev denounces Carter's attacks on USSR regarding Afghanistan	O
	January 13	USSR vetoes UN call for sanctions on Iran	O
	January 21	Carter wins Iowa primary	L
	January 23	State of the Union address; warns USSR about the Persian Gulf	O
	January 25	Bani Sadr elected president in Iran	O

APPENDIX C-1. Continued

Year	Date	Event	Rating
	January 26	Carter's Olympic stand gains support from other countries	L
	January 29	Carter says US needs allied help to protect western interest in Persian Gulf	O
	January 29	Canada helps six US diplomats escape Iran	R
	January 30	Carter predicts moderate recession for 1980	O
	February 3	US vows aid to Pakistan	O
	February 7	US postpones economic sanctions to discuss hostages with Bani Sadr	O
	February 8	FBI probes corruption in Southwest	C
	February 10	Carter wins Maine primary	O
	February 12	Announce US to dispatch assault troops to Arabian Sea following Afghanistan crisis	L
	February 12	International Olympic Committee says Olympics will be held in Moscow	L
	February 13	Hostage negotiations continue	O
	February 22	US restricts number of USSR diplomats allowed in US	L
	February 23	UN commission arrives in Iran	O
	February 25	Carter embargoes sale of phospates to USSR	L
	February 26	Carter wins New Hampshire primary	O

APPENDIX C-2. Events Rating (bimonthly)

Date	R	L	C	Date	R	L	C	Date	R	L	C
6502	0	0	0	7004	0	-2	0	7506	+1	0	0
6504	+1	0	0	7006	0	-1	0	7508	0	0	0
6506	0	0	0	7008	0	+1	0	7510	+1	0	0

APPENDIX C-2. Continued

Date	R	L	C	Date	R	L	C	Date	R	L	C
6508	0	+1	0	7010	0	0	0	7512	0	+2	0
6510	0	+1	0	7012	0	-2	0	7602	0	+2	-1
6512	0	0	0	7102	0	-1	0	7604	0	0	0
6602	0	+1	0	7104	0	-1	0	7606	+1	0	0
6604	0	0	0	7106	0	-1	0	7608	0	+1	0
6606	0	+1	0	7108	0	-1	0	7610	0	-2	0
6608	0	-1	0	7110	0	-1	0	7612	0	-1	0
6610	0	+1	0	7112	0	0	0	7702	0	+1	0
6612	0	0	0	7202	+1	+1	0	7704	0	0	0
6702	0	0	0	7204	0	-1	+1	7706	0	0	0
6704	0	+1	0	7206	0	+1	-1	7708	0	+2	-1
6706	0	+1	0	7208	0	0	0	7710	0	0	-1
6708	0	-2	0	7210	0	0	-1	7712	0	0	+1
6710	0	0	0	7212	0	+1	0	7802	0	0	0
6712	0	0	0	7302	0	-1	-1	7804	0	+3	0
6802	+2	0	0	7304	0	0	-3	7806	0	0	0
6804	0	-2	0	7306	0	+2	-3	7808	0	-1	0
6806	+1	+1	0	7308	0	0	-4	7810	0	+3	0
6808	0	-1	0	7310	0	0	-3	7812	+1	0	-2
6810	0	0	0	7312	0	0	-1	7902	+2	+1	0
6812	0	0	0	7402	0	+2	-2	7904	0	0	+2
6902	0	0	0	7404	0	0	-3	7906	0	+4	-1
6904	0	+1	0	7406	0	+2	-8	7908	0	-2	+1
6906	0	0	0	7408	+1	0	-3	7910	0	0	0
6908	+1	+1	0	7410	0	-1	-2	7912	5	3	3
6910	0	+1	0	7412	0	0	-1	8002	0	4	-4
6912	0	-2	0	7502	0	0	-1	8004	0	-1	2
7002	0	0	0	7504	0	-3	0	8006	0	1	-1

R = Rally
L = Leadership
C = Corruption

APPENDIX D

APPENDIX D-1. Group Support for Democratic Presidents: Coefficients for all Unemployment Groups

	Aggregate	Married Men	White Collar	Blue Collar	Male	Female	Youth	White	Nonwhite	N
National	3.54*	8.96*	4.31*	3.37*	4.84*	3.05*	2.55*	4.41*	1.25	42
Party Identification										
Republican	-3.91*	-9.56*	-4.81*	-3.78*	5.35*	-3.46*	-2.73*	-4.87*	-1.38	42
Democrat	-4.05*	-5.39*	-7.13*	-2.70*	-4.19*	-4.72*	-2.37*	-4.38*	-2.57*	42
Independent	-5.78*	-12.95*	-7.82*	-5.37*	-7.35*	-5.54*	-3.75*	-6.98	-2.41*	42
Occupation										
Professional	5.40*	11.88*	7.12*	4.86*	6.84*	5.11*	5.53*	6.53*	2.13*	42
White Collar	4.72*	10.63*	6.43*	4.35*	6.03*	4.61*	3.12*	5.74*	1.85*	42
Blue Collar	4.65*	10.32*	5.92*	4.18*	5.98*	4.31*	3.08*	5.60*	1.83*	42
Income**										
5	3.78*	8.95*	4.85*	3.55*	3.77*	3.48*	2.49*	4.63*	1.46*	42
5-10	4.09*	10.29*	5.21*	3.92*	3.62*	3.69*	2.78*	5.07*	1.50	42
10-15	9.86*	17.07*	15.55*	8.80*	6.60*	11.34*	5.48*	11.23*	5.10*	31
15+	19.41*	36.21*	28.41*	17.36*	16.96*	19.86*	11.66*	22.24*	9.60*	19
Sex										
Male	3.86*	9.27*	4.62*	3.47*	4.99*	3.25*	2.52*	4.59*	1.31	42
Female	4.30*	10.79*	5.46*	4.11*	5.82*	3.87*	2.92*	5.32*	1.59*	42

	(1)	(2)	(3)	(4)	(5)	(6)	(7)	(8)	(9)	N
Race										
White	4.53*	10.94*	5.85*	4.23*	5.99*	4.13*	3.00*	5.56*	1.73*	42
Black	13.01*	15.78*	19.90*	9.05*	10.82*	11.42*	6.70	13.98*	6.90*	19
Age										
Under 30	13.25*	26.15*	18.98*	11.97*	15.80*	13.30*	8.23*	15.38*	6.32*	42
30-49	5.62*	13.15*	7.48*	5.20*	7.39*	5.19*	3.65*	6.80*	2.30*	42
Over 50	3.34	8.87*	4.18	3.25*	4.64*	2.86*	2.25*	4.17*	1.17	42
Region										
West	4.37*	10.76*	5.55*	4.14*	5.85*	4.01*	3.02*	5.40*	1.60	42
South	6.60*	14.37*	9.10*	6.16*	8.23*	6.46*	4.10*	7.87*	2.89*	42
East	1.33	5.66	0.99	1.48	2.51	0.73	1.93	1.98	0.03	42
Midwest	-3.73*	-4.91*	-6.63*	-2.43*	-3.88*	-4.18*	-2.39*	-4.02*	-2.37*	42
Religion										
Catholic	1.82	5.97	1.73	1.86	2.84	1.22	1.79	2.42	0.41	42
Protestant	5.74*	12.81*	7.48*	5.29*	7.30*	5.24*	4.04*	6.88*	2.35*	42

*Significant at the 95 percent level

**Income in thousands of dollars

279

APPENDIX D-2. Group Support for Republican Presidents: Coefficients for all Unemployment Groups

	Aggregate	Married Men	White Collar	Blue Collar	Male	Female	Youth	White	Nonwhite	N
National	-3.79*	-5.00*	-6.61*	-2.52*	-3.94*	-4.31*	-2.35*	-4.10*	-2.40*	48
Party Identification										
Republican	-4.05*	-5.39*	-7.13*	-2.70*	-4.19*	-4.72*	-2.37*	-4.38*	-2.59*	48
Democrat	-2.93*	-3.69*	-5.14*	-1.89*	-3.01*	-3.26*	-1.97*	-3.15*	-1.90*	48
Independent	-3.44*	-4.44*	-6.02*	-2.27*	-3.55*	-3.93*	-2.19*	-3.72*	-2.22*	48
Occupation										
Professional	-2.67*	-3.31*	-4.72*	-1.75*	-2.67*	-3.12*	-1.67*	-2.86*	-1.72*	48
White Collar	-3.89*	-5.02*	-6.89*	-2.49*	-4.00	-4.42*	-2.42*	-4.19*	-2.47*	48
Blue Collar	-3.58*	-4.63*	-6.26*	-2.35*	-3.73*	-4.02*	-2.28*	-3.86*	-2.34*	48
Income**										
5	-4.93*	-6.67*	-8.47*	-3.32	5.12*	-5.49*	-3.08*	-5.35*	-3.12*	48
5-10	5.05	-6.71*	-8.86*	-3.32*	5.26*	-5.78*	-3.17*	-5.47*	-3.23	48
10-15	-4.71*	-6.16*	-8.28*	-3.10*	4.72*	-5.29*	-2.93*	-5.10*	-2.98*	48
15+	7.55*	10.20*	14.04*	4.69*	4.37	8.06*	4.69*	8.25*	4.83*	44
Sex										
Male	-4.73*	-6.20*	-8.31*	-3.05*	-4.92*	-5.36*	-2.94*	-5.08*	-3.07*	48
Female	-3.22*	-4.23*	-5.65*	-2.10*	-3.35*	-3.59*	-2.06*	-3.47*	-2.05*	48

									N
Race									
White	-3.39*	-4.26*	-5.81*	-2.23*	-3.44*	-3.75*	-2.36*	-3.62*	-2.22*	48
Black	-0.98	-1.10	-1.58	-0.57	-1.02	1.04	-0.74	-0.98	-0.75	44
Age									
Under 30	3.56*	4.72*	6.49*	2.13*	3.74*	3.99*	2.24*	3.84*	2.42*	48
30-49	-2.84*	-3.55*	-4.78*	-1.92*	-2.89	-3.16*	-1.86*	-3.06	-1.86*	48
Over 50	-4.16*	-5.49*	-7.19*	-2.75*	-4.32*	-4.68*	-2.56*	-4.47*	-2.70*	48
Region									
West	-4.02*	-5.20*	-7.07*	-2.62*	-4.17*	-4.48*	-2.61*	-4.34*	-2.89*	48
South	-5.16*	-6.95*	-9.18*	-3.37*	-5.43*	-5.87*	-3.09*	-5.57*	-3.28*	48
East	-4.66*	-6.09*	-8.47*	-2.97*	-4.85*	-5.27*	-2.84*	-5.01*	-3.00*	48
Midwest	3.39	9.01*	3.78	3.28	4.76*	2.83	2.46	4.32*	1.09*	48
Religion									
Catholic	-3.50*	-4.41*	-6.31*	-2.20*	-3.56*	-3.93*	-2.30*	-3.45*	-2.30*	48
Protestant	-4.02*	-5.21*	-7.17*	-2.58*	-4.17*	-4.52*	-2.55*	-4.33*	-2.60*	48

*Significant at the 95 percent confidence level

**Income in thousands of dollars

281

Index

About the Author

Kristen R. Monroe is Assistant Professor of Politics at New York University and is currently a Visiting Assistant Professor in Princeton University's Department of Politics. She is also a member of the faculty at New York University's School of Law. Editor of *The Political Process and Economic Change,* she has written extensively on the economy's political impact. She is currently constructing a microlevel theory of how expectations and uncertainty affect political behavior, a theory that integrates the economist's emphasis on rationality as a conscious calculation of costs and benefits with the social psychologist's concern with preconscious and subconscious motivations and impulses.